THY WILL BE DONE

A Spiritual Portrait
of
TERENCE CARDINAL COOKE

THY WILL BE DONE

A Spiritual Portrait
of
TERENCE CARDINAL COOKE

BENEDICT J. GROESCHEL, CFR
and
TERRENCE L. WEBER

ALBA · HOUSE   NEW · YORK

SOCIETY OF ST. PAUL, 2187 VICTORY BLVD., STATEN ISLAND, NEW YORK 10314

C/B

Library of Congress Cataloging-in-Publication Data

Groeschel, Benedict J.
   Thy will be done : a spiritual portrait of Terence Cardinal Cooke
   / by Benedict J. Groeschel and Terrence L. Weber.
         p.   cm.
   ISBN (Hardback Edition): 0-8189-0591-3
   ISBN (Paperback Edition): 0-8189-0595-6
   1. Cooke, Terence, 1921-1983.   2. Cardinals — United States —
Biography.   I. Weber, Terrence L.   II. Title.
BX4705.C7763G76   1990
282'.092—dc20
   [B]   90-917
                                                                      CIP

Nihil Obstat:
James T. O'Connor, STD
Censor Librorum

Imprimatur:
Patrick Sheridan
Vicar General, Archdiocese of New York
May 18, 1990

Designed, printed and bound in the United States of America by the Fathers and Brothers of the Society of St. Paul, 2187 Victory Boulevard, Staten Island, New York 10314, as part of their communications apostolate.

Printing Information:

Current Printing - first digit   1   2   3   4   5   6   7   8   9   10   11   12

Year of Current Printing - first year shown
  1990   1991   1992   1993   1994   1995   1996   1997

TABLE OF CONTENTS

FOREWORD

by

JOHN CARDINAL O'CONNOR

I saw Cardinal Cooke become angry twice in ten years. In each instance, his anger lasted for a fraction of a moment; a sudden flash and it had come and gone. The aftermath was a complete restoration of his habitual, unruffled calm — no seething acrimony, no residual bitterness. Given my own volatility, his calmness impressed me deeply.

It was in search of the reason for that calmness that I discovered how truly charitable this man was. It was extraordinarily difficult for him to see evil in anyone, regardless of the provocation. He would be quite likely to say of a convicted killer: "The poor fellow must not have known what he was doing."

I learned early in my relationship with him, however, not to mistake kindness for naiveté. I would never have tried to sell him a sick horse. He had a shrewdness about him that could have made him a baron of Wall Street, had he chosen. The financial stability of the archdiocese I inherited as his successor was in major part a function of that shrewdness.

Yet he was first and foremost a holy man. Long before it became public knowledge that he had cancer, he was suffering without a murmur of complaint, going about his daily responsibilities with saintly cheerfulness. Few other than his doctor knew

vii

that between appointments he would have blood transfusions to keep him going. He might justifiably have been a down man, ill-humored, cantankerous. Never was such the case. The weakness and pain were always masked by the most winsome smile.

I am pleased that Father Benedict Groeschel and Pastor Terrence Weber have written this book, and I am equally pleased by the book they have written. It is as unpretentious as was the cardinal himself. And it's a gentle book that tells us just enough about the cardinal's own gentleness, without becoming maudlin.

It is more than six years since I first sat at Cardinal Cooke's desk, moved into his residence, took his place in Saint Patrick's Cathedral. Yet it is unlikely that even this very day will pass that I will not be introduced as, or referred to as "Cardinal Cooke." That says a great deal about the impact he made on the Archdiocese of New York and the world at large. This little book will help assure that such impact will perdure, as it deserves to. More importantly, it will undoubtedly encourage a multitude of readers to follow the cardinal's gentle way of kindness and love.

May, 1990

ACKNOWLEDGMENTS

*A*n endeavor such as this is never the sole product of the author, or in this case, the authors. In order to paint an accurate portrait of our subject we had to consult many people who knew Cardinal Cooke. Without their insights, observations and anecdotes our spiritual portrait would have been rather drab.

We are indebted to those who agreed to be interviewed for this book whether their story was used or not. Through a whole host of interviews, ranging from the cardinal's tailor all the way to those who walked with him in the inner circle of intimate friends, the authors have gained a broader perspective of their subject. For those who contributed to this work in that respect we will always be grateful.

Likewise, once a manuscript is finished you need a group of people who will check it for accuracy and readability. We would like to thank Bishop Patrick Ahern, Lawrence Kenney, and James McHugh. We also thank Monsignors Eugene Clark, Joseph Murphy, James Murray, Patrick Sheridan, James Wilders and Fathers Thomas Shelley and William Reisig. Their comments on the manuscript greatly aided us in putting the finishing touches on our spiritual portrait of Cardinal Cooke.

We are deeply grateful to Sister Aloysius McBride, O. Carm. and the volunteers of the Cardinal Cooke Guild for so much assistance. Without the efforts of Sister Aloysius it is doubtful if this book could have been completed.

The superb cover art was created by John Lynch, a young

artist who has produced several other portraits for publication of religious biographies. We are grateful to him and to the Ladies of Charity who provided the sponsorship for this lasting contribution to the memory of the cardinal.

We do not want to forget Claudia McDonnell, who with her "fresh eye," reviewed the manuscript for proper use of grammar and punctuation.

Finally, we wish to thank John Cardinal O'Connor who set aside the time needed to write our Foreword. Throughout this project Cardinal O'Connor has offered the support and encouragement needed by the authors to continue on. He has done much himself since becoming Cardinal Cooke's successor to make known the life and faith of his predecessor.

A spiritual biography such as this one is really the collective work of many individual people. We have only taken the various themes and brought them together on the printed page.

The Authors

INTRODUCTION

by

BENEDICT J. GROESCHEL, CFR

*W*hen I met him I recognized him as one of a dying breed: almost extinct, like the rhinoceros. In fact, he had the same expression as a rhinoceros. He was an old-fashioned, tough, New York taxi cab driver, complete with peaked hat and cigar. When I asked him to take me to Saint Patrick's Cathedral, he shot back the question, "You going to the cardinal's funeral, Padre?" When I answered that I was, he answered, "I wish I could park this hack and go in myself. I knew the cardinal, you know. He came up to the Bronx where I live. Me and my wife — we met him twice. Our best friends are Italians and they introduced us to him. He was great. It didn't make no difference to him that we was Jewish — everybody was the same to him."

As we dodged the heavy city traffic and crowds gathering around the Cathedral the driver told me of his admiration for Cardinal Cooke because of his concern for the ordinary people.

As I stood by his window and gave him his fare he said to me, "You mark my words, Padre, that cardinal was a saint." As I turned toward the gate in the police barricade to go up to the side steps of the Cathedral I met the popular columnist, Bill Reel. He asked me what I thought. Tears were welling up inside me because I had come from open heart surgery to bid good-bye to the cardinal who had made me his friend. I had not seen him since

xi

the day before my surgery a month ago, when he was already confined to bed. The memories of that precious hour filled my mind. I could hardly talk to Bill, but managed to say something while the words of the taxi cab driver echoed in my mind. "A saint!" Of course, a saint! After the solemn pontifical funeral Mass I met Sister Aloysius, a Carmelite Sister of the Aged and Infirm and a mutual friend of Cardinal Cooke. She remarked to me, "If people were canonized by popular acclaim as they were in the ancient Church, then the cardinal would have been declared a saint today." "A saint." A saint, of course!

I was not surprised when John Cardinal O'Connor, the successor of Cardinal Cooke as Archbishop of New York, announced that he would soon begin an investigation to determine if there was serious support for the beginning of a cause of canonization.

When the letter arrived asking me to undertake the work of investigating the possibility of a cause I waited a while before responding to it. Not only was I already in over my head with responsibilities and cutting corners, but this would be a personally painful task. The tears were not over and the wounds had not yet become scars. Other people, some of them even closer to the cardinal than I was, would feel the same. Then, there was the question of privacy. A potential candidate for sainthood loses a lot of privacy, and Terence Cardinal Cooke was a very private man.

On the other hand, saints are eventually canonized because of the direction of Divine Providence. The Church not only insists on popular support and enthusiasm for the cause but also on miracles. If it should be God's will, did I or anyone else have the right to stand in the way? I asked myself what Cardinal Cooke would have done. The answer was clear. If asked to take on such a responsibility and burden the cardinal would have said, "Yes." I had no valid excuse. I thought he could be a candidate for canonization. I thought it then, and after five years of investigation I am more convinced than ever that his cause should be opened. He, indeed, appears to be a saint to me.

Every step along the way has been cleared for our work. Unexpectedly, Sister Aloysius was able to become the coordinator of the Cardinal Cooke Guild; she has been very effective, using her years of vast experience as an administrator in New York. A fine young Lutheran pastor, The Reverend Terrence L. Weber, wrote asking to be a volunteer worker. He was so enthusiastic and so well organized that he was to become the first Lutheran pastor in church history to be appointed archivist of a possible cause of canonization. Pastor Weber became co-author of this book by doing all the research and organization of the cardinal's personal and public papers. Many of the interviews with people who knew Cardinal Cooke were done by him. The numerous revisions of a text which are needed before publication were also done by Pastor Weber.

Thousands of supporters have joined the Cardinal Cooke Guild and hundreds of volunteers have given their services. Remarkable reports of favors through the intercession of Cardinal Cooke have been reported. As we shall see, so far this endeavor is what Cardinal Cooke wanted everything to be — a source of edification and strength for the faithful. In death as in life, he still preaches the love of God and the love of our brothers and sisters of the human family because of the love Christ has for them.

Why This Book

The goal of the authors in writing this spiritual biography is to make known to the people of God as far as possible the faith and inner life, the struggles and virtues of His Eminence Terence Cardinal Cooke. Our purpose is not to present a complete historical biography which would explore his accomplishments and his significance in Church history. This needs to be done by an historian, and it is too soon after the death of Cardinal Cooke to attempt it now. Rather, our hope is to present a spiritual portrait which communicates some of the inner life of this great Christian, who so deeply touched thousands of ordinary people and who faithfully attempted to fulfill his challenging duties in difficult times. Carl Gustav Jung has pointed out that the most important events of a person's life are unseen and take place in the mind and soul. These inner events are only known from what the individual chooses to reveal of self, or from external behavior which reflects these inner events. A biography which attempts to reveal these inner events might best be called a spiritual portrait. As with any portrait, the painter cannot include every detail, but rather he leaves the viewer to creatively respond to what is significant but necessarily incomplete.

In this time of total media coverage, the biography of a public person has become more difficult to write. A multitude of external events are known, reported and summarized at the time of the person's death. This was certainly true of Cardinal Cooke. When we began our task we were determined to search beneath these media events and to see what evidence there was of the inner motives, struggles and attitudes, even the defects of our subject. We undertook this task with the definite goal of presenting a portrait that delineated the personal spirituality of Terence Cardinal Cooke. We became more and more convinced of his consistent, deep and heroic dedication as we reviewed the evidence. It is said that biographers should love their subject, and the authors of this biography certainly do. If and when the Archbishop of New York "instructs"the cause of canonization, that is, calls for a formal investigation into the life of the cardinal, we expect that this biography will provide much of the necessary documentation. We were advised that it is wise to do this within a few years lest memories fade and documents become lost.

It was obvious to us that we must produce an honest — and when necessary — critical portrait. To be critical is no small task, since family and friends of the cardinal may feel that such a study intrudes upon their privacy and may be critical without sufficient reason. When a person's work in this world is finished no criticism can be called constructive, since it is no longer possible for the person criticized to change. However, criticism can be gentle and respectful. When we encountered what appeared to be some of the shortcomings and limitations which beset all human beings we did not hesitate to discuss them. We also described good qualities which others might see as limitations or faults. For example, Cardinal Cooke had a well known tendency to avoid confrontation. He deeply disliked being critical. Some biographers might choose to interpret this more negatively than we have done, but at least we have tried to provide future biographers with accurate information.

It is interesting to note that Cardinal Cooke had few enough enemies. It has been observed that even they came to his funeral and apparently mourned his loss. They appeared to recognize that seldom had they met so fair and chivalrous a foe in the lists of life. Cardinal Cooke also had his critics even among his fellow clergy and religious. Administrators must choose to give responsibilities and recognition to those whom they think can best contribute to the work at hand. Inevitably, others who think themselves equally or better qualified may resent that they were not chosen. The Catholic Church during the time of Cardinal Cooke's public life was involved in profound change, with many resulting conflicts. Like everyone else Cardinal Cooke was guided by his own intellectual convictions and vision. We shall see that he conceived this vision broadly and endeavored to include persons with widely ranging views among those with whom he chose to work. In the Archdiocese of New York there were many capable men and women, and Cardinal Cooke chose some and not others to work with him. We are not aware that anyone has accused him of having based his selection on unworthy motives. A problem of writing a biography so soon after a person's death is that there are always people around who are bruised. In our investigation we have not encountered one informed person who was incapable of seeing beyond his own feelings and recognizing that the cardinal was trying to do his best to be honest and just in the midst of conflicting responsibilities.

During the last weeks of his life, the various themes of the life of Cardinal Cooke came together in a startling crescendo as the hidden details of his battle with terminal cancer began to emerge. It became more widely recognized that his years of service were characterized by activity completely beyond any reasonable expectation. These years of serious illness were accompanied by extremely painful symptoms which should have been incapacitating.

The last days of the cardinal's life were like a symphony in which the various themes were repeated, augmented and harmoniously related to each other. The volume of this symphony was greatly amplified by the outpouring of deeply felt personal concern for the cardinal on every side in New York City. This worldly and competitive city, known for its harsh and at times inhuman treatment of its inhabitants, paused in its tracks to express concern and gratitude for the humble, gentle man who had risen to be one of its most illustrious and caring citizens. Catholics and non-Catholics, believers and unbelievers, rich and poor of every race and background in great numbers and in varied ways expressed their concern and esteem. It appeared that hundreds of thousands of people felt that they knew the cardinal personally, and in a way they did. He had met them along life's path like our taxi cab driver, and as he had done, they saw the cardinal as their friend. His personal ideal of love of God and of every human being expressed in the course of his life had left its mark on tens of thousands of lives. This had been done at tremendous personal cost in the face of sickness and pain.

As the facts of the cardinal's illness became known, people began to ask, "How did he do it?" How and why did he stand there for hours after a Mass to greet people and to pose for a picture with a newly confirmed child or with senior citizens on an outing? How did he keep going, graciously, kindly, always smiling when he was still recovering from that morning's blood transfusion? A word begins to emerge as an answer. The word is *heroic*. How was he always recollected, always prayerful, always putting the things of the spirit first? How did he remain faithful, gentle and responsive to the needs of the Church and of everyone he met? The word again is heroic. In this book, we the authors, a Lutheran pastor who never met him and a Catholic priest who was one of his companions on the inner journey, invite you, the reader, to share what we know and to ask yourself these questions: "Was Cardinal Cooke really heroic in season and out of season? Was he consistently faithful in the face of immense personal discomfort? Does this fidelity and concern for others reflect the power of grace and the gifts of the Holy Spirit consistently sought after and received?" These are the questions this book addresses. These are the questions of the Church. They become ultimately the questions of sanctity.

> *March 17, 1990*
> *Feast of Saint Patrick*
> *Patron Saint of the Archdiocese of New York*

INTRODUCTION

by

THE REVEREND TERRENCE L. WEBER

E very now and then there comes into an individual's life 'someone' who makes a significant impact on his or her growth, development and understanding of life. The impression or example made by this 'someone' on the individual can be either personal, professional, moral or spiritual. This 'someone' may be a person from the past, perhaps one of the saints. It may be a person we knew rather closely, like a relative or a teacher. It may also be someone we never knew at all. Nonetheless their effect is always the same: to give a lasting example that we may imitate in our day-to-day life.

Terence Cardinal Cooke has become that kind of a 'someone' for me. I never knew the cardinal. Throughout his years as Archbishop of New York thousands of people in deference for his office kissed his episcopal ring. I never kissed his ring or even shook his hand. During his life that bright twinkle in his eyes and boyish smile on his face graced everyone he met. I never saw that smile myself. It is said that Cardinal Cooke never forgot the name of someone he met. He did not know my name, to be sure, though we share the same baptismal patron. Our paths in life never crossed.

Yet, in a way, I have met him. I have met Cardinal Cooke and I have come to know him and I have come to love him deeply. I have come to know the cardinal through my research in his archives and through the countless hours of interviews I have conducted in order to assemble this spiritual biography. I have come to love him and the kind of person and priest he was through the people who knew him best. Terence Cardinal Cooke has become for me what a priest should always be — an imitator of Jesus Christ Our Lord.

It is odd even in this ecumenical age to think that a Lutheran pastor should be asked to serve as co-author with a Roman Catholic priest of a biography about a Catholic prelate. But that is the beauty of it. Cardinal Cooke, in death as in life, has a way of bringing people together regardless of their background. He brings us together so that through our united efforts the Church of Jesus Christ may be edified.

I am delighted to be a part of this special and unique project which has in countless ways edified my own spiritual life, my own Lutheran priesthood. Along the way, while preparing this book, I have been privileged to meet some remarkable people. People who themselves stand in need of an example in order to get through the day. People who themselves stand in need of strength in order to bear the load. People who themselves stand in need of redemption in order to enter the fullness of eternity. People who themselves, like our beloved cardinal, saw their lives rooted in the death and resurrection of Jesus Christ. From that all-embracing event we receive whatever we need in order for God's will to become our will.

You may have known Terence Cardinal Cooke very intimately. Or you may have seen him once or twice in public. Perhaps you never met him at all. Through the pages of this spiritual biography I hope you will come to know him and love him, that he will become for you that 'someone' who every now and then comes into an individual's life.

March 17, 1990
Feast of Saint Patrick
Patron Saint of the Archdiocese of New York

THY WILL BE DONE

A Spiritual Portrait
of
TERENCE CARDINAL COOKE

In using the word "saint" or other similar terms, and in describing reports of favors apparently received from Divine Providence, we in no way intend the anticipate the judgment of the Holy See whose decision is respectfully awaited. In all matters we wish to conform completely to the decree of Pope Urban VIII "Coelestis Jerusalem" of July 5, 1634 and all other ecclesiastical legislation pertinent to this subject.

The Authors

CHAPTER ONE

THE BACKGROUND

The West Side

*T*he background for any portrait of Terence Cardinal Cooke is as complex and discordant as his figure was simple and integrated. This idealistic and uncomplicated man lived all of his life, except for two years of graduate studies, either in New York City or within an hour's drive of this incredibly dynamic and confusing environment. To appreciate the spiritual journey of this man we must place him not on a farm or in a country town where one would expect to find a saintly person, but rather in the swirling and commercial port city which will in many ways, some obvious, some obscure, determine the course of his life. Occasionally in this biography we must stop and reappraise the background because the great city, like a Leviathan, will have turned and changed its position, and this movement will require reappraisal and readjustment of our portrait. As it has done for all of its inhabitants, the City of New York will place new challenges in Terence Cooke's path. When you are the shepherd of millions of New Yorkers, the ability to recognize these movements and to respond creatively to them becomes a critical issue, not simply for the success of your work but even for the authenticity of your mission.

Terence James Cooke was born on March 1, 1921, on the edge of a world that had grown a generation beyond the one described by O. Henry. New York at the end of the First World War was a city made up principally of recent immigrants to America who clung to their national identities as a source of solace and mutual protection, and yet who all yearned to become part of the thriving, victorious nation that had awaited them beyond the golden door. New York, perhaps more than any other port city in the world, was in reality a noisy conglomerate of a thousand ethnic villages overlapping each other, inter-relating, sometimes peacefully, always competitively. It was and still is, like any other port, a city where idealism and cynicism clash while quiet families live out the dramas of every day life a block away from corruption and crime. These two worlds rarely encountered each other except when the family men told stories at the supper table of the strange characters they met in their work as policemen, taxi drivers or salesmen.

Religiously, the New York where Terence Cooke grew up was an extraordinarily devout place filled with magnificent cathedrals, churches, synagogues and religious schools. At the same time, it was the home of some of the religions' most vociferous critics. Yet even before the days of ecumenism and religious understanding, all these believers and unbelievers managed to gather in peace, except for skirmishes when the ethnic competition of aggressive teenagers adopted the mask of religious controversy. For the most part Catholics, Protestants and Jews went their own separate ways religiously, while the prejudices of the old world were gradually shed and the wounds of religious persecution were slowly healed. Terence Cooke was deeply part of the vibrant Catholic life that the immigrants brought to New York, but he was also part of the time of healing sectarian wounds. As a young man he would reach out to those whose immediate ancestors had opposed his own family in Ireland, and to Jewish friends whose parents had been forced to hide from Christians on Good Friday in Eastern Europe. This varied array of believers and unbelievers, of decent folk and villains of all persuasions, came together to cheer the Giants in the Polo Grounds. Babylon and Jerusalem wrapped up in a hot dog roll is still the best description of New York.

The parish where Terence Cooke was baptized was a fascinating symbol of all that New York could be to her millions of children. Corpus Christi Church on 121st Street was made up mostly of Irish, German, and Jewish immigrants who lived in respectable tenements clinging to Morningside Heights. If you went up on the roof, as all imaginative city children love to do, you could look south and see the imposing mass of the Episcopal Cathedral of Saint John the Divine. This no doubt reminded the Irish of the government they all detested as the oppressor of their homeland. In fact, Terence was given the baptismal name of Terence MacSwiney, [1] the Lord Mayor of Cork, who had died in a hunger strike to protest the treatment and execution of the Irish patriots in the 1916 uprising and the continued occupation of Ireland by the British Crown. [2] Little did the young immigrant couple, Margaret and Michael, ever think their son would attend solemn ecumenical services in that great Episcopal cathedral when Archbishop of New York.

Between Saint John the Divine and LaSalle Street, where the Cookes lived on the edge of Harlem, was the old Catholic church, Corpus Christi. The new pastor was Father George Barry Ford, who built a bright new church after the Cookes had moved to the suburbs. The new church in the New England classical style, reminded many of the Irish parishioners of a Protestant church. Union Theological Seminary to be built across Broadway, looked for all the world like a Benedictine Abbey.

The great bulk of Columbia University rises between Saint John the Divine and Corpus Christi; Father Ford, would become a renowned chaplain of the university and a feisty pioneer in the early days of the interfaith movement. Cardinal Cooke's two predecessors occasionally found this movement awkward but he himself would enjoy it thoroughly. When Cardinal Cooke presided at the funeral Mass of Father Ford in 1978 and this writer preached the sermon, the cardinal and I chuckled together after the liturgy about how our long-time friend had been a prophetic spirit in so many ways and had managed to fulfill an important, and at times, disconcerting role in the life of the Church in New York. In fact, it was the building of the Morningside apartment houses, spearheaded by Father Ford, that led to the demolishing of the tenement buildings where the Cooke children were born.

Before concluding our picture of this little corner of New York we should mention for those unfamiliar with the scene that the Jewish Theological Seminary now dominates the corner just above LaSalle Street where the Cookes lived. The old seminary building (replaced in 1929 by an impressive new structure topped by a lantern) reminds us that Terence Cooke grew up in the then largest Jewish community in the world. He always had many close friends in the vibrant Jewish community of New York. His predecessor, Cardinal Spellman, would provide an essential push for the admission of the new State of Israel to the United Nations[3] and would be the first Catholic prelate in New York to have close ties to its thriving Jewish community.

Beyond all these buildings rises the imposing tower of Riverside Church, the closest thing to a Baptist Cathedral in the world. The only thing missing in this montage of religious buildings is a mosque.

Finally, to complete our painting of this remarkable neighborhood, it is important to note that only two blocks from the apartment on LaSalle Street was the beginning of Harlem, a fascinating neighborhood of upper Manhattan then largely Irish, Italian, Jewish and German with a growing Black community. This Black community was made up of immigrants from the West Indies as well as a great number of Black Americans from the South. The Motherhouse of the Franciscan Handmaids of Mary, one of America's three communities of Black sisters, is almost parallel with LaSalle Street but several blocks east. The main avenue, 125th Street, where Terence's mother bought their food and his father caught the elevated train to work, would become the most famous center of Black life and culture in the world. The eastern end of that busy street would be, a few decades later, the northern border of Spanish Harlem, a vibrant and expanding Puerto Rican and Latin American community. Sixty-three years after his birth both Black and Hispanic communities expressed profound grief and loss at the death of a beloved friend when Terence Cooke died after years of service to them as the Archbishop of New York.

In 1921, at the end of the First World War, the young Irish immigrant couple, Michael Cooke of Knock Moy in County Galway and Margaret Gannon of Athenry in the same county welcomed their third child as they did everything else — with gratitude to God. They were gentle, devout, country people. In hopes of finding employment and a better chance for their children, they had left the beautiful green countryside to be plunged into the largest city in the world. The City of New York had a safe corner for them; a neighborhood with aspects of a village, a church where they felt at home, a thriving Irish community which boasted a great cathedral named after their patron saint, and a civil rights demonstration turned into a celebration — the Saint Patrick's Day parade — the largest to march annually up Fifth Avenue. The sights and sounds of New York greeted a little boy, intelligent, curious and filled with a vital love of life. Decades later he could even recall the number of steps both up to the apartment house entrance and up to the family door, and other details of his early life. [4]

His father, Michael, was the formative influence in the life of Terence. Known to everyone as a kindly, devout and friendly man, Michael was a faithful member of the Third Order of Saint Francis, who went regularly to the monthly meetings and spent considerable time kneeling each evening saying his nightly prayers. His daughter, Katherine, recalls the family dog would nestle for a nap across the calves of Michael's legs while he knelt, confident that he would not be disturbed until his master's prayer time was over. Michael Cooke could deal successfully with wealthy and important people, the "swells" as they were known in those days. Starting out as a tile setter, he moved up to being a chauffeur and then a civil servant. Perhaps the most telling memory of him comes from a neighbor about Terence's age. He remembered Mr. Cooke organizing the children of the neighborhood to pick up broken glass in the street so no one would get cut playing stick ball or tag. [5] Apparently, he did this kind of thing quite regularly. Terence would remain very close to his father, who was also his model, until his death in 1961.

Margaret Gannon, the cardinal's mother, also a quiet and gentle person, was really an innocent Irish colleen transplanted to America. She gave birth to her three children in her little apartment on LaSalle Street: to Joseph in 1917, to Katherine in 1919, and finally to Terence two years later.

The family constellation was filled out by several uncles and aunts on both sides who all "stuck together" as wise immigrants do, knowing that survival and upward mobility in a great metropolis is best assured by family ties. Tragedy would soon prove the wisdom of this intuitive reliance on family support.

Each of the relatives had a special place. In a letter Terence wrote to a priest friend as a seminarian when he was eighteen, this comes across quite clearly.

> The whole family went down to see Uncle Michael off on Saturday. Indeed, it was a sad sight. As you know he was with us only a couple of months but endeared himself to every one he met. Everybody felt bad because such a lovely character was leaving them. I can see him now, a solitary figure waving a green handkerchief and many times cover-

ing his weeping face. The boat was pushed out of the harbor very slowly and everybody made themselves hoarse yelling good-bye. Most of us will not see him again. [6]

Among the members of the extended family, two people stand out, who could have found their places in the short stories of O. Henry. Uncle Jimmy who would have so profound an effect on the character and personality of Terence that many times people unknowingly quote this man's words when describing the cardinal. James Gannon had been a horse trainer in Ireland; he became a police sergeant in New York and was responsible for training the famous New York City mounted police. Annually, Sergeant Gannon and the police cavalry put on a demonstration at Madison Square Garden. A dashing photograph of him taking a horse across a hurdle belies the fact that this man had lived through an unthinkable tragedy. He had returned home from work one day to discover his wife and three children had been asphyxiated in a gas leak. The Cookes and Gannons stuck together and Uncle Jimmy moved in with the family. Jimmy not only put together the pieces of his broken life but eventually remarried and regained his old vitality. Uncle Jimmy advised his nephew to treat everyone the same way — and that was with cheerful courtesy and respect whatever their station in life.

Uncle Jimmy's philosophy of life is clearly reflected in the life of Terence Cardinal Cooke. Indeed, it would become the quality that most people would remember about him. Prelates and diplomats, waitresses and kitchen hands, opera stars and housewives, the Dalai Lama and the nun who cleaned the sacristy, were all treated the same way — with a loving friendliness and unobtrusive courtesy that expressed a powerful belief in the dignity of every human being. Many people would be puzzled after meeting the cardinal for the first time. "He seemed as though he were impressed to meet me," they would say. Michael Cooke and James Gannon had left their mark on the personality of the future cardinal.

The other great influence in the cardinal's life (perhaps one more reminiscent of the stories of Flannery O'Connor than O. Henry) was Aunt Mary. Mary Gannon was not a gentle Irish colleen like her sister, but a witty and determined single woman whom life had given a tough vocation and who fulfilled it with total dedication and absolute faith. To appreciate the role of this remarkable woman who embodied the selfless dedication of so many single Christians we must move on.

The Bronx

Little did the old Dutch Calvinist farmer named Bronc ever dream that his farm on the edge of civilization would give its name (spelled in an art nouveau form) to the first step of upward mobility to millions of Catholics and Jews — and many Protestants as well. The Bronx, an unusual form of a proper name with a definite article before it, shares this linguistic eccentricity with other Dutch names like "the Hague" and "the Hook." The extensive neighborhoods of the upper Bronx became filled with thousands of modest homes on tree-lined streets far away from the roar of the elevated trains and the society atmosphere of Manhattan. By united family efforts, hard work and frugality, the Cookes moved to the Throgs Neck section of the northeast Bronx in 1926 to the parish of Saint Benedict, conducted by the monks of Saint John's Abbey, Collegeville, Minnesota. The Cookes fell under the influence of Father Laurence Schmidt, who would be a support to the family and to young Joe and Terry, who would eventually leave for Saint Joseph's Seminary from this suburban home. Those who attended Cardinal Cooke's episcopal ordination recall that he introduced Father Laurence to all the clergy. The three children would be educated by the Dominican Sisters of Blauvelt, New York, and the names of Sister Anthony, Sister John Dominic, Sister Virginia and others would become household words for the Cookes during the next half century. At Saint Benedict's Terry received the sacraments and became a very active altar boy. It was here he thought of becoming a priest. His sister recalls that, as a youngster, he got involved with many playful pranks and developed his lifelong sense of humor. As a result he once got a grade of sixty percent in arithmetic. A visit by Mr. Cooke to Sister Anthony quickly followed.

All seemed to be going very well for the family in its slow but consistent rise up the ladder taken by almost all immigrants. Then in 1930 something happened to Terence Cooke that is the worst thing that can ever happen to a little boy.

His mother died apparently of peritonitis leaving behind in profound grief her husband and three children, ages nine to thirteen. The young father, supported by his extended family on both sides and deeply rooted in the faith and piety which had withstood tragedy for centuries, responded in the only way he knew how. He communicated to his children that somehow with God's help they would get through this terrible darkness. Even this tragedy would not overcome them. With the help of God, things would work out.

The three children cried together with their father but in the midst of their tears a message was written into the mind and heart of the bright little boy: "Even this will not be the worst. God knows best and God will see us through. God's will be done." This lesson remained at the center of the life of Terence Cardinal Cooke. It colored everything he did, inspiring his motto as a bishop: "Thy Will Be Done." It stayed with him in difficult years as archbishop, guiding him through years of terminal illness. It was on his lips as he lay dying and it echoes in the memory of those who knew him. It was the spiritual message given to others by his life. The reader may be thinking this is not a very original message. As old as Abraham, it has been reiterated millions of times even by the martyrs of the twentieth century. This message of confident acceptance of the divine will and the belief that

God will bring good out of evil is called in Christianity the *Doctrine of the Cross.*

This ancient message needs to be reaffirmed in every age, not only by words but by example, especially in our time. In the case of Terence Cooke, this message, the hope that had guided the disenfranchised and persecuted Irish people for four hundred years, was passed on by a gentle chauffeur to his three mother-less children on that dark day which must have seemed to a little boy like the end of the world.

Father Laurence who had cared for her during her illness offered the funeral Mass for Margaret Cooke. Life got started up again with a lunch after the burial. Soon, along with Aunt Mary and Uncle Jimmy, Uncles Peter and Pat moved in with the little family.

Decades later the cardinal would tell Sister Anthony she had been a mother to him.[7] He would tell Katherine, his sister, how much she did for him in the years after their mother's death. Joe, his brother, became an admired big brother and guide. However, the most important person to emerge in this situation was Aunt Mary.

Mary was everything that an Irish working girl was supposed to be. She worked hard at Wanamaker's Department Store where she earned her living and a bit more to send back to Ireland. These Irish working girls were tough, deeply religious, and at the same time street-wise, careful with their hard-earned money, but generous to the Church. The Cathedral on Fifth Avenue was sometimes referred to as the glory of the Irish working girl. The fearful challenges of immigration, the fact that many of the Irish boys stayed at home to care for the family farms while their sisters went to America, Canada or Australia to earn their living and send something "home," all came together to create a kind of woman whom everyone respected and whom perceptive people loved in spite of their toughness.[8] Mary Gannon was one of these. When she left her job at Wanamaker's and with no fanfare took up the task of rearing her sister's three children, she accepted it as a part of God's plan for her. She was very different from her gentle, retiring sister, Margaret. Although she only came to live with the Cookes after Margaret's death, she was a friendly and outgoing person and got to know everyone in the neighborhood quite soon. She had an opinion on almost every subject and expressed it freely to those who would listen. She apparently was a bit of a "cross" for Michael Cooke to bear, but one he received gratefully, knowing he could not keep his family together without her help. She was generous, self-sacrificing and demanding all at the same time. She insisted on what she thought was right and she was usually correct in her assessments. Although she was afraid of no one, there was apparently only one person she would not take on — her nephew, Terence. One has the impression the bright little boy, always thoughtful and polite, was more than a match for Aunt Mary.

The boyish pranks for which Terry had a reputation stopped after his mother's death. It was a time of profound grief for the little boy. Sleepwalking episodes made it necessary for him to move his bed downstairs where he was safer. The boy grew closer to the Church and spoke always of being a priest. He conscientiously studied to be an altar boy when this required recitation of Latin prayers and a hint of semi-military precision. While he was studying for this a characteristic episode took place. Since no full-fledged altar boy had come, Father Lyons asked the apprentice Terry to light the candles for Mass. He lit all fourteen of them and was bursting with a proud sense of accomplishment, then the monk explained only two were necessary.[9] Those who knew the cardinal in later life will recognize a familiar characteristic: enthusiasm to do the best job possible. Throughout his life he was a stickler for details, making sure everything was handled properly and courteously until the day he surrendered the care of the archdiocese to his vicar general, Bishop Joseph T. O'Keefe, the day after he learned he was soon to die.[10]

Cathedral College

Upon graduation, Terry followed his brother Joe to Cathedral College, a high school and two-year junior college with a strong liberal arts curriculum to prepare young men for the seminary. The boys commuted every day by bus and subway. Joe was more carefree than his brother and would often go through his weekly allowance prematurely. Terry would remind him and his sister that they should learn to manage their money better. An able administrator was in the making who would keep the archdiocese both solvent and extraordinarily supportive to the poor.

In the summer, like most "junior seminarians" Terry would have a full time job. He worked for Berger's used furniture store on Third Avenue and 146th Street in the Bronx. He was a conscientious worker and learned quickly to be a good businessman. Mr. Berger grew to treat him as a son and Terry remained a close friend of the family for many years.

Terry's classmates at Cathedral College remember him as someone energetic and completely loyal to the school and its regulations which by today's standards were severe. He enjoyed sports and school activities. He edited the student magazine, *The Chimes,* and played the violin. [11] Letters he wrote to priests at this time show a young man who saw life in optimistic and uncomplicated ways with a blend of street wisdom and naiveté. [12] Terence Cooke followed the rules of life with little or no difficulty and related as well to older people as he did to his peers. When an adult, these qualities would leave him at times puzzled by the complex feelings of others who lived with complicated emotions of love and hate. Though he learned to cope with people who did not share his uncomplicated vision of life, he never quite understood them. He found it difficult, perhaps impossible, to really think ill of someone, even someone who disagreed with him and hurt him. The following talk, given to the Alumni Society of Cathedral College when he was sixteen years old, although written with a boyish simplicity, is remarkably consistent with his attitudes forty years later.

> When we love God perfectly we love Him above all things because He is infinitely good in Himself and this is the kind of love to which we should aspire. Imperfect love of God, on the other hand, is had when we love Him for His favors and benefits to us.

> Both in our mental appreciation and in our voluntary resolve, God should stand above all the rest not excepting father and mother. Love of God is a principle of moral perfection. When persecutions were and are going on, the thing which burns in the hearts of the martyrs and strengthens them against all kinds of pain is the beautiful and supernatural virtue of the love of God. Missionaries go to foreign lands to spread the word of God because of their great love for Him. The love of God draws millions of people all over the world to church on Sundays and weekdays to worship God and to talk with Him.

> When Christ came on earth after the people of the world had waited for centuries and centuries, He taught the Golden Rule (Do unto others as you would have them do unto you.) Our Lord gave many examples of love of neighbor, no demand or plea went unheeded. Our Lord gave us the command that we should love our neighbor, "A new commandment I give unto you: That you love one another as I love you, that you also love one another." Love of neighbor is the way of acting towards our neighbor. We must respect his rights, his possessions, his life, his honor, his dignity, and his home. When our neighbor is in need we should assist him as we would a brother. We should not do anything to harm or injure our neighbor, but rather we should do everything to help him. Our love of God is not a true one unless we love our neighbor, for God tells us clearly that the

least thing we do to our neighbor we do to Him. Whosoever sees in his fellowmen not the human peculiarities, but rather the God-given and God-like principles is really the one who loves God and his neighbor.

Our Lord urges us to forgive our enemies, to be reconciled with them, to assist and love them. Christ Our Lord, has given us a supreme example of love of neighbor by His mercy and kindness to the sick, the crippled, and the afflicted. Why can't we follow His example?[13]

To readers of our day this talk and several like it may suggest an age of innocence gone by. The war had not yet begun. Hitler was a name most people did not take very seriously or perhaps even recognize. America was coming out of the depression. The complex view of life which characterizes the young people of our era was practically unknown when figures like Pat O'Brien, Shirley Temple and Tyrone Power were the popular conveyors of cultural values. In New York City everyone had his place and few people protested about the place assigned to them. They all wanted to rise and there seemed to be an opportunity for all to rise somewhere.

We see another side, however, of this idealistic and apparently naive young man, one that deepens our appreciation of his awareness of conflicts and problems quite beyond the scope of his own environment. In his senior year of high school in 1938, Terence Cooke wrote a fine, perceptive essay called, "Meet General Smuts." It was about the South African leader who had been a more progressive governor than many of his fellow Boers. The following revealing paragraph which could have been written fifty years later, gives us insight into the development of a man we know from his long concern for the plight of people of every race.

To my mind the most interesting and powerful thing in South Africa is how the government is going to treat the blacks and what the blacks are going to do about it. Government by and in the interests of the whites alone has not saved them and shows signs of ending in still worse disaster. The blacks are definitely a part of the whites, and segregation is impossible. Sheer domination may serve for a season — for twenty, fifty years, maybe more, since Union, native self-consciousness has grown as it never did in a century preceding. The blacks must have a secure place in the country, peacefully and easily at once, or later by violent contention. Their problem cannot be solved at a blow, or without their own help. However, we shall see. [14]

The Seminary

Wearing the traditional black suit, white shirt and black tie that identified the seminarian of the times, Terence Cooke went off with his classmates from Cathedral College to Saint Joseph's Seminary in September of 1940. Although this was an occasion for the Cookes, it was not a noteworthy event beyond their little circle. Almost every parish in the city had several young men attending the seminary at the time. The huge old building dominating the hill in Yonkers had stood firmly on its foundations for fifty years. It served notice to all who passed by on the new parkways that the Catholic Church in America was here to stay and that its priests were going to have the education and scholarship they had been deprived of by the persecutions and revolutions of nineteenth century Europe. The old seminary, like a veteran school teacher, received the new class but scarcely took notice of it on a campus already crowded with almost three hundred seminarians.

Far away from the pleasant green hills of Westchester County, the first sounds of war were shaking the foundations of industrialized and enlightened Europe. The naively-held belief that scientific progress and technological achievement were inevitably going to bring a more civilized world was being blasted away as the armies of the Third Reich invaded Poland and much of the rest of Europe. Men were learning painfully that science and progress without morality can be very destructive. The preceding years in New York had been marked by the arrival of terrified Jewish refugees who told incredible tales of religious persecution in Germany. The Nazi-Soviet Non-Aggression Treaty had been signed by Molotov and Von Ribbontrop, leaving much of the New York Jewish community bewildered and deeply frightened. The United States teetered on the brink of war for two more years while the Holocaust and the enslavement of much of Europe went on.

Years of Destiny

Other momentous events preceded the quiet entrance of the entering class of 1940 into the seminary. In September of 1938 the gentle and kindly old Archbishop of New York, Patrick Cardinal Hayes, had died.[15] This distinguished and charitable man was the only ordinary the seminarians had ever known. He epitomized the Catholic position in New York. The archbishop was no longer expected to be the controversial defender of the down-trodden as the first archbishop, John Hughes, had been. With the financial success of some of the earlier Catholic families, the increased representation of Catholics in triumphant Democratic politics, and the success of the labor unions, the Church no longer had to fight for existence. It merely had to continue to grow. Schools, charitable institutions, social agencies staffed by a growing army of religious sisters, brothers and priests, and well staffed parishes all suggested that a Catholic prelate maintain a dignified silence except on purely religious and moral issues. This Cardinal Hayes did, and he was appreciated for it.

In 1940 the needs of the times were different and the men

who would be called to fill these needs would be different too. Deeply troubled by the situation in Europe and highly critical in two encyclicals of the rise and activity of the Fascists, Pope Pius XI had died on February 10, 1939. When he was succeeded on March 2nd by Pope Pius XII a new era in the history of the Church began. [16]

The character of this remarkable man had been forged in the struggles of a family which had remained loyal to the Church in the face of fierce anti-clericalism. He by no means saw the office of pope as simply presiding over the Church. Pope Pius XII, although a man of his times and steeped in the conservatism of the loyal Catholic aristocracy of old Europe, would open up in the Church deep questions and powerful currents. These would effect the everyday life of the young seminarians who donned their black cassocks in those fateful days.

Another event which profoundly affected the life of Terence Cooke had occurred on April 12, 1939. Auxiliary Bishop Francis Joseph Spellman of Boston was appointed to succeed the late Cardinal Hayes. He was a very different kind of man for very different times.

Cardinal Spellman, as he was to be known after his elevation to the College of Cardinals in 1945, was one of the most important influences on the life and spiritual development of Terence Cooke. "The Cardinal," [17] as he was better known in and around New York, worked incessantly. He was personally modest and even self-effacing, loved by some, including Terence Cooke, respected by many, feared by his enemies and often maligned by his critics up until the present time. The memory of this astoundingly dedicated and prodigious worker has been besmirched by John Cooney in recent years. [18]

Such attacks deeply pained and distressed Cardinal Cooke, who knew his predecessor better than anyone else. No one ever said Cardinal Spellman was a saint, including Cardinal Spellman. Terence Cooke knew him to be a hard working and dedicated servant of the Church, a devout man, a more than able administrator and a staunch supporter of the country that had provided personal freedom and economic opportunity to millions of European immigrants. Cardinal Cooke also knew him to be a shy and somewhat lonely man in his old age. Like many people, he needed someone to care for him, and Terence Cooke sought nothing except the satisfaction of doing so. Later, as the cardinal's secretary, Terence Cooke would even decline dinner invitations on Sunday evening, his only free time, so the old cardinal need not dine alone. [19]

The enthusiastic and vibrant young man who walked down Seminary Avenue in 1940 with his brother and his classmates from Cathedral College was probably not thinking anymore than anyone else about the new pope and the new archbishop. He was probably thinking and praying about the storm that was breaking over the world — the storm that ominously began to resemble what people still call "The Great War."

The Cookes were members of the new middle class, many of whom were generally so concerned about their own survival that they had few resources or time for concern about the people right behind them on the ladder of upward mobility. The Cookes and many other devout Catholics were different. For motives that were primarily religious, they were concerned for others. Despite his own obviously devout and unworldly ways, Terence Cooke was both involved in social concerns and deeply aware of the danger that ideological and social conflicts could generate.

Young Terry was much involved in Casita Maria, a pioneer outreach program established as a youth-oriented service agency for the newly arrived Puerto Rican community in New York. Casita Maria continues to develop programs in cultural heritage, indigenous leadership training, family counseling, and high school drop-out prevention. Cardinal Cooke, one of an illustrious line of bishops, priests and religious who at one time served as counselors and teaching volunteers at the Casita, always highly regarded these vibrant volunteers as an important facet of the life and faith of the Church of New York.

During the summer and fall of Terry's first year in the seminary, the United States was daily drawn closer to war. It is difficult for younger readers to realize the underlying fear people had on the eve of America's entrance into the Second World War. The Allied powers suffered almost irrevocable losses during the first months of the German attacks. Entire countries, many devoutly Catholic, had been swallowed up in a few weeks.

The war with Japan, somewhat unexpected by most people, began with the attack on Pearl Harbor in 1941. Three powerful nations — Germany, Russia and Japan — stood poised against the Allies. Hitler had made it clear that his war on the Jews would become a war against Christianity and all religions. In several speeches, Hitler claimed that among the crimes of the Jews was the crime of establishing Christianity and giving Christ to the world. More and more, the Nazis were openly espousing a bizarre kind of Nordic paganism, a sort of revival of the ancient gods.

As one of the scholarly students of this era, Dr. Joseph Lichten of B'nai B'rith, has observed, these were most dramatic times in which it was difficult for anyone to accurately assess what was going to happen even within the next few days.[20] The Christian world was largely in a state of confusion and horror as the first photographs came through of the demolishing of synagogues and churches in eastern Europe.

Every thinking New Yorker considered the possibility of the war coming to his doorstep. The city was actively preparing to be bombed. The attack on the Church of Poland left little doubt that the Dark Ages had returned and that Christian clergy, religious and laity might have to suffer for their faith.

It is not surprising, then, that the possibility of persecution and martyrdom captured the mind of the young seminarian. Thirteen years before Terry went to the seminary, on November

23, 1927, a young Jesuit, Father Miguel Augustin Pro, had been martyred by a firing squad in a Mexico City police station.[21] Pro was a dynamic young man who had become a seminarian and a priest in secret because of the religious persecution of the Mexican dictator Calles. The following description of Father Pro, written by Terence Cooke, reveals much about the seminarian, his own self image, and his ideals. Almost prophetically, it also suggests the development of his attitudes toward sickness and death. When writing of Father Pro, the young seminarian reveals himself:

> Soon after he joined the Society of Jesus, his natural gaiety became supernatural, when even his brother novices became discouraged the incomparable Miguel came forth as the joy-maker. Yet under the mask of his laughing countenance he endured the first attacks of that mysterious illness that was to be his constant companion to his death. His passionate love of life was conditioned by his love for man and most of all by his love for God. Father Pro's love for man was exemplified by the long awaited day of his ordination and in the eventful days of his priesthood. When he received the Sacrament of Holy Orders on August 31, 1925 his only wish was "to be of use to souls." His illness did not seem to be an impediment to a fruitful priesthood; three operations came immediately after ordination. Calles had thrown his country into the turmoil and battle of persecution. A reign of terror existed because terror was the only weapon he had to consolidate his position. The Mexican people bravely fighting for their faith cried out for the aid of their priests. Father Pro did not fail them. Broken in body though he be, he compelled that body to perform every religious and charitable and educational activity.[22]

After describing the daily exploits of Father Pro — well-known throughout the world because they were so remarkable — and his many escapes from the secret police, Terence Cooke asks the question,

What was the secret of Father Pro's extraordinary love for life and man; it is this and nothing more — his love for God. From the day when he made that stirring retreat — a retreat that changed the whole course of his life — an ever-deepening love of God enabled him to love life and man more deeply. In his simple childlike faith he loved life because God made life. He loved man because God made man and in life and men he saw a reflection of the glory and majesty of his first love — God. Why did he endanger his own life by attending the sick, caring for the poor, teaching the Word of God, ministering the sacraments and celebrating Holy Mass? Why was he willing to die for his fellowmen — the answer is simply this — he wanted to lead souls to God. This was the man who now faced the savage wrath of the modern Nero, Calles. This was Father Pro, St. Francis of the twentieth century — whose sickly body bursting with the passionate triple love of life, man, and God radiated strong courage and Christian faith. [23]

Terence Cooke was deeply moved by the description of the execution of Father Pro and by his final words, "Hail, Christ the King!" He was also deeply moved, as was the Catholic world, by the twenty thousand people who, in the face of religious persecution, attended the burial of Father Pro.

Very few things will give us a better insight into the spirituality of Cardinal Cooke than his own description of Father Pro: idealism, youthful joy, vibrancy, concern for others even in the face of illness and danger. The spirituality of the young Terence Cooke was not what people ordinarily consider a contemplative spirituality. It was not based on a profound inner recollection or awareness of the Divine Being in the center of the soul. Although he was a very loyal member of the Third Order of Saint Francis and wore the cord and scapular of that Order for many years after he left the seminary (sometimes to the amusement of others), Cardinal Cooke never expressed any desire to be a monk. [24] He was very much a man of an active and joyous and outgoing spirituality.

Terence Cooke's admiration as a young seminarian for Miguel Pro probably tells us more about him than anything else. At times it was disconcerting when Cardinal Cooke visited a Jesuit community and announced to everyone he was really a Jesuit at heart. One can be sure this reflected not only his profound respect of Father Pro and a number of the Jesuit heroes whom every young Catholic American boy admired in those days, but also his own personal outgoing and energetic spirituality. He was definitely someone who loved life, loved human beings, and loved God. These qualities were apparent in his early twenties. They deeply marked the letters he wrote while he lay dying in the archbishop's residence in that "grace-filled" time before his death.

CHAPTER TWO

THE FORMATION

The Seminary Years

*T*he Second World War loomed ominously over Terence Cooke's time in the seminary. Those in school in the United States during those years will recall the war was ever present and yet far away. Every aspect of life was deeply affected by the war effort and by constant apprehension over the fate of loved ones overseas. During the first three years of the war the possibility of a victory by the "Axis powers" was on everyone's mind.

For the devout, and certainly for Terence Cooke, the war meant a time of constant prayer and petition for peace. Even before the outbreak of hostilities, the Nazi's presented such a diabolical picture to the world (a picture that later proved to be true beyond all human imagining) that for religious Americans the war became a sort of holy war, a crusade. Even the breaking of the Nazi-Soviet Alliance in 1941 and the Allies' unexpected joining of forces with the atheistic government of Soviet Russia did nothing to dispel the religious fervor of American Catholics.

Patriotism is at its best a blend of fortitude and loyalty. These virtues shone brightly in the eyes of young men and women wearing khaki uniforms as they marched in long somber parades down Fifth Avenue. Clergy of all denominations supported the war effort as a holy cause. No one was more consistent in his support, nor more involved personally in assisting the cause than the Archbishop of New York, Francis J. Spellman. The influence of Cardinal Spellman's loyalty to his country and enthusiasm for its democratic government would do much to shape the thinking of the young student who would be his successor.

The Nazi atrocities, the unbelievable dimensions of the Holocaust, the enslavement of whole nations in eastern Europe and in the Far East, the persecution and murder of hundreds of thousands of people because they were clergy, religious or dedicated laity — these became known at the end of the war, and verified that indeed this war was not only a just war, but a battle against evil. The forces under Hitler were so inhuman, so contrary to nature and humanity, so devoid of all decency or human feeling that history passes an ever more severe condemnation upon them.

Like almost all Americans, the young seminarians at Dunwoodie prayed both for peace and for victory. Those who would criticize Cardinal Cooke in later years for his loyalty to his country and accuse this gentle and peaceful man of militarism might do well to remember that his formative years were spent during what almost all would admit was a just war. Even though his ideas about war changed over the years, especially during the conflict in Vietnam, the cardinal would always see the men and women who went into conflict as brothers and sisters trying to defend human rights. But he would see the military personnel on the other side, the enemy, as well as the ordinary people who believed what they were doing was right, as brothers and sisters too, no matter how much they had been deluded by the sinister forces which led them. Cardinal Cooke had a rare capacity even in the midst of conflict to see the enemy with a human face and recall that he was also a child of God.

While the war raged on, Terence Cooke continued to study diligently as a seminarian. His classmates and friends from the seminary all agree he was a conscientious, hardworking and enthusiastic student. For several years he was in charge of the seminary bookstore, a fairly large operation serving the needs of almost three hundred students. Having learned the retail business at Berger's Furniture Store, [1] he now put to good use the talents which later made him an excellent fiscal organizer. Several important people in the business world would comment in later years that the cardinal would have made a first-rate financial manager.

According to his classmates, Terry was not one to question the system. His home and family background suggest he accepted authority and felt a personal obligation to support it, even when authority was not used as well as it might be. While not possible to find among his fellow students any who criticized Terry for his acceptance of the seminary system, there were certainly those who could mix loyalty with criticism, and even with the touch of ironic cynicism for which New Yorkers are so well known. While Terry did have a comic sense of the absurd, it never went so far as to be severe or cruel. Considering the mix of ethnic humor that blended on the sidewalks of New York to create its awesome street-wise comedy, Terence Cooke would have to be described as a very mild-mannered citizen of the "Big Apple." He was also most personally committed to trying to make "the system" work rather than tearing it down. Perhaps his attitudes toward authority both civil and ecclesiastical, would be best epitomized by this sentiment typical of so many immigrants: "America has been good to us. It has given us a chance we did not have in the Old World. Let's work together and make it better."

This attitude toward the country and even the Church was dominant in the America of the 1940's and 1950's, and it was totally consistent with Terence Cooke's personality, upbringing and seminary training. He would be a source of controversy in the late 1960's and early 1970's when this very attitude would become for some an idea to be rejected, mocked and even ridiculed.

In the eyes of all observers Terry Cooke was a fine seminarian. He kept the rules, worked hard, and was friendly in a quiet
sort of way. Each year he immensely enjoyed working with
children in summer camp. He loved to set up recreation programs, take youngsters to the park, direct athletics and keep his
eyes open for the poor kids who fell behind. Both priests and
laymen who were seminarians at that time laugh to recall stories
of the Badger Camp in New Rochelle and other programs for
children where Terry took the lead in organizing things with
humor and fun.

He also continued his involvement in the Casita Maria after
he left Cathedral College. The Casita was now thriving because
the Hispanic population was growing. His volunteer work began
an involvement with the Hispanic community and lasted to the
very end of his life. Little did the young Irish-American volunteer
realize his efforts at the Casita Maria would lead him to be
honored in a special way. *El Diario,* the Spanish language daily
newspaper in New York, carried on its front page the headline,
"Adios, Amigo," accompanied by his picture in a beautiful engrav-
ing the day after his death.

Anyone interested in the spiritual life of the cardinal must
now look beneath the surface and ask, "What made this young
man tick?" Was he simply a good natured conformist with little
inner spiritual depth? He has been described as the ideal type to
be an eagle scout, which he was not, or a senior altar boy, which
he was. Was there something more?

A Priestly Way of Life — Sacrifice

One of the future cardinal's classmates and very close
friends, Monsignor Edward Dugan, responded to questions
about his inner life by saying, "We did not talk about such things in
those days; all of this was kept very private."[2] Fortunately, we do

have the private notes of the young seminarian, Terence Cooke. These notes were written for himself and are not unlike the notes that many literate seminarians of the time might have written. They reveal an intense, totally honest, idealistic young man who saw his life as an act of service to the crucified Savior, the most important and real influence in his life. The most interesting thing about these notes is that they suggest the shape of the spiritual life of a man the world came to know as Cardinal Cooke. While many people have high ideals in adolescence, only few will consistently hold on to them through life. These thoughts of the young seminarian will consistently define his expressed attitudes and behavior for decades to come and will characterize his response to the monumental challenges life had in store for him.

The young Terence Cooke saw himself struggling on the road to perfection. In 1942, citing Archbishop Alban Goodier, S.J. and Cardinal John Henry Newman, two English spiritual writers, as well as the Belgian hero, Cardinal Mercier, we find the following revealing notes:

Methods of Perfection

Goodier — lose yourself in God — simply trust entirely
Mercier — submission to the Holy Spirit
Newman — do the work of each day perfectly in accomplishment and motive, these are necessary to do the will of God.

The essence of the plan of perfection is to take the will of God and make that the standard of your life, "I want God to make me." Although the spiritual life is simple we must not exaggerate its simplicity. The spiritual life can be summed up in these notions.

On the way to perfection —

1) we must trust ourselves less and trust God more
2) the Holy Ghost will give us the gifts of courage, wisdom, and fortitude

3) on every way I can go toward perfection
   "In the beginning it was written that I have come to do
   thy will, O Lord."[3]

In another set of notes, probably written in the same year,
we read the following words which, to those who knew Cardinal
Cooke in later years, seem to have a prophetic ring. They
express many qualities which the cardinal would later display in
his own life.

Sanctity - Perfection

1) we must have a desire for perfection
2) we must contradict our weakness with God's strength
3) we must trust in Him

Our desire must be an efficacious one, ever conquering all
obstacles. Our desire must be supernatural in motive. This
desire for perfection should dominate all my actions.
Perfection should be the pearl of great price for me. My
desire for perfection must be uniformly persevering. The
quest for perfection must begin now and continue until
death. The spirit of sacrifice must be eternally ours. Just
like Isaac, we must prepare ourselves to be sacrificed on
the altar of God.[4]

The reader can envision an earnest young man of twenty-
two, the somber atmosphere of war around him accentuated by
the discipline of seminary life, with his strong conscience and
powerful Irish-American super-ego. We can picture him sitting at
his desk in his black cassock, writing words which would be
challenging even to a cloistered monk. Few around Terence
Cooke suspected that he was taking the spiritual life so seriously.

Things were not easy for the young seminarian. His closest
friend at this time was his brother Joseph. He-had followed Joe
into the seminary, and when his brother decided that the priest-

hood was not for him it was a keen disappointment to Terry.[5] However, characteristically he accepted his brother's decision with total graciousness and continued to be his closest friend until Joe's death in 1973.

Perhaps the person who knew Terence Cooke best was his close friend, Father William Reisig. He tells of long walks around the seminary grounds when they would talk about "life, politics and the war."[6] Although Father Reisig recognized his high ideals, he would say it was only in later years that they spoke "about themselves."

The following note written in December of 1943 suggests that the man who would suffer so bravely later in life was already beginning to feel the brand of suffering.

The Virtue of Fortitude

In the beginning of training a novice — fortitude is required more than humility — said the founder of the Carmelite Order. Fortitude is a moral virtue making man willing to undergo dangers of life. It hits a medium between the fear that paralyzes and the recklessness that makes us foolhardy. We can show fortitude by patience. When troubles come our way, we should not immediately tell our neighbor, seeking consolation. It is better simply to say more to Jesus Christ. Fortitude is also shown in perseverance. Fear of failure or fear of being alone often inhibits us in the service of God. There is a danger as a man approaches the priesthood — that he might fear being alone. We are never alone, Christ is with him to help him along the way. Another feature of fortitude is a willingness to admit failure. It requires heroic courage.

You want to be a priest — then you must die to self and live for God. On ordination day — you lie on the floor of the sanctuary — offering yourself as a victim to be immolated; as you move to the altar you receive the chasuble the

priestly vestment — signifying charity. The priest must be
a man of charity. As you touch the chalice of salvation so
also you must also drink the chalice of suffering in your own
life — you will offer with the bishop your first Mass. Just as
the consecration takes place you must change and become
like Christ. In the Mass the priest is also a victim.

The very theme of the priest's life is sacrifice. He follows a
master who sacrifices — he feeds on sacrificial food. Sacrifice must be something instinctive to him. The priest
cannot be like the rest of men. He who offers the Mass must
imitate Christ. [7]

This strong emphasis on sacrifice as an element of the
Christian life has diminished in recent writings on spirituality. As
the foundation of the piety of the nineteenth and early twentieth
centuries, it was the school in which Cardinal Cooke was formed.
It was not only deeply linked with the suffering of the Catholic
immigrant people before and after their arrival in the United
States, but it was also something the great spiritual writers of the
times focused upon.

Those influenced by contemporary spirituality, which tends
to be more "positive" and focuses on the Resurrection, will find it
hard perhaps to appreciate the sacrificial element in the spirituality of the young seminarian. Sacrifice is a word which means to
make something holy by giving it to God. It implies pain and
suffering, but also implies joy and fulfillment. The sacrifices
parents make for their children are often seen as joyful ones. As
Our Lord Jesus says in the Gospel, "When a woman is in travail
she has sorrow, because her hour has come; but when she is
delivered of the child, she no longer remembers the anguish, for
joy that a child is born into the world" (John 16:21).

Thus, despite its being out of vogue, the sacrificial element
in Christian spirituality is very much rooted in the Gospel of Jesus
Christ. Again, Our Lord says, "If any man would come after me,

let him deny himself and take up his cross and follow me. For what will it profit a man, if he gains the whole world and forfeits his life" (Matthew 16:24-25).

The French school of spirituality which sought to reform the life of the clergy before and after the French Revolution was highly focused on the idea of the priest as a sacrificial victim in union with Christ. In no popular figure was this sacrificial nature of the priesthood more clearly embodied than the humble French curé, Saint John Marie Vianney. In his seminary days, Cardinal Cooke acquired a small statue of John Vianney. This would accompany him along with the crucifix and a statue of the Blessed Virgin Mary all of his life. The statue of the sacrificial curé, who gave himself to God unstintingly despite his limitations, would be standing on the little night stand in the cardinal's bedroom when he died.

The idea of priestly sacrifice which he developed in his seminary years would stay with Terence Cooke all his life. It would color every aspect of his priesthood, and make the last days of his final illness into a beautiful gift of courage and prayer to God, for the people whom he loved and served.

The Heart of a Young Man

The contemporary reader who has been exposed to popular psychology may find the following revealing passages difficult to appreciate. Popular psychology has tended to use such naive and "positive" formulations that the central ideas, or heart, of Terence Cooke's spirituality may appear distasteful and even neurotic. The reader is warned not to take our own historical moment too definitively. Our very positive and supposedly humanistic time will pass away too and soon come to be considered just another period itself.

Older readers may find the following passages either pleasantly nostalgic or deeply aggravating. It would be most helpful to the reader to recall that these passages were written in time of war, after a severe economic depression, and in the atmosphere of an immigrant Church which had led people to bear their real sorrows by an imitation of the crucified Savior. There are not wanting, even in the behavioral sciences, those who would see such a devotional life as more genuinely reflective of the human condition, and more functionally useful, than a naive and overly optimistic religiosity which ultimately denies many real aspects of the human condition.

Before reviewing the following notes found in the papers of Cardinal Cooke, it is also important to bear in mind they reflect the thinking of the spiritual directors of the seminary at that time, Monsignors Francis Shea and John Dougherty. These dedicated men, along with others such as Monsignor Daniel Dougherty (brother of John), had served as spiritual guides and directors of an army of priests and seminarians over the years. They epitomized a piety tough in its demands and yet kindly in its presentation. They had very clear and definite ideas of what it meant to be a priest. They saw the clergy as simply the successors of the apostles and their collaborators. Priests were to be in the world, but not of the world. They were to be totally dedicated to the work of the Lord. Every aspect of their lives was to be defined by that identity — even recreation. To emphasize their point the Dougherty brothers in later years even ran their own summer camp for priests and seminarians, Clairvaux, in Stowe, Vermont.

To understand Terence Cooke, one must understand this very special approach to Christian spirituality, which was given an added dimension of priestly piety and propriety. His roots reached into difficult historical eras — into the experience of the Irish clergy in the penal days, into the piety of the reformist French clergy before and after the revolution, and even back to the experience of the Italian clergy at the time of the Catholic

Reformation. Names like Saint Oliver Plunkett, the martyred Irish bishop, Saint Vincent de Paul, and Saint Charles Borromeo, the reformer cardinal of Milan, were very familiar to seminarians and shaped their ideals. The young contemporary Catholic can hardly imagine the power, the self-confidence, and in this case, the total dedication that flowed from this piety. Many who knew it regret it has all but disappeared.

The following note on spiritual reading gives some idea of the seriousness with which Terence took his responsibilities.

Picture:
Saint Ignatius sick in bed doing his spiritual reading.

Purpose:
1) to strengthen our sense of duty, reveal the processes of sin and clarify our steps in following Christ
2) unless a priest is interested in his own soul he will not be interested in saving other souls
3) for something to be real it must be organized into one's life[8]

The message is clear — not only has one to read, but one has to make this reading a vital part of life. This required courage. The lay reader may wonder why courage is necessary for a clergyman. In any sub-culture, including the clergy, the power of the group process may cause the individual to deny reality, to accept mediocrity and to minimize the effects of the call of grace. Nothing illustrates this better than the Gospel itself. Courage is necessary for anyone seeking to accept the inspirations of grace. Terence learned this lesson early. He sought to be unmoved by human respect. He repeated to himself:

What God thinks is what counts. Hold fast to the principle. My life must be guided by principle. Courage requires detachment from trifles. Show courage by persevering in the task that is assigned to us.

Motto — "It shall be done." Courage overcomes the excessive fear of failure. It makes men men when the job is to be done. We must have stout hearts and strong souls. [9]

One is inclined to smile at an almost boyish attitude toward the struggles of life, although his ideas are absolutely sound. The lines were, after all, written by a very young man who would someday show great courage in the face of terminal illness. Taken by themselves they could suggest an almost shallow self-reliance and optimism — like Nelson Eddy singing "Stout Hearted Men." But there was always the other side. In a meditation for the Tenth Sunday after Pentecost (in the old missal) Terence writes,

> Tomorrow is the Feast of Blessed Humility. This is the basic virtue. In the Epistle, "no one can say Jesus is Lord save by the Holy Ghost." The Pharisee was the personification of pride. Prayer — May Jesus lift pride out of our souls.
> 1) A proud man has no real friends or friendliness. He does not have the charity of Christ. Pride turns one's gaze inwardly — one is self sufficient. We must cooperate with one another by prayer.
> 2) He (the proud man) disrespects others. Do not make odious comparison. God has given us sufficient grace. Forget self.
> 3) The proud man is always involved with externals, not internal things. Christ called them "full of dead man's bones." This is a possibility in the lives of each one of us.

The Humbling of the Publican

Jesus humbled Himself — in the crib, on the cross, in the ciborium. (St. Bernard)
1) Humility shows us our place.
2) A person realizes his dependence upon God and his debt to God. God does not need me, I need Him.
3) A publican makes no comparisons. [10]

Beyond these serious attempts at understanding humility there is another theme beginning — The Mystery of the Cross. Here the real values of the mature Terence Cooke begin to emerge out of the boyish piety of another era.

Monday of Holy Week

The way of the Cross is the only way to God. "It is impossible to get to heaven in any other way than that by which Jesus trod — the way of the Cross."

St. Teresa — "to suffer or to die"

St. John of the Cross — "to suffer and to be despised."

Sickness is the touchstone of character — enduring pain without complaint and accepting God's Will — is a way to sanctity.

Prayer is something that can make us more like Christ.

Discouragement — after sin. Have confidence in God. Lift the cross and say, "O crux ave, spes unica!"

How to bring the cross into your life?
1) By limiting type and amount of food you eat on fast day.
2) A shortening of sleep.
3) Deny yourself of some legitimate pleasure.
4) Do extra work. [11]

As Terence made progress toward the priesthood the tenor of his meditations and reflective notes bears the strong marks of Monsignor John Dougherty. This dedicated man was referred to at times as "John the Baptist" because of his tough and practical theology. Terence, on the eve of his ordination to the sub-diaconate, took the following notes, probably derived from Monsignor Dougherty. It is interesting that in later life these very practical suggestions were a consistent part of the entire demeanor of the cardinal.

January 25, 1945 — Practical Suggestions —

You can help your people only if you get to know them.
These things cannot be subordinated to your recreation.

Drinking makes the priest a problem to himself and to
everyone else.

Close friends should only be priestly friends, but do not
spend too much time going around visiting. The fewer lay
people that you have for intimate friends the better. People
know where you go. Do not have favorites in the parish and
thus cause scandal to others.

January 25, 1945 — Afternoon Conference —

Learn the lesson of humility, do not be self-centered. Can't
we ever come to the point of giving everything to God? Let
God work through you — forget yourself. Let God work in
you. [12]

It may strike the reader that the image of the priest that
emerges from these reflections is one who would be distant from
the laity. Everyone who knew Father or Bishop or Cardinal
Cooke knows he was open, engaging and most friendly. He
obviously had many friends and enjoyed them all. The fact is when
he took time off for relaxation it was almost always with his old
friends from the seminary. Even for Cardinal Cooke, what little
relaxation he enjoyed was with fellow priests and members of his
own family.

The most frequently repeated theme in the personal spiritual
notes of the young seminarian as he approached the priesthood in
1945 was humility. He did not see this elusive virtue in any abstract
terms at all. Terence's idea of humility and his living of it were very
practical and much related to people in the real world.

Humility is perfected by submission to almighty God.
Prayer helps us to acquire it. Practice of humility can be
animated by an internal spirit of humility.

1) Attitude towards superiors — they are God's representatives and we should overlook their imperfections

2) Attitude towards equals — defer, submit to the judgment of others

3) In our relation to those who are inferior in some way — never lord it over them, be a servant to all, keep in mind who you are — a man subject to sin, never publicly reprove an individual — if possible, you are to save souls and not to show off authority

4) Don't live richly, keep your furnishings simple, don't be fastidious about your appearance, always be neat and clean

5) Have a candor in your speech, don't just go around with a tendency to put others in their place, be yourself — in the sense of posing something you are not, better still, be Christ-like

6) Practice external positions which are not showy, less of self and more of God, if you have humility of spirit it shows itself clearly in your external demeanor. [13]

If ever there was a consistent personality trait of Terence Cooke it was a friendly, deferential manner to all. It would mark his life every step of the way. How many people would say, "He made so much over me and I'm a nobody." No one was a "nobody" to Cardinal Cooke because everyone was important to God. If people were in an inferior situation, he saw them as inferior only in some unimportant way. He saw all stations of life, all signs of importance or unimportance, as entirely relative. The absolute was that the individual was a child of God.

A person who believes this is very vulnerable in a world where people can be forceful, competitive and demanding. How does a person who is striving to be humble in the terms described above manage to cope with the arrogant?

The following account drawn from a letter of testimony

reveals that thirty years after he wrote the above resolution, Terence Cooke was still pursuing humility.

During the height of the Vietnam war Cardinal Cooke went to Fordham University for what was thought to be a typical ordination ceremony. It was anything but typical. The ordination Mass proceeded as usual through the rite of ordination itself and the vesting of the chasuble. When it came time for the greeting of peace from the cardinal to the newly ordained, two of these new priests would not greet the cardinal. One of them walked over to the lectern and stated that he would not offer "the peace" to Cardinal Cooke unless he resigned as the Military Vicar. The other priest also said something to the effect that "I too have difficulty making peace with war." The cardinal stopped the ordination ceremony at that point and attempted to explain his own views on the military ordinariate. After that he walked towards the two newly ordained men with his hands extended to offer the peace to them. [14]

But one must look even deeper than the conscious efforts of humility. After all, even these efforts can arise merely by imitating the behavior of significant persons in one's life. The spiritual director or psychologist must not be impressed by mere efforts; he is looking for values.

On retreat before being ordained a deacon, Terence wrote the following lines. While they reflect a very traditional spirituality, they are also strangely similar to the famous discourses of Sóren Kierkegaard, the Danish spiritual writer and philosopher almost unknown in the Catholic Church when Cardinal Cooke was a seminarian.

> God and Myself. Recollection is of paramount importance. We need silence of the tongue and heart. In your resolutions forget the past. Give yourself completely to Christ and see what He will do for you.
>
> Recollection — finding out what's wrong with me

Order — arranging things according to one plan, that plan is the Will of God, Christ is the mediator, He squared His human Will with His divine Will

Repair the past. Prepare for the future. Get the intellectual realization that you have gone wrong in the past, but that you hope you are going to go right in the future

Meditation — The Blind Man, "Son of David, Have Mercy On Me . . . Lord, That I May See." Lord, let me see myself as I really am . . . unless we make our human wills subordinate to God's will we will find no peace. [15]

Ordination to the Sacred Priesthood

Terence Cooke completed his training in the seminary in December of 1945. It seemed to many this time was the beginning of a brave new world. The war had ended and people prepared for a time of peace and prosperity. The United Nations Organization had come to New York and its charter was proposed as a promise of universal peace. Victory had been achieved in the summer and people everywhere in the United States were getting back to a normal life. There were many signs of gratitude to God — the "good guys" had won for a change, even if hanging over all their victories was an ominous mushroom-shaped cloud.

Terence and his classmates were ordained in the Cathedral of Saint Patrick on December 1, 1945 at the hands of Francis Cardinal Spellman. A photo of the occasion shows a thin, very serious looking priest in the old-style vestments. His sister, Katherine, recalls that he was very ill that day with "the flu" and had some difficulty getting through the three-hour ceremony. [16]

Perhaps his illness explains why no notes or reminiscences can be found in his papers. His ordination card included a picture of the crucified Lord with the caption, "Today, you will be with me in paradise" — the Lord's words to the dying thief.

Looking at the drawn, serious face of the young priest kneeling at his ordination Mass, one may speculate that the temporary sickness was a sign of things to come. Most of the years that Terence Cooke spent in the priesthood were marked by illness. In a meditation made the previous May, the deacon warned himself, "Don't exaggerate your difficulties."[17] Then, he cited the inscription from the Massachusetts School for the Blind, "Obstacles are things to be overcome." The years in the seminary had not been marked by great obstacles. In fact, as the saying goes, he had sailed through. But his own ill health and the difficulties of the decades following the war would indeed prove obstacles to overcome.

Prayer, recollection, the pursuit of humility and charity to others — these words, so difficult to accomplish but so easily spoken, served as the ideals of the newly ordained priest. He saw life ahead as "a spiritual combat with himself." The following lines written in the year of his ordination sum up this battle for him.

> Holiness is an essential requisite for a priest. The holiness of a priest's life is the necessary means for the conversion of many. "Let your light shine before men." Imitate what you teach. If we offer an oblation daily yet offer no oblation of our own life, we fall short of our calling. A priest must be holy. Humility is the foundation of all virtues. Jesus said, "Learn of me because I am meek and humble of heart." We are free men only when we are free from sin.
>
> To be free from sin, we must be humble. Worldliness always seeks self and it is satisfied with our own horizons. All the virtues are grounded in humility. Humility is a virtue which reveals the truth about ourselves and God. It implies knowing the truth about ourselves and about God. The greater virtue we have, the greater is the danger of our pride. We forget the source of all goodness in our life is from God. When we are all pleased with ourselves, pride walks in. If we have accomplished anything worthwhile it is God working in us. The spirit of always putting our best foot forward to get places has no place in the priesthood. We must be Christ-centered rather than self-centered.[18]

CHAPTER THREE

THE YOUNG PRIEST

Difficult Beginnings

*F*ather Terence James Cooke had been temporarily assigned to Saint Thomas the Apostle Church and Our Lady of Mount Carmel Church, both in Harlem. While there he was notified on December 11, 1945, by Archbishop Spellman that he had been scheduled to go on to post-graduate study at the University of Chicago, beginning with the spring semester. A note attached to a carbon of Archbishop Spellman's terse letter, and apparently written in his own hand, reads, "Terence Cooke very capable. Good all around ability. Good student. Chosen for post-graduate work. Did very good work in catechetics."[1]

It sounded like a promising ecclesiastical career was to begin — not that this would have meant a great deal to the young priest. But the cross was waiting for him at Saint Sabina's Church in Chicago, where he was welcomed by the cardinal archbishop, Samuel T. Stritch. A severe eye condition which had begun in the seminary grew acutely painful in Chicago. It made it impossible for him to read.[2] By January 18th he had returned to New York, and on January 22nd was assigned by a kindly letter from Archbishop Spellman as temporary assistant at Saint Athanasius Church in the South Bronx.

Although it was almost impossible for him to read the words of the missal, Father Cooke was happy at Saint Athanasius. At that time this was a thriving Italian-Irish parish under the care of the popular and devout priest, Father Joseph Mastaglio. These years brought in a trickle of Hispanic Catholics who had been moving into the parish. Saint Athanasius is now a center of urban renewal in the Hispanic South Bronx. As one would suspect, Father Cooke immediately was involved with the CYO and with other parish activities. In a brief basic biography published by the Chancery Office in 1978, the following paragraph appeared.

> He has since maintained a personal interest in his first parish, seeing in it a microcosm of the large shift of white parishioners to the suburbs and the influx of Black and Puerto Rican Catholics into urban parishes. Throughout his pastoral and administrative work he has paid careful attention to social and demographic movements looking to the assimilation of new members into parish life. [3]

But there was another side, a hidden side, to Father Cooke's activities as there had been in the seminary. For many years there had been on a tranquil hilltop in Saint Athanasius parish, a convent of cloistered Dominican nuns. These enclosed sisters had chosen for their vocation a life of prayer and intercession for the clergy of New York. Since the convent was dedicated to the perpetual adoration of the Eucharistic Presence of Christ, it was called Corpus Christi Monastery. Almost immediately the convent became a haven for the young priest whose cheerful ways disguised his painful and dangerous eye condition. The older sisters recall that each week on his day off, he offered Mass in the quiet chapel and spent the rest of the morning in private prayer before taking the subway north to visit his father and his aunt in Throgs Neck. [4]

Throughout his life Cardinal Cooke had a special love for cloistered sisters and a special relationship to this convent. Among his personal effects are several beautiful medieval-style illuminated cards and scrolls made for him by the nuns of Corpus Christi. Years later he would direct this author to initiate a center of spiritual development for the archdiocese at a convent of cloistered sisters (in this case Blessed Sacrament Convent in Yonkers), so that the work would be sustained by the intercession of the dedicated religious whose apostolate was prayer for the Church.

One of the sisters at Corpus Christi recalls that the young priest was so friendly and devout that she recommended to him a man who was having some questions discerning his vocation.[5] The man was grateful to receive his help and is still a religious brother today. Since his eye symptoms continued, Father Cooke was transferred after a year to the chaplaincy of Saint Agatha's Home for Children in Nanuet, New York, conducted by the Sisters of Charity. This large facility for children without parents or homes profits to this day by the impact of Terence Cooke's presence, according to Sister Rose Mary Commerford, who was the administrator at that time.[6]

Sister Rose Mary recalls that Father Cooke arrived in March of 1947 and left in September of that year. The former chaplain, an older man, had provided basically a sacramental ministry. Resurrecting his old skills as a camp director, Father Cooke immediately organized a summer program for all students that included trips to amusement parks and cultural sites, as well as on-campus activities.[7] He made himself available to the staff, supported the administration in effective ways and managed not to be a busybody with all of this. In fact he remained a friend of several staff members for years. The children at Saint Agatha's Home some thirty-five years later are still enjoying some of the summer programs that he initiated.

Recovery and on to Social Services

While doing all this Father Cooke was visiting the Knapp Eye Institute under the care of Doctor Raymond Pfeiffer. Dr. Pfeiffer found that corrective lenses were the solution to his visual problems. He improved so much that in late July he was assigned to Catholic University School of Social Work in Washington, D.C., where he attended classes the following September.

Long after his eyes returned to normal, and in fact for the rest of his life, Cardinal Cooke would remember a severely handicapped friend who had offered her suffering for his recovery. With his help this remarkable person, Ruth Arreche, founded the Fordettes — a prayer group of severely handicapped people who met for prayer and mutual support.

Terence Cooke no doubt had mixed emotions about his transfer since he was so obviously enjoying Saint Agatha's. He was now part of the Catholic Charities Staff, and the letter of assignment was signed by the Executive Director, Monsignor Patrick A. O'Boyle, who was later to become the cardinal archbishop of Washington.

On October 31, 1947, Terence Cooke wrote to Monsignor O'Boyle the following letter, which was very characteristic of his enthusiasm and his concern for others.

Dear Monsignor O'Boyle:

Everything is going well at the National Catholic School of Social Service. Our weekly schedule consists of two full class days and three days in the field. The courses that I am taking at present cover some of the basic areas of social work. My field work assignment with the Bureau of Rehabilitation in Washington presents many opportunities. The assignment that I have gives a whole view of the field from the standpoint of a non-Catholic agency. This should be helpful for the future. Our main work is with prisoners, many of them quite young. Case social histories are prepared and plans of adjustment with their families are worked out for the purpose of parole. Last week I enjoyed a visit to the National Training School. Our school is attempting to give the best social techniques grounded on sound scholastic philosophy . . . I would like to take this opportunity to thank you for your kindness to me. It has been very encouraging and very helpful.

Somewhat aware of the great responsibility that is yours, I assure you and your work a daily "memento" in the Holy Sacrifice of the Mass.

Respectfully yours in Christ,
Terence J. Cooke [8]

After a year it became clear to the faculty of the School of Social Service that they were dealing with an outstanding candidate. The dean, Monsignor John J. McClafferty, wrote to the new director of Catholic Charities, Monsignor Christopher J. Weldon, later bishop of Springfield, Massachusetts, the following:

Dear Monsignor Weldon:

You will recall at the Wednesday evening dinner, I mentioned to you briefly that our faculty member in case work, Miss Lucille Corbett, thought that the Reverend Terence Cooke manifested unusual knowledge and skill in the social work area of case work. At this time and in this letter, I wish to give you, verbatim, the observation of Miss Corbett, who is Father Cooke's case work instructor.

". . . Father Cooke has demonstrated unusual ability in understanding the case work process and extremely rare skill in practicing it. In other words he is a 'natural,' which is not often met within case work practice. I, for one, am reluctant to see him go into group work his second year, but as he is to be assigned to youth activities in the diocese on completion of his course, that will be indicated — unless this decision is reconsidered. Father Cooke is very ready to accept his superior's decision as to where he is to be placed and expresses himself as equally interested in group activities as in case work."[9]

Monsignor Weldon wrote a memo for review on March 29, 1948, concerning Father Cooke.

I saw Father Terence Cooke today and spoke to him about his assignment. He indicated a willingness and a genuine interest in the assignment to group work which I proposed to him so that he will major in that. He does understand, however, that he is to take some courses in administration and that he is not to narrow himself down too much to the field of group work.

He impressed me as having a very sound approach to the whole situation and aside from a willingness to accept any assignment or "take orders" with regard to his future, he was intelligently cooperative in discussing his personal responsibility in carving out that future. He acknowledged the developing importance of the group work field and we discussed in particular the Catholic responsibility in New York as of the present moment.

I discussed with him his financial situation and informed him that as of the 1st of April his monthly stipend would be reduced from $75.00 to $50.00. He felt that he could manage on this successfully. I further instructed him that if he ran into financial difficulties he should not hesitate to bring them up with me and we will discuss the matter further. [10]

This last statement suggests that indeed we are talking about a very dedicated man. The reports of the impact of Terence Cooke on the Catholic University School of Social Work are not difficult to summarize because they are so uniformly positive.

This was in fact a springtime for social work and for a religious involvement in the behavioral and social sciences. The bright young man with outgoing ways and a kindly manner made a profound impression. His intelligence made his impact more substantial. Rather than trying to summarize this impact, it might be best to cite the following observation made by Professor Dorothea F. Sullivan in 1969 at the request of Mrs. Charles Ridder of the *Catholic News.*

Terence Cooke — Graduate Student 1947-49

Those of us who were at the National Catholic School of Social Service, Catholic University, during the two years Father Cooke was a student quite well recall as one of his outstanding characteristics the ability to establish easy relationships with those whose lives he touched.

Faculty, fellow students and clientele recall the young priest as one with whom it was a pleasure to talk, never overbearing with clients nor subservient with faculty, he carried himself with grace and distinction.

In his academic work he made a signal contribution to the field of social work when he selected as a topic for his master's thesis "Thomistic Philosophy in the Principles of Group Social Work." Faculty members felt that this research would make a distinctive addition to the professional literature written from a Catholic point of view, but perhaps no one foresaw what a wide readership it would have. In the spring of his first year of study Father Cooke made plans to interview knowledgeable social workers from coast to coast during the summer vacation. (Many students talk about collecting data for their thesis during the summer but not all get around to it.) He set himself a demanding schedule which he carried through to completion before the academic year opened in the fall.

It is customary in schools of social work to publish the titles of the master's theses among the various schools and it is permissible to borrow the document from one school to another on inter-library loan. As soon as the title "Thomistic Philosophy in the Principles of Group Social Work" appeared on the list, requests for inter-library loans came so frequently that the Catholic University Press decided that the thesis should be printed in off-set form. This is routine for doctoral dissertations, but a great rarity for master's theses which many regard as "an exercise in research" and not a significant contribution to the body of knowledge. As the copies became available for purchase, faculty members in other schools armed themselves with it, particularly when they went out to work in other countries. The readership was by no means confined to Catholic institutions. Schools of social work in Europe wrote for copies and schools in South America translated it into Spanish. There is little possibility of accurate measurement but it would not be hazardous to state that it had the widest distribution of any master's thesis written in a school of social work. The topics dealt with in the thesis include the ultimate basis of human group formation, group membership and group process, cooperation and competition, democratic atmosphere and democratic goals, the social group as a training ground for virtuous living.

Father Cooke traveled from coast to coast to interview leading social group workers in his collection of data. Few of these were Catholics but all were cooperative, and interested in his scholarly approach. In all probability they still remember the zealous student, and rejoice in his current elevation. [11]

As soon as Father Cooke returned to New York he was appointed to the youth division of Catholic Charities. He had to fill out a questionnaire in which he included the following items:

Special Interests — parish work, religious instruction,

youth work, day and overnight camping, music, sports and reading

Ambitions — to be a Christ-like priest working effectively for souls through Catholic Charities and my other assignments [12]

He was assigned to live at the Cenacle of Saint Regis, 62 West 140th Street in Manhattan. This was a retreat house conducted by the Sisters of the Cenacle. Here he made friendships with the sisters which would last all his life.

His schedule was a busy one and he often went to meetings until late at night. He was mothered by an older lay sister of the community, Sister Seraphina. Many of the retired sisters tell stories of his dedication, humor and spirituality. Sister Elizabeth White, who is now retired, recalls that having him as a resident and part-time chaplain was a special privilege and a source of much help for the sisters and the retreatants. [13]

We get a glimpse of Father Cooke from two people who knew him at that time. The staff member in charge of finances at CYO, Mary Bierbauer, writes that "it didn't take much time to work with Father Cooke because he was so alert and informed." She continues, "Father Cooke was very considerate to the staff and knew when they needed help or any sympathy. My mother was very ill at the time and he was exceptionally kind — he visited her at the hospital many times. He was very good to me at this time and even brought me home the Friday before Mother's Day and gave my mother his blessing. I retired in 1967 but always remembered him. Cardinal Cooke inquired about me even after I retired and remembered me every Christmas with a card." [14]

Another woman, Barbara Johnson, who had to leave the Dominican cloister because of illness, reports that Father Cooke got a job for her at Catholic Charities when she left the order. He was also her counselor and spiritual director during very difficult months of readjustment. She recalls that Father Cooke, at the

Catholic Charities Christmas party, secretly taped the whole staff
singing "Rudolph, the Red-nosed Reindeer." He then played the
tape, to the staff's great amusement. Most of the people had
never before heard their own voices on the newly invented tape
recorder. [15]

Father Cooke was also a part-time assistant at Saint Jude's
Parish in upper Manhattan. He coached baseball and basketball,
counseled young people and organized things in the newly established parish. He also began a seven-year stint as an instructor
in the Fordham School of Social Services. His thesis from
Catholic University continued to be very popular. Father Thomas
Lacey of the CYO in Oakland, California, wrote,

> Your book has been studied, re-read, underlined, kicked
> around and quoted. I've done everything except the build-
> ing of a shrine . . . Terry, you are the first CYO man I've
> ever met who recognized the fact that other people outside
> the field of group work have good ideas. You're certainly the
> first one to point to St. Thomas and say, "Okay, clerical
> wise guys, if you don't believe me look at the master." [16]

When Father Cooke came to the Department of Youth
Activities he was assigned as assistant to the director, Monsignor
Harold S. Engel, who also resided at the Cenacle. The memories
of Monsignor Engel provide insight into the character of the
young priest. The picture is one of consistent and total dedication
and of phenomenal activity.

Monsignor Engel describes his experience, "Since we lived
together at the Cenacle, I could not understand how he kept his
busy schedule and yet found time enough to prepare for the next
day. At the Cenacle, at night, he would always be doing work.
Every single evening was in preparation for the following day. He
would be preparing talks, drawing up schedules, filing reports.
He worked unceasingly at his job. To me, it was a wonderful thing

to have someone so faithful and conscientious in my department."[17]

Although he was very busy with his work, he took on new activities. It bothered Father Cooke that the only place for young adults to meet was in bars. He organized and ran a dance for singles at the Hotel McAlpin every week. These dances went on for years and led to many happy Christian marriages.

Despite all this activity, Monsignor Engel remembers two very important things about his assistant. "I never had an experience where I saw him angry. He was such a humble person that somehow he always knew what to do at the right time."[18]

Monsignor Engel also recalls that Father Cooke easily integrated the social and spiritual aspects of his work. It was not always easy to coordinate social and recreational activities with spiritual goals. Monsignor Engel felt that the future cardinal could do this because the spiritual life was the center of his existence. The celebration of the Mass was the focus of his life and activity. According to his former supervisor, this was recognized by all who knew him well.

There is a saying that if you want to know what someone is like, you ought to ask his boss. Monsignor Engel, who died in 1988, summed up his long experience with Terence Cooke in these touching words, "I could place complete trust in him. I have no recollection of ever having to correct or admonish him for what he did. He was one of the most faithful assistants that anyone could ever have or hope for."[19]

A Question of Motivation

We return to the question — what was behind this excellent performance? Was it simply a need to excel, to avoid criticism? Was it ultimately simply a kind of compulsive neurosis — a workaholism as it is called — with no other foundation than the satisfaction of knowing that one has done a job well? Was it simple ambition, nicely tailored in a clerical suit, but ambition nonetheless? Or was his motivation something deeper and more spiritual?

In this decade of remarkable activity as described by his immediate superior, Monsignor Engel, did Father Cooke manage to keep alive the idealism, the youthful spirituality that was reflected in his personal notes during his seminary days? Anyone who has moved in the clergy or religious life from the idealism built up by years of formation to the engaging activities of the apostolate knows that this is a decisive moment. It would have been very easy, very understandable for a person of Terence Cooke's energy and ability to lose track of the initial spiritual motivation of his life, and to replace it with acceptable but much more self-centered goals and ambitions. We could all forgive him for doing that because we have all done it ourselves, at least to some degree.

If Terence Cooke had done just this, if he had replaced the kingdom of God with the respectable kingdom of the Church, we would not be proposing his cause for canonization. In the lives of many Christians — clergy, religious and laity — there is a desire for the reign of God preached by Christ to take deep root in one's soul. This desire often co-exists with moderate ambition, a melancholy toleration of one's own sins and shortcomings, a willingness when there is a question of serious sin to "seek first the kingdom of God," but a willingness to make compromises in other situations. This is what decent religion is all about. Perhaps there is even a kind of second-rate virtue in persevering when one recognizes one's own mediocrity.

There are, have been, and always will be, in parts of the Church and indeed among many people, those who do not settle for less. They push on, as Saint Paul says, "toward the prize." They strive with all the vitality of youth, even into old age. We often dismiss their sincerity as naiveté, their zeal as fanaticism, their genuine holiness as a kind of sublimated narcissism. But we are wrong, and sometimes in the gray light of dawn we know that we are only deceiving ourselves to avoid confronting our own mediocrity. We deny the existence of purgatory even when we are in one of our own making.

We ask the question now about Terence Cooke — were his fervent ideals sustained or did they get lost in the maelstrom of a busy life, with all the positive ego-enhancement of youth work successfully done and appreciated? Are we studying another re-run of the myth of the Pied Piper — or the life of a holy man?

Fortunately in the papers of Terence Cooke, among summaries of lectures and sermons and some personal notes which he expected no one else ever to see, there are many indications of his real motivations and desires. The very private expression of Father Cooke's spiritual expectations of himself can be found in notes that he wrote only for his own consideration. The following document with multiple dates from June 1952 to June 1953 indicates what these expectations were during that very active year of his life.

Surrender to the Will of God

Jesus must be the life of my work. "I do not call you servants but friends."

1) Monthly day of recollection - Thursday before or after first Friday or Manhattan Day of Recollection

2) At least - a weekly Friday Holy Hour

3) Weekly Confession - Friday or Saturday morning, try to get a definite director

4) Anticipate Divine Office - after breakfast, before or after supper

5) Daily Schedule —
   a) Rising one hour before Mass for prayer and meditation;
   b) Holy Mass - Thanksgiving, Visit, Particular Examen;

c) Read Divine Office (as above);
d) Visits and Rosary - Chapel of Our Lady of Charity;
e) Prayers during the Day - Angelus, Aspirations, Rosary - Have the mind of Christ, good example, bring others to Christ, work for His Glory, for souls;
f) Evening visit at the Cenacle;
g) Spiritual Reading - after breakfast, if possible and in the evening;
h) Evening - Prayers, General Examen, Meditation Points [20]

This energetic schedule coupled with his statement of goals on "Surrender to the Will of God," not only suggests a life of committed virtue, but of vibrant simple faith in the midst of many activities. Terence Cooke was thirty-one years old and he had already been a priest for seven years. Later when he was twenty-three years a priest and forty-seven years old he made a similar schedule for himself on the stationery of the cardinal's residence. [21] As we will see this later schedule was even more demanding. Consistency was an important part of his spiritual efforts. The public expressions of these motivations are revealing in that they are a direct expression of the Gospel values without any apology or hesitation. Writing about the purpose of Catholic social agencies, Father Cooke said,

> The Catholic social agency realizes that man's ultimate objective is God, but frequently material and temporal problems are obstacles in man's quest for that ultimate objective. By assisting man with the material things and temporal problems, assistance is given in attaining his ultimate objective. [22]

Father Cooke had no hesitancy at all about comparing the function of a social worker to that of a priest.

> The social worker in a Catholic agency is a participant in the Church's apostolate in the salvation of souls. How does the

social worker differ from the priest? The priest ordinarily works for the salvation of souls directly: by administering the sacraments, preaching, etc. The social worker ordinarily works for the salvation of souls indirectly: by ministering to the temporal needs and by helping man with his temporal problems. The social worker cuts the strings of temporal obstacles so that man can be free to move more freely toward God. Man's temporal welfare is the proximate concern of the social worker; man's eternal welfare is the ultimate concern of the priest. [23]

Even in the 1950's such a direct expression of spiritual values in the field of social work would have caused some to snicker. In our secularized atmosphere of today, it might be dismissed as simply naive and pietistic. Without entering into the debate about whether such a view of social work as a "secular vocation" is accurate, it suffices to say that it does demonstrate how the future cardinal conceived of his own vocation and the vocation of the lay staff with whom he worked.

He goes on in the same article to reveal even more about himself. Writing of the opportunities of the Catholic social worker, he observes:

The motive of each act of the working day can be Christian charity — the love of the neighbor for the love of God. By this motivation, which is an act of the will (not the feelings or emotions), the entire day can be one great act of love of God.

Social work can be a very effective way of self-sanctification for the worker. If the worker sees Christ in every client, he or she will be working for and with Him constantly. Work will be supernaturalized: every act will be gaining grace from God; every act will be an act of virtue.

Pray for the clients. This will help the client, because the worker's prayer will call down God's grace and assistance.

Talking to people about God, about the cross; teaching the
client how he can sanctify his temporal problems, and how
he can advance his eternal welfare by bearing his temporal
sufferings and misfortunes. A life of voluntary actual poverty, under spiritual direction. [24]

In these very idealistic principles, especially the last, Terence Cooke is speaking about his own motivation. He is talking
about himself. He did all of these things, including living with
actual poverty. Even as Archbishop of New York he personally
resembled a poor man. His room was tiny, his recreation was that
which could be enjoyed by anyone of the middle-class, his
personal clothing most modest. While he had to be properly
attired for his job, his own personal items were simple in every
way. When this author collected his personal effects as part of the
cause of canonization it was obvious that one would have had
difficulty in getting rid of them at a yard sale. While not the
furniture and clothing of the poor, they were certainly of the
quality of things used by people who belong to what is called the
middle-class.

During his years at the CYO, Father Cooke found much of
his spiritual strength and expression in giving retreats and confer-
ences to religious sisters, especially to the Sisters of the Cenacle
and the Presentation Sisters at Saint Jude's Convent, where he
continued to help out. The following is an outline of a conference
for the Sisters of Saint Jude's. It reveals much of Terence
Cooke's own attitudes toward life.

Consequences of the Love of God

Kindness towards our fellow human beings. Kindness
should flow from a deep interior life, the real love of God. It
should flow from mortification, sacrifice and reparation.

When we are kind we place ourselves in the other person's
place. We begin where the client is — where the group is.

We take the time to hear the question before giving the quick answer.

When we are kind, as apostles of charity, we radiate goodness and joy. Kindness goes about doing good. We do this not sometimes but always with a sense of mission.

The more sick and the more painful it is for a person, the more we should be kind to that person.

The kind apostle of charity is easily approachable, inspires confidence by his appearance, manner, tone of voice. He realizes it is not easy for people to discuss their personal problems.

When the kind apostle of charity is worn and tired out he will still serve generously. To do this we must be detached and mortified. [25]

Outlining some themes of social work, Father Cooke wrote,

The only way to be happy in social work is to be truly kind. Kindness is for the selfless. There is nothing as selfish as a selfish social worker. Kindness makes us happy at our work. It gives us a sense of achievement. We are not in the work for what we can get out of it — we are in the work to become saints, serving Christ in others. [26]

The reader may wonder if all of this altruism is really a kind of people-pleasing, a kind of sublimated narcissism which leaves the person who practices it alone and detached. Father Cooke definitely was not heading in this direction.

Kindness permits us to help others, to form strong relationships with them. Our kindness helps them to be truly free, to become aware of their problems and to solve them. [27]

Long after writing his thesis and after years of toil and at times failure, Father Cooke could still write, "As a social worker we are apostles, apostles of kindness working with the mind of Christ under the protection of the Blessed Mother. We work as members of the Mystical Body, in a spirit of charity, gratitude and kindness."[28]

There was another side to this spiritual life of the future cardinal. Anyone who was as optimistic and generous as he was is bound to have disappointments and to suffer. The world is not an easy place for anyone who is as upbeat as he was — especially the world of a huge commercial port city such as New York.

In a talk called "The Forgotten Virtue — Hope," Father Cooke paints a picture of the other side of reality.

> There are many depressing facts that stare mankind in the face today — the growth of communism, the cold war, juvenile delinquency, family disruption, dishonesty in public office, inflation, tension, unhappiness, unrest. History will undoubtedly describe the present age as filled with anguish for a large portion of the human race, an era shot through with justifiable forebodings. There is a great need today for men to practice the forgotten virtue of hope.
>
> Hope is a theological virtue and we have an obligation to practice it. We have an obligation to foster hope in our own souls and in the souls of all with whom we come in contact.[29]

We can hear the young priest speaking to himself in the next line and unwittingly he reveals the source of his own optimism.

> The lack of conscience in this matter is seen in the fact that few ever confess faults against hope or examine themselves on it. Saint Paul startles us by saying, "We are saved by hope." This principle is applicable to every field of human endeavor. For example, a football coach and team, a metropolitan opera performer, a doctor and a man gravely ill. This is true in the natural and the supernatural spheres. We are most likely to accomplish our best performance

when we are relaxed, confident and hopeful. The basis of
our hope is the almighty power and infinite benevolence of
God. "To one who does what in him lies, God gives grace
always." "Grace is never lacking to a man of good will."[30]

After giving several biblical examples of hope — the centu-
rion, the blind man of Jericho, Simeon and others — Father
Cooke again reminds himself,

One common obstacle to the growth of hope is excessive
self-consciousness. We are too sensitive to the chance of
failure — the possibility of criticism and a host of petty
thoughts. A retreat master said one who keeps looking in
the mirror will find a good reason to become discouraged.
We should keep the eyes of our minds fastened on God —
trust in God. For example, Peter walked on the waters until
he became afraid. Our Lord gave us the Our Father. First
our attention is directed to Our Heavenly Father and then to
our needs. The first thing that is necessary is to praise,
thank and adore God.[31]

As one reads these lines on hope one can only think of this
same writer facing serious illness for nineteen years — nine of
those years living with a terminal illness. He had faced tragedy in
his young life with the death of his mother and of his aunt and her
three small children. He had already had some taste of illness. In
this talk on hope he suggests a practice which is all the more
revealing.

Another practice to develop hope is to study the unpleasant
and painful situations in order to discover in what way they
can be utilized as aids to progress. Remember the story of
the Jewish prince in Ben Hur imprisoned in the slave galley.
Our Divine Master went about doing good and encouraging
hope. Our Blessed Mother and Saint Joseph lived by hope—
Nazareth—Bethlehem—Egypt—Cana and Calvary.[32]

He then mentions one of the great classics of western spirituality, "Abandonment to Divine Providence," by Jean-Pierre de Caussade.

> If we are properly disposed we may count upon recurring grace at any time, in any place, amid any set of circumstances. We grow in holiness by first learning to see God in all things and then later by learning to see all things in God — who is both the center and circumference, the beginning and the end. Contemplate God and be at peace. [33]

Then Father Cooke quotes the famous lines of Saint Teresa of Avila, "Let nothing disturb thee, let nothing affright thee, all things are passing, God never changes."

Thirty years later, facing the certainty of a excruciatingly painful death, Cardinal Cooke could easily find the proper term for this experience. He called his terminal illness "a grace-filled time." That phrase had been germinating inside him for at least half a lifetime.

A Fateful Encounter

Monsignor Engel records one of those apparently unimportant moments which deeply affect lives and easily change the destinies of many people. The reaction of Terence Cooke to the outcome demonstrates that his heart was not set on anything other than serving God's people, especially the young.

Those who knew Francis Cardinal Spellman will unanimously attest that he was a shy man who disliked public appearances. He much preferred to hear a sermon rather than to give one. Nonetheless the Director of Youth Services finally persuaded him to make an appearance on television, which was still in its infancy. The whole enterprise was a bit chancy because of the cardinal's shyness. Father Cooke was placed in charge of the event and served as master of ceremonies. He explained everything to the studio audience and spoke directly to the television audience.

Monsignor Engel recalls, "He was doing such a wonderful job in his presentation, that is, his sincerity was so evident that I could not help but notice Cardinal Spellman paying a great deal of attention to Father Cooke. I know that that was the first time that Cardinal Spellman realized the ability of Father Cooke. After that meeting he started to 'move up the ladder.' "[34]

Terence Cooke was really not interested in "moving up the ladder." It simply was not his philosophy of life. He threw himself into whatever he was called upon to do. He obviously enjoyed doing it; in time he came to love it. It became part of him.

The following testimony of Monsignor Engel bears this out — to show how he loved his youth work, "I remember the day so well when Father Cooke came into my office and told me that the cardinal had just called him and appointed him as the procurator at the seminary. I must say that he was so unhappy to give up his youth work that he actually cried when he told me. That shows you what he thought of the work he had been in. I felt that Cardinal Cooke was always humble, right to the last day of his life. In all of his activities, I never thought that he took advantage of his position in order to get something. If it happened, I never noticed it. He showed nothing but great humility in all ways."[35] It is not easy for anyone to accept and live the challenge of Christ — "to seek first the kingdom of God." Paradoxically, it is all the more difficult for a cleric — for a priest or minister — because one's life and career are so closely joined with the kingdom of God. As Saint Augustine says, they are "inextricably intertwined."

In 1954 the Catholic Church in the United States — and certainly the Archdiocese of New York — was approaching the pinnacle of its prestige. It was also approaching the most turbulent and difficult years of its history. The man whom Providence would choose to be the shepherd in those difficult years struggled between his own preferences and his desire to follow the command of authority. He wept to give up not prestige or power, but the chance to be a Catholic social worker, a priest with endless kindness and indefatigable energy seeking to serve the youth of New York. Being procurator of the seminary, an elegant title for a business manager, was by no means as appealing as his work with youth.

It was probably the most painful sacrifice that Terence Cooke made in his whole life. He had offered to make it before, in 1950, when Cardinal Spellman had asked for volunteers for the military chaplaincy.[36] That task would have suited him better. In his adult life we know of only one other time when he wept openly because of an assignment. As we shall see, it was when he was notified of his appointment as the Archbishop of New York.

When Terence Cooke left Catholic Charities, he left behind him the vivid memory of his service and zeal, of his courtesy and hard work. The memory of Terence Cooke's contribution has not dimmed over the years. It is possible, however, to reach back in time to 1954 and to measure the powerful impression the young priest had made on his contemporaries. One of his fellow-workers, Monsignor James J. Lynch, writing to apologize for not being able to attend the farewell dinner given by the priests of Catholic Charities in his honor, writes the following,

> Your tremendous facility for being liked has drawn to you, as ambassador of Christ, the priests of the archdiocese and thousands of its youth. This coupled with your terrific drive and dedicated service has made you, the priest, a unique instrument for the furtherance of the great cause of charity. The reaction of the priests of the staff is gratitude, not for your service, but for the privilege of having served with you.
>
> Tonight you look around a room filled with warm and close friends who have a manly affection that will abide. As you leave you may take with you a full realization of the great amount of good you have wrought.[37]

CHAPTER FOUR

INTRODUCTION
INTO OFFICIAL LIFE

The new year of 1954 ushered in a new life for Terence Cooke — official life as a representative of the large Archdiocese of New York. His work with youth at Catholic Charities had mostly been in direct service and organization of activities on or close to the grass roots level. Although he officially represented the archdiocese at this level, he was delighted to be directly involved with coordinating spiritual, educational and recreational activities for young people. His former colleagues suggest that he knew full well that he was moving away from this direct pastoral involvement as he returned to his seminary in Yonkers.

During the three years that he was procurator of the seminary, he continued his part-time assistantship at Saint Jude's Church, although he certainly was not expected to do so. One suspects that he always hoped to return to parish work and to the direct service of people. In fact, he never would. But the desire was always there which had been expressed on a small card filed away among his papers when he was a seminarian — "I only want to be a parish priest."

Those who knew him well were always aware that even when he was cardinal archbishop, he preferred the role that demanded the friendly and engaged devotion expected of a young parish assistant. Sometimes, to the annoyance of clergy who take a more serious interest in liturgical propriety and homiletic elegance, he would speak to a congregation at a crowded function in Saint Patrick's Cathedral in a most informal way. During one of these dialogue-type encounters where the congregation responded to the cardinal's questions by clapping, a priest who is a distinguished liturgical scholar observed to this author, "I feel like I'm at a CYO camp." In retrospect that remark is quite revealing. Perhaps the cardinal himself wished that he were still offering the liturgy on a wooden porch at a camp for kids from the city.

The first office Terence Cooke held in what was then called "official life" in the archdiocese was the apparently tedious, demanding and possibly dull job of procurator of the seminary. He was in charge of the general maintenance of this huge stone building which was then over fifty years old. He had to purchase everything necessary for this thriving institution which was crammed with about three hundred seminarians. He also had to deal with its financial problems. His business sense, memory for details and energy enabled him to do this very well. Twenty-five years later, when new windows were being installed, the procurator at that time mentioned that they needed four hundred windows. The cardinal kindly corrected him, "There are four hundred and twenty windows." He mentioned that his successor had probably miscalculated because he forgot the twenty windows in the laundry.

Father Cooke enjoyed one phase of his work the most, and that was working with the seminarians, even in a limited way. He escaped from his desk to engage in sports with them, especially baseball. He valued the opportunity to counsel those who came to him and he enjoyed preaching occasionally in the packed chapel — although as most clerics know, there is no congregation more demanding than the faculty and students of a seminary. There must have been days that challenged even the bubbling, innate optimism of Father Cooke.

Perhaps only a cleric who has lived through the seminary experience can really appreciate the full impact of the following scene. The seminary chapel was then a grim place with dark oil paintings, tarnished gold leaf and dulled brass. (Cardinal Cooke made sure that he refurbished it before his death.)[1] The congregation was made up of New Yorkers, a tough cast of characters who work at never being impressed. It has been suggested that New Yorkers will submit critical reviews of the music used at the apocalypse. Father Cooke was giving a sermon on "Joy and Holiness." Only a very brave man could attempt that in the seminary, and in fact he gave this talk after he had two years to scout out the territory and win some support. The following outline is one that he made for this sermon in the seminary.

"I will go to the altar of God, to God who gives joy to my youth." These are the words with which the priest begins the Mass every morning.

When we see the expectancy of a parish — awaiting the arrival of a new pastor — we gain some realization of how much it depends on the pastor. If he is joyful, kindly, affable, approachable, they welcome him in return. Parishioners will come to Church with greater joy. Curates will co-operate with enthusiasm. Acolytes will trudge more willingly through the snow to early Mass. The janitor will shake the fire with more zest. The choir will try to sing in tune. The housekeeper will hum a song over the morning bacon and eggs. If, however, the pastor's greeting is a scowl, the people will hurry to pass him by . . . . The same process takes place when a new teacher arrives at school or when new officers are elected in an organization. Since an optimistic, joyful personality has such an effect on an organization, it might be helpful to give further thought to this matter.

Since your smile, your kindness, your friendliness affects people so much, that which gives rise to these qualities must be very important. These qualities come from a joyful spirit. The question is — are you an optimist or a pessimist? There are many amusing definitions of the optimist and the pessimist. The optimist looks at the oyster and expects a pearl. The pessimist looks at the oyster and expects ptomaine poisoning. The optimist has a positive and constructive attitude towards life — while the pessimist has a negative and destructive attitude.

A sunny disposition is a great blessing. Some people are born with it and others develop it. The optimist, who is a person with Christian joy, keeps his sunny disposition going strong.

Joy preserves and fosters optimism and averts pessimism. It is useful to virtue, useful in the transaction of business, useful in society, useful for all good things.

There is a difference between the moderate optimist and the exaggerated optimist. To be an optimist is not to be a Pollyanna who covers all the realities of life with a sugar coating — refusing to realize that life has its serious moments. (Example of the man who fell out the window of the tenth floor and as he came down past the fifth floor, he said, "So far so good.") To be an optimist is not to turn away from sickness, suffering and death or to refuse to talk about things that are unpleasant. To be an optimist is not to be careless or to muddle through things somehow. To be an optimist is not to let others make the effort and bear the burden of work and worry while we sit idly by. [2]

The reader can only appreciate how revealing — and not simply amusing — this quotation is by reading the next paragraph. These few lines will tell us of the consistency of Terence Cooke's spiritual principles and attitudes. They reflect ideas and traits which we saw previously in the idealistic young student at Cathedral College. In fact, they reach back to that terrible day when the young Irish immigrant laborer had to tell his three children that their mother was dead and that "somehow they were going to make it through." The optimism of father and son was based on a stripping away of self, a profound but simple spirit of self-transcendence.

> Optimism that is genuine is made of a tougher fiber. It has behind it courage, confidence and resolution. It is stripped of self, yet warm with the love of life and of those who live it — warm, most of all, with love for the Giver of life. The optimist is brave because he trusts in God. He is strong because he builds his viewpoint on God. He is cheerful because he has faith which throws light upon all things. He rejoices in the Lord. He is kind because joy and charity have a natural and supernatural tendency to overflow from the human heart and communicate themselves to others. [3]

If you, dear reader, are more inclined to pessimism and are annoyed by all of this, prepare yourself now for something worse. Father Cooke for some reason identified pessimism with discouragement. One could quibble with him on this point, but one cannot dismiss this particular optimist as unrealistic because he was in fact a very practical and informed man. There are people in the financial world who have said that his blend of optimism and practicality would have made him a millionaire many times over on Wall Street.

The next line of this sermon on what he calls pessimism is most revealing.

> Pessimism turns everything face downward and it ignores the best in people and things in order to find the worst. The pessimist is much too busy with his gloomy reactions to be sympathetic towards others.

> The story is told about a priest who built his philosophy of life on what he called the "Three Great Refusals" — refuse to be disappointed, refuse to be discouraged and refuse to be offended. This is worth thinking about.

We can help ourselves not become discouraged by refrain-
ing from wasting vital forces or worrying about things that
have gone amiss. A doctor knows how discouragement can
hamper the cure of a patient. Discouragement paralyzes
ability and self-confidence. It destroys efficiency. It hides
God's means and methods. It hides God Himself.[4]

Now if you are one of those people who believe that the
biggest difference between the pessimist and the optimist is
information, then you are definitely going to disagree strongly
with the following points in this sermon. (One can see several
people in Saint Joseph's Chapel back in 1956 squirming in their
seats when they heard the following:)

It is necessary to be of "good heart" if we are going to live
peaceful lives. The essential characteristic of a saint is
joyfulness. When we are joyful — we are peaceful, patient,
gentle and serene. This disposition shines from our eyes,
lights up our face and puts music in our voice.

Joy is a powerful means of drawing grace from God. "Rejoice in the Lord and He will give you what your heart
desires" Psalm 36:4. Joy implies trust and child-like submission to God. If we are joyful in our generous offering to God,
we will receive the grace to accept all things from the hands
of God and give Him what he asks. Joy is also a requisite for
true brotherly love. "How good and pleasant it is when
brothers dwell together in unity."

We must not be burdensome. My neighbor may bear it
patiently but I have no right to burden him with my
unfriendliness.

Joy is a requisite for the service of God. Neither Our Lord
— nor His service — nor the reward He promises gives
cause for dejection. To serve God is to rule. God loves a
cheerful giver. We can make every day a joyful day — by
rejoicing — by willing it. The will to rejoice is essential.

"Rejoice in the Lord always." The state of grace is not just a state of avoiding sin. It is a state of joy.

In our daily effort to be joyful, we might remember that a strong will discovers causes for joy, for example, God's many gifts to us. Joy is kept as holiness by means of a permanent attention to God's presence, constant performance of His will and a continuing union with Him in prayer. "The kingdom of God is within you." The kingdom of joy is within us.

In offering Holy Mass we have a reminder to be joyful. We are reminded that he who is joyful, remains eternally young as we say with the priest in the prayers at the foot of the altar, "I will go unto the altar of God, to God who gives joy to my youth."[5]

There is no doubt that in all of this Terence Cooke was revealing the sources of his inner strength. His optimism, his joy, his heartfelt friendliness, his love of others which was the hallmark of his private and public life were not a posture or even a good resolution. They were an integral part of his life. He was by no means a "hail fellow, well met." There was nothing of the public relations man in his friendly approach to people. All his life he believed that how he acted to others was how he treated Our Lord Jesus Christ.

A Personal Flaw?

This is perhaps the moment to raise the question of a personal flaw which many who knew and loved Terence Cooke thought they identified. It was a consistent tendency in the personality of a man who would become a cardinal to avoid controversy or confrontation. One close associate put it very well when he said, "He had no stomach for controversy." He rarely confronted people, and when he did it was obvious that he was very uncomfortable. Those who criticized his work as cardinal, both liberals and conservatives, will cite different situations when they believed that he should have been more forceful and confrontational. We will come to some of these situations when we focus on the last sixteen years of his life, spent as Archbishop of New York.

It may be wise at this time, however, to recognize in the frequently repeated themes of his sermons and talks that Terence Cooke was an innate optimist. He was not simply optimistic about things, but also about people. He found it difficult to conceive that a person might have bad motives, that someone could be impelled by hatred or revenge or mere cupidity. He tended to dismiss faults as human weaknesses. His training as a social worker taught him to try to talk things through. Perhaps he was even touched unconsciously with the thought that given a chance to be himself or herself, everyone would act decently.

This can be a dangerous way of thinking for any leader. It leaves one very vulnerable. Terence Cooke was saved from the worst dangers of his optimistic world vision by his own sense of sin and his theological commitment to the doctrines of grace, original sin and the need for redemption. He had grown up with people who accepted the fall of the human race, but who placed more emphasis on redemption and its moral consequences. The Cookes were simple people who tried to live lives of gentleness and honesty. Sometimes this caused Terence to forget Our Lord's reminder that "from within, out of the heart of man, come evil thoughts. . . ."

In a talk he gave to the Dominican Sisters at Blauvelt in 1961, he described the sisters who taught him at Saint Benedict's as "joyful, kindly, affable and approachable." He went on to say that their joy was contagious. "The priests went about their duties with greater enthusiasm. As altar boys we trudged through the snow to early Mass to find our cheerful sisters there before us. The joyful spirit of the sisters even kept Tony, our over-burdened janitor, in fairly good humor. Joy illuminated our prayers, works and deeds. The dedicated, cheerful life of religious will always be a factor in fostering vocations."[6]

Whether in the long run this optimistic way of looking at people should be considered a strength or a weakness is something that the readers will have to decide for themselves. The question is worth keeping in mind because Terence Cooke's friendly smile is of substantive importance for this spiritual portrait. This smile remained on his lips until the hour of death. His belief in joyous friendliness will account for what some have judged to be weakness. After his death, one bishop who ideologically did not have much in common with Cardinal Cooke commented to this author, "I missed him at the last bishops' conference. He was always there to give you a smile and to make you feel good about yourself."

The Presence of God

The secret of Terence Cooke's outward kindness and gentleness is revealed by these personal notes, written while he was procurator and later chancellor. Among his notes is another "Rule of Life." It is originally dated June 27, 1958, but it is renewed and re-dated each June until 1965. He begins this personal spiritual program with the following: "Special effort to live in the presence of God — to make Jesus the life of my work and to really surrender to the Will of God." He continued his resolution of the past, including his visits to the Blessed Sacrament, and ends with the words in Latin, "O Lord, make haste to help me."

Another little note is also very revealing of how he saw his responsibilities. It reads, "A challenge — to priests. Our flocks cry out — if you want me to be a saint — show me how by your example." In 1955 he writes this note: "Charity is the distinctive mark of the Christian life. This love is shown by gratitude, kindness and sympathy. We must always give thanks as Christ did in gratitude to benefactors, parents and teachers. Grateful for the opportunity that we have to serve others and exercise charity."[7] The peace and charity of Terence Cooke were founded on very deep convictions.

A Portentous Moment

On a Sunday morning in the early winter of 1957, Francis Cardinal Spellman came into the sacristy of the Cathedral to prepare for Mass. An assistant was waiting to vest him when the cardinal startled him by asking, "Do you think that Father so-and-so would make me a good secretary?" The priest agreed because the name suggested was that of a capable and intelligent man. The cardinal asked his assistant to please call the priest and ask him if he would come for an interview that afternoon. The cardinal then offered Mass, but at the end of the liturgy he said to the same assistant, "No, don't call Father so-and-so. Rather, call Father Cooke up at the seminary." Father Cooke was appointed the cardinal's secretary that afternoon.

This office required that he learn all the pontifical ceremonies and be able to guide the cardinal through these complex pre-Vatican II rites. It also required that Father Cooke meet and deal effectively with large numbers of ecclesiastical and civil dignitaries from around the world. He also had to elicit the cooperation of vast numbers of people in the service professions, from housekeepers of the austere residence on Madison Avenue to cab drivers and bell-boys around the world, because Cardinal Spellman was a man of world-wide interests and influence.

Terence Cooke did all of these tasks the same way he ran the summer camps and the seminary — efficiently, quickly and constantly. But efficient though he was, this office was by no means an easy position for him to fill. As a social worker, Father Cooke was accustomed to working with people. Now as the cardinal's secretary, he would not deal directly in the day-to-day affairs of people in need. Cardinal Spellman knew most of the important people of the world. He had crossed swords with some and was a powerful ally of others. He was really the first Archbishop of New York who had strong ties outside the Catholic community. The ecumenical movement had not yet arrived in the Catholic Church, and yet Cardinal Spellman cooperated with all who were interested in making New York and the world a better place to live. He built up a huge system of schools, hospitals and social institutions. He played an integral part in the acceptance of the newly-founded State of Israel into the United Nations. As we have already noted, despite vicious calumnies years after his death, Cardinal Spellman was a deeply dedicated priest whose personal life was above reproach. As he grew older he came to depend on his associates, including his secretary more and more. He relied on Father Cooke to know how to treat even difficult people kindly.

At Work in the Chancery

Father Cooke was elevated quickly through the two ranks of monsignor. His sister reports that he did not make much of these honors. When he was named "monsignor" he did arrange a dinner for his priest friends, but did not care to have it at a restaurant. He asked his dear friend, Sister Aloysius, to arrange something for them at the Carmelite Convent so as not to attract attention. He was appointed vice-chancellor of the archdiocese less than a year and a half after becoming secretary. Along with his many administrative duties, he was especially entrusted with encouraging ecumenical activities by working with Christian and Jewish organizations.

Three years later, in 1961, Monsignor Cooke was appointed
chancellor. This meant that he was in charge of the finances and
temporalities of the vast archdiocese, which at that time was at
the height of its prestige. Those who can remember that time will
recall that almost every week, and often twice a week, Cardinal
Spellman dedicated a new building — either a school, or a church,
or a hospital, or a religious house. Large numbers of young men
were entering the priesthood and virtual armies of men and
women were entering the religious life. Catholics were preparing
to move off the top step of the ladder and to enter as first class
citizens into the life of the nation, which up until that time had
been predominantly Protestant.

People spoke of the possibility of a Catholic president, which
did indeed happen, and an American pope, which did not. In the
late 1940's, people like Paul Blanshard and other critics of
Catholicism predicted that the Church was going to take over the
country. [8] That didn't happen either. It was a perfect time to be an
optimist, and Monsignor Cooke was the right man, in the right
place, at the right time — but it was a difficult place for someone
who was struggling to be a saint. Did he manage to keep the ideals
of his early years in the midst of all this activity and success? If he
did keep these ideals of humility, service, charity and love of God,
how did he preserve them? These are the most important questions in the study of his life.

Preserving Values and Ideas

The young secretary who entered the whirl of activities
around Saint Patrick's Cathedral — with its average of five or six
thousand visitors a day — was probably unaware that he was
being watched. At first he was one of the "low men on the totem
pole," to use a famous New York expression, garbed in his black
cassock and surrounded by monsignori and bishops in purple. At

Saint Patrick's Cathedral, as at any large place of worship from Saint Peter's in Rome to the Temples of Bangkok, there is a permanent government. It is made up of the people who provide the services necessary for the orderly carrying-out of religious worship. If they do their job well they survive for decades. They are all observers of the passing scene, which activity constitutes a suitable form of occupational therapy. Even if the New York equivalent of the fictional English butler, Jeeves, gives some of their secrets away, the members of the permanent government still manage to keep an unobtrusive eye on everything that goes on in Saint Patrick's Cathedral. They are perhaps of all mortal men and women the best reminders of the all-seeing eye of God.

One of the most noble of this tribe of sacristans, vergers, shammosim, ushers and Rosarians is Mr. Bernard Carroll, who since 1936 has kept things in order at Saint Patrick's Cathedral. Bernie welcomed Father Cooke with open arms not only because he had been his brother's classmate at Cathedral College, but also because he often borrowed the priest's old car. Bernie and Father Cooke had joined forces to make it possible for each priest on annual retreat at the seminary to offer his own Mass. Previously, the priests had to attend one liturgy. From the vast stores of the Cathedral, Bernie had gathered all the chalices and linens necessary to equip a hundred so-called portable altars.

Sitting in a little chapel off the sacristy, Bernie recalled many things about his friend, but the most important details for our portrait are the following.[9] Terence Cooke, from his first day at the Cathedral to his last liturgy there in August 1983, showed the greatest respect to the presence of Christ in the Holy Eucharist. According to Bernie, Father Cooke never entered or left the Cathedral without a prayer of adoration at the tabernacle. Bernie continued, "He was a wonderful example of what a priest truly is. The full essence of the priesthood came through his life and example day in and day out as I knew him. He was an inspiration to me. You could be out in the woods with him, and him in a pair of overalls, and still you knew he was a priest."

Bernie also remembered that he responded to suggestions such as the one to put the names of deceased priests on the same page in the liturgical calendar on the day they died, rather than in the last pages of the book. "He would listen to you with a big ear." Bernie had seen Monsignor Cooke rise to the rank of cardinal. When asked if he ever changed, the answer was immediate: "He never changed; he never thought he was any more important than any ordinary priest. He was always the same way, always gentle. Of course, he could get mad and he showed it at times. You could always tell when he was angry. His face would tense up and he might snap, but never in a vindictive way. He would often return and explain the situation."

The following story will illustrate that even when he had risen to higher office, Monsignor Cooke had not changed his ideals of kindness and cheerfulness. Bernie tells the story in his own words: "There was a religious order priest, now deceased, some time ago who lived in the rectory of the Cathedral and was going to get the 'boot' because he was a little over-indulgent. I thought very highly of the man and saw only the good side of him. He came out one day and started to cry. He said, 'I need somebody to help me.' I liked the man very much. I went to Cardinal Cooke, who was then the chancellor, and asked him to help that priest. Without any hesitation he gave him another chance. Because of Bishop Cooke's compassion, that priest was able to straighten himself out. That was the end of his problem. But that was the way the cardinal always acted towards others. If you wanted a job for someone, or if someone needed a place to live, as long as you were truthful with him, he would try to give you the benefit of the doubt. He wanted to know the truth no matter how bad it was."[10]

Another person who remembers the dedication of Cardinal Cooke is Matthew Smith, who served his Mass daily from 1961 until he became archbishop in 1968. Characteristically this simple task was rewarded in many ways. The Smiths still treasure an autographed photograph which the cardinal gave them when he was ordained bishop. He celebrated Matt and Alice's thirtieth wedding-anniversary Mass in the Lady Chapel at Saint Patrick's Cathedral. When their son, Gerard, entered the Marine Corps in 1967, Bishop Cooke gave them his own rosary, made of ebony and mother-of-pearl, with the inscription, "Reverend T.J. Cooke." It was characteristic of Terence Cooke that he kept very little for himself. It can be parenthetically noted that this has not made it easy to collect his personal items. He had given many things away.

The Influence of Two Fathers

Two most important forces in the future cardinal's life come sharply into focus during this period — his relationship with his own father and with Cardinal Spellman, who would become in many ways a second father to him. His relationship to both of these men did much to preserve the ideals that he had formed as a young man. And yet, Michael Cooke and Francis Spellman were themselves very different.

Terence Cooke always smiled whenever he spoke of his father. The picture we presented early in this biography of a cheerful and humble workman with great faith remained unchanged for the rest of Michael's life. He, of course, enjoyed immensely his son's unexpected recognition by the Church. His life reached a pinnacle of happiness when he accompanied the future cardinal and a few friends on a visit to County Galway in Ireland. His son offered the liturgy in the parish community of Knock Moy where he had grown up. His eyes grew moist when they went to New Castle, the home of his wife, Margaret, "who had gone home to God" thirty years before.

Michael moved with his daughter Katherine up to West Nyack in 1951, and he himself "went home to God" in 1961. Michael had prepared his son for suffering by his own example over the years. We have some insight into the cardinal's attitudes toward human suffering and death from a sermon which he preached to the Ladies of Charity in 1954. Preaching on the text, "For as we share abundantly in Christ's sufferings, so through Christ we share abundantly in comfort too" (II Corinthians 1:5), Terence Cooke stated,

Sympathy has been described as winged charity. Sympathy is the nurse for the illness of the soul. It is the feeling compassion for another's suffering. Sympathy anticipates the slow mind. It is prophetic. It foresees. Sympathy is spontaneous. It is the promptness of charity. Just as charity is of the heart, so sympathy is nothing more than winged charity. The passage of Isaiah describing a lack of sympathy helps us to understand the true nature of sympathy. It is quoted by Saint Matthew, "And the prophecy of Isaiah is fulfilled in them, who saith, 'By hearing you shall hear, and not understand, and seeing you shall see and shall not perceive. For the heart of this people is grown gross' " (Matthew 13:14). The heart that is gross is dull in feeling, such a heart is not sympathetic. Instead of being sensitive the gross heart is callous; instead of being prophetic it is blind. Such a heart is not winged charity. It is tied to itself and caged in the narrow limits of selfishness. There are three requisites for a truly sympathetic heart: 1) unselfishness; 2) knowledge; 3) experience. Sympathy is essentially unselfish. It does not walk with pride. It is the charitable heart looking outward. Besides unselfishness, sympathy calls for knowledge. We must know another's sorrow and pain to feel for him. The richest sympathy is produced by knowledge, vivified by experience. No one is so well able to give sympathy as one who has known the want of it; as one who wishes to save others from drinking the cup which he himself has deeply drunk . . . [11]

In an earlier version of the same talk when he was in the fourth-year theology class, the young Terence Cooke gave the following meditation probably to his fellow-students at the seminary:

The Sacred Heart is the model of every priestly heart. Since His Heart was filled with sympathy for fallen humanity this virtue should play an important part in the life of each one of us. There is hardly a greater power than sympathy in changing great sinners into the most devoted and self-sacrificing saints. We are too often like the coldly repellent Pharisees and too little inclined to help those who have fallen. We should let our Master's example stimulate and help us to be tenderly sympathetic towards discouraged and disappointed men. [12]

No doubt the death of his father in his old age was deeply moving to Monsignor Cooke. However, those around him realized that although grieved, he quietly accepted God's Will and was concerned and considerate about the needs of his immediate family, especially his aunt. He comforted all those who mourned and did not think much of his own comfort and pains.

A biographical sketch released by the archdiocese in 1978, and apparently approved by the cardinal, states that his father, along with Cardinal Spellman, was the greatest individual influence in his life. The cardinal recalls, "We never saw him (Michael Cooke) annoyed at anyone. We were poor and happy and eventually were even able to have piano lessons for my sister and brother, and violin lessons for me."[13] The cardinal always remembered his father's oft-repeated advice, "Whatever you do, do it with all your heart!"

According to the same biographical sketch, Terence Cooke looked on Cardinal Spellman as his second father. He lived in the cardinal's residence and dined with him every evening. [14] After Cardinal Spellman's death, Cardinal Cooke said, "It was a rich experience and an education being around him. His memory was incredible. He knew how to take the best of the past and the present. His consideration was unfailing and so was his courtesy. I can still see him helping every visitor on with his or her coat and accompanying them to the door." [15]

This detail of Cardinal Spellman's courteous way with people needs to be stressed because of the calumnies against him in recent years. The author was told the following incident by Father George Barry Ford, the late chaplain of Columbia University and pastor of Corpus Christi Church in Manhattan.

Father Ford was a colorful figure of mid-century New York and an outspoken liberal priest of the times. He was also occasionally critical of Cardinal Spellman and most of the hierarchy. Nevertheless, Cardinal Spellman respected him and prevailed upon him to retract his resignation as pastor of Corpus Christi when Father Ford had an altercation with Monsignor James F. McIntyre, then the chancellor and later cardinal archbishop of Los Angeles.

When Cardinal Spellman had a run-in with a Protestant bishop, Father Ford was quoted in a news magazine as saying something to the effect that mediocrity is a quality shared by bishops of various denominations. He was summoned promptly to the cardinal's residence. When Cardinal Spellman entered he took Father Ford's coat and sat down and asked if he indeed had said this. Father Ford shot back that he had and said, "It's true, isn't it, Your Eminence?" Cardinal Spellman looked sad and responded, "I suppose it is. Thank you for coming down." He rose, helped Father Ford on with his coat, accompanied him to the door and thanked him again for coming.

Cardinal Cooke recalled a particular piece of advice from his mentor. "You can't say 'yes' to everything. But when you say 'yes,' say it quickly. Take a half an hour to say 'no' so you can show sympathy for the other fellow's side." This lesson on being sympathetic was not lost on Cardinal Cooke in the case of Father Ford. Many years later, when the new chaplain of Columbia University dedicated a residence in honor of Father Ford, Cardinal Cooke not only attended but spent the better part of an hour chatting with the venerable old gad-fly, who still had plenty of sting left.

Those who knew Father Ford will perhaps be surprised that whenever he recalled this unexpected conversation and the tribute that Cardinal Cooke paid him, tears would come to his eyes. In a way it was a recognition that Father Ford had never expected to receive. Cardinal Cooke commented when he celebrated Father Ford's funeral Mass that he had made his own unique and colorful contribution to the Church of New York for half a century. One suspects that he may have believed that Cardinal Spellman would have wanted that compliment to be given to his old critic.

Chancellor and Bishop

From June of 1961 until February of 1965 Monsignor Cooke served as chancellor of the Archdiocese of New York. He was responsible for the finances of the rapidly growing archdiocese as well as an immense amount of administrative detail. Among his effects is a large loose-leaf folder with hundreds of samples of letters and notices appropriate for all kinds of occasions, ranging from permission to have a non-Catholic sponsor at baptism to the appointment of honorary papal knights. The Church at this time was evolving from a tightly structured canonical self-image to the much more egalitarian and broad image which is accepted today. During the years Monsignor Cooke was chancellor the Second Vatican Council took place, causing ecclesiastical administration to become very complex and at the same time more fluid.

This author received dozens of letters from Monsignor Cooke giving the permission required at that time to preach in Protestant and Orthodox churches and in synagogues. Each of these letters was courteous, exact and gracious. When a phone conversation was necessary, Monsignor Cooke was always most cordial. It is now embarrassing to realize that this man was burdened with the care of immense projects and responsibilities, yet took time out to make suggestions on the phone about how to deal with this or that ecumenical relationship.

We finally met when Terence Cooke kindly invited me to his ordination as auxiliary bishop on December 13, 1965. When I identified myself, he threw his arms around me and thanked me for my ecumenical endeavors. I was startled that he would recall this small detail at the great occasion of his ordination to the episcopate. Later I would come to realize that it was character- istic of him to take the attention off himself and put it on others in a most self-effacing way.

Several other similar incidents took place at Bishop Cooke's episcopal ordination. He showed great deference to Bishop Wil- liam J. Moran, the other bishop ordained with him for the military ordinariate, referring to him as his "Gemini space twin," an allusion to the two astronauts. Father Laurence Schmidt, OSB, the parish priest from Saint Benedict's Church who had inspired his vocation, was also presented to everyone present at the reception at the Waldorf-Astoria Hotel. The elderly priest beamed as the young bishop spoke glowingly about him. Little did the assembled clergy realize that in three years Father Laurence would be introduced again, this time at Bishop Cooke's installa- tion as the new Archbishop of New York.

Unfortunately for biographers and readers alike, the period between the announcement of his elevation to the episcopate as titular bishop of Summa on September 15, 1965, and his ordina- tion in December was a very busy time for Bishop Cooke. As a result, he left no notes about his feelings during these months.

The visit of Pope Paul VI to the United Nations — the first visit of a pope to the United States — took place on the Feast of Saint Francis, October 4th. It was a time of innumerable details and preparations in which the newly appointed bishop participated. The aging Francis Cardinal Spellman relied more and more on his assistant. Those who were in Yankee Stadium on October 4th may recall that at one point when the pope circled the stadium, the old cardinal shuffled along some distance behind him, leaning heavily on the arm of a tall, young man. It was Bishop Cooke.

Although no personal reflections can be found in the notes of the bishop recording his thoughts at this time, Katherine, his sister, recalls that while he was not much impressed at receiving ecclesiastical titles, [16] he was deeply moved at becoming a bishop because it constituted "the fullness of the priesthood." This term, which may sound clerical or even ostentatious to some of our contemporaries, meant something very special to Terence Cooke.

In notes that appear to have been written in June of 1967, when he was vicar general and was giving a talk to a group of young Catholics, apparently on the responsibilities of a bishop as shepherd, he began with this text: "Be then a father — love, protect, serve your sons and daughters. Let no harm come to them. Let nothing impede them on their way to salvation."[17] He told them that they filled him with hope at a very difficult time. He enumerated the problems of the era: war, work for peace, poverty, family disintegration, juvenile delinquency, drug addiction and injustice. He spoke as he often did of hope based on God as necessary for the success of any truly human endeavor.

One wonders if Bishop Cooke were thinking of his own troubles and burdens when he said, "To grow in hope we must think more of God and less of ourselves, and contemplate God and Christ at peace. We are a family. We need each other. We lean on each other. We love each other." There is a special poignancy in these words; they were spoken at a time when he himself was deeply aware of his need for hope and the need to rely on other people for support, because serious illness had come back into his life.

Illness Again

It was during his busy years as chancellor that Terence Cooke again had an encounter with the disease that would deeply affect the rest of his life and eventually cause his death. It has been difficult to discover his reactions to his illness because he kept it secret, and he did not relate to illness, even terminal illness, in typical ways. In a conversation a few weeks before his death, he explained his motives for secrecy about his condition to his close, personal friend, Bishop Patrick V. Ahern. "If I had not done it, and let everybody know what I had, I would have been a lame duck as archbishop. I would never have been able to get done the things that I had to get done."

Bishop Ahern has provided the most intimate, personal account of the future cardinal's early illness and response to it. [18] It all began at breakfast on the morning of November 11, 1964. The two priests were old friends and had worked in the cardinal's residence together for a number of years. Bishop Ahern recalls that Terence Cooke mentioned a lump on the side of his face and then allowed his friend to touch it. It was very small and very hard. Bishop Ahern suggested that he go to see a doctor instead of going to New Orleans as part of the delegation Cardinal Spellman was sending to the funeral of Archbishop Joseph Francis Rummel.

The next day Monsignor Cooke agreed. He canceled his ticket and went to Saint Vincent's Hospital, where in a few weeks he was operated on by Doctor William F. Robbett, a well-known surgeon. Bishop Ahern was able to deduce that all was not well when an urgent call came to Cardinal Spellman from Sister Anthony Marie at Saint Vincent's. In his own words, he describes the scene that evening and his friend's reaction to the news that he had cancer.

"That night I walked into the hospital room and tried to be as jovial as possible. I tried to be all smiles and light-hearted. I didn't make any reference to the outcome of surgery. He was also being as casual as he could be; however, I could see that he was deeply affected. I would say that his eyes were wet. He was trying to put up a brave front, but wasn't doing much better than I was. He said, 'You know, I'm going to have to take radiation.' So I said, 'Ah, that's only because you're the chancellor and very important to them.' He said, 'Absolutely!' Each of us was kind of deceiving the other. Then I recall he said, 'The problem is, Aunt Mary is going to be very upset. So would you be sure in telling Aunt Mary to explain it gently.'

"I remember going home and feeling extremely sad. I was sad to tears. That night I waited for Monsignor Vincent Kenney to return home. He was closer to Cardinal Cooke than I. When he arrived home, I rang him and asked if I could come over. I did. We sat and talked. In telling him what I just told you, I said, 'Terry has cancer and we're going to lose him.' For me, in those days, cancer meant that it was probably all over. But I can never forget what Vinnie said. 'Terry Cooke is not going to die. The reason why he's not going to die is because he is a saint. God has some very special work for him to do.' That's verbatim: 'God has some very special work for him to do.' And then he added, 'I'm going to die before Terry Cooke.'

"The following May, Monsignor Kenney died of a heart attack. That almost sends shivers down my spine because it was terribly prophetic. But what prompted Vinnie to say that? He said it without the slightest doubt. Vinnie was something of a saint himself. He was immensely admired.

"Terry came home and did not miss a day in the chancery office. He went down at a certain hour every day to get his radiation. He worked like a guy who did not have a thing wrong with him."[19]

Monsignor Cooke was only able to return to work about a week after he was discharged from the hospital. During the period of his recovery, he stayed with his sister and his Aunt Mary in their apartment in Stuyvesant Town. The day after his discharge he called Sister Aloysius and asked if he could arrange to offer Mass at the Mary Manning Walsh Home. Sister offered to send the car to pick him up. He responded, "Oh, no, that won't be necessary. I'll work my way up there myself." Suddenly, Aunt Mary broke in on the phone, "Sister, I'm glad to know you're a woman of intelligence. You send the car immediately." Monsignor Cooke then responded, "The boss has spoken!"

This small vignette suggests how Cardinal Cooke would manage his life for the next nineteen years, during which he was watching for a recurrence of cancer or experiencing what proved to be a fatal cancer. He went about his duties and he never expected people to make special arrangements for him.

One is forced to ask whether this event marked a spiritual turning point in the life of Terence Cooke. It is a well-documented fact of the spiritual life that in order for there to be true progress on the road to holiness, there must also be an abiding and ever-growing acceptance of God's Will. This acceptance, an ever-deepening and more comprehensive attitude, goes by many names. In different circumstances it can be called hope, trust, abandonment to divine providence, obedience, even love. It lifts a person above the self-concern which is so necessary for growth in childhood and adolescence. It lifts the individual beyond the narcissism to which we are all prone to some degree. For the disciple of Christ, it is the willing acceptance of the limitations of mortality and of individual pathology. In accord with the teaching of the Gospel that "one must take up one's cross daily," it was what Michael Cooke had taught to his little children when they stood by their mother's casket.

In some respects Terence Cooke would find it easier than most people to practice this acceptance. As we have seen, he came from a family sustained by faith and hope. He preached about hope and acceptance often, and believed in the saving power of the cross. However, the struggle to accept a dangerous and ultimately fatal illness was more difficult for him in another respect. He loved life. He loved it with an innocence that only the unworldly can have. He enjoyed many aspects of life — music, art, the vitality and great diversity of a teeming metropolis. He enjoyed the poor and even the rich. He enjoyed baseball and having company. Astonishingly, he even enjoyed going to meetings. He loved to laugh. He was literally compelled to be sympathetic to those in trouble.

Bishop Ahern interrupted his account of his friend's recovery from his first bout with cancer to mention parenthetically, "Terry enjoyed himself. He enjoyed a good hamburger. It had to be done in just a certain way. He loved to supervise the cooking of a hamburger or a steak. There were always a million instructions to follow. He was a real manager. But people did not resent it. I think people just saw it as part of the innocence of his nature."

Terence Cooke loved life and he loved hamburgers, but he was also growing in holiness. Holiness is universal in its essential aspect. The universal and indispensable aspect of holiness is an acceptance of God's Will as it is manifested in the painful events of life. It would be wrong to say that God sent cancer to Terence Cooke. He contracted cancer for the same reasons that many other human beings do. He lived a life of stressful work. He lived in one of the most polluted environments in the world where the incidence of this mysterious disease is very high. God did not give him or anyone else cancer, but God was with him during his trial and he will be with anyone who calls upon him.

Thy Will Be Done

When Terence Cooke was appointed auxiliary bishop ten months after his first encounter with cancer, he chose as his episcopal motto the words, "Thy Will Be Done." We do not have available any of his thoughts on this choice, except that it was thoroughly consistent with his life. When he was appointed archbishop three years later, however, he made these remarkable observations, which are all the more significant since we now realize how ill he was.

> When I was asked, as all new bishops are asked, to choose a motto, I selected from the Lord's Prayer the phrase "Thy Will Be Done." These words are very much in my mind and heart today. I think I feel them more deeply than ever before. Today and tomorrow and for whatever time God chooses that I remain Archbishop of New York, I must devote all my efforts to doing God's Will by being a good bishop serving my fellowmen. If God's Will is to be done, we must have the will to chart a course of action that is independent of all fears. If our heavenly Father's Will is to be done on earth we must then achieve above all an even more full consciousness that we are our brother's keeper and that our brother is every man. "Thy Will Be Done" — a motto, a design for life, a prayer, a noble hope. I pray that God will strengthen me to be a good instrument of understanding, love and peace to my fellowmen. I pledge today that I will work each day of my life to accomplish God's message of goodwill for all the members of the human race. [20]

Holiness is a quality that is frequently unrecognized. Cardinal Newman suggests that for the most part, truly holy people are seen by their contemporaries as very much the same as the rest of us. As we have seen, a few of Terence Cooke's close friends, like Monsignor Vincent Kenney, recognized his holiness. Apparently, Cardinal Spellman shared this appreciation of his assistant and passed it on. The letter which Monsignor Cooke received on September 15, 1965 from Pope Paul VI was rather remarkable in that it contained an untypical and extraordinary recognition of a candidate to the episcopate. "So now our cherished brother, Francis Cardinal Spellman, bearing as he does concerns which increase daily, has asked that a priest might be appointed with whom he might share this heavy burden of guiding his flock. We have decided that you are capable of sharing this burden because of your wisdom, but even more importantly because of the true holiness of your life."[21]

Pope Paul VI did not forget his words. When he wrote to Bishop Cooke concerning his appointment as Archbishop of New York three years later, he reiterated his observations about the candidate, "You are outstanding not only for your intelligence, but also for your holiness of life, your prudence and your experience."[22]

Holiness of life is something that was desperately needed at the end of the 1960's. Confusion was everywhere, in the Church, in the state and in all of society. The elderly Cardinal Spellman was confronted by sweeping changes some of which he thought were too rapid and others he thought unwise. The Vatican Council required change in almost every corner of the life of the Church. Often this change was brought about injudiciously and too rapidly. The changes became new patches on an old garment. The old garment was tearing. Good things long overdue were demanding to be done, especially in New York with its immense Black population seeking civil rights. Almost no one was able to grasp the breadth of change and the power of the forces unleashed, or to distinguish positive and negative, creative and destructive trends which affected every diocese, religious order, parish and indeed every living person.

Bishop Cooke worked along with the late Archbishop John J. Maguire and a very well-trained staff of highly motivated men and women to keep the ship on course, while the old cardinal struggled with ill health, old age and deep concern about the times which no one really understood. As Cardinal Spellman's health began to fail, people naturally spoke about his successor. No one spoke about Terence Cooke.

Bishop Cooke himself very much believed that the appointment of bishops was the work of the Holy Spirit. He felt that his appointment as auxiliary bishop was the work of divine providence. He neither sought it nor refused it. At times this spiritual view of the workings of the Church on earth amused or even exasperated some of his colleagues. When one of his close friends suggested that he might succeed Cardinal Spellman, he replied with a laugh, "You're crazy!" He confided to his sister, Katherine, that when Cardinal Spellman died he expected to be transferred as a bishop to a smaller diocese, so that the new archbishop would be able eventually to appoint his own choices. [23] Later he told another close friend that when the apostolic delegate informed him that he had been chosen by Pope Paul VI to succeed Cardinal Spellman, he suggested a much more obvious candidate and offered to support him in every way, since they had worked together in the past. The choice was not to be altered.

Francis Cardinal Spellman died unexpectedly on December 2, 1967. Archbishop Maguire became the administrator of the archdiocese. Cardinal Spellman's funeral Mass was one of the great ecclesiastical events of the age, attended by the President and Vice-President as well as a host of ecclesiastical dignitaries, Catholic, Orthodox, Protestant and Jewish. The funeral would mark the end of an era of unparalleled growth and success for the Church. As the black-robed Father Robert I. Gannon, S.J. gave his eulogy, one was able for the moment to lose sight of the very serious challenges facing both the Church and the nation. Speculation ran high about Cardinal Spellman's successor. One evening in March of 1968, Bishop Cooke was walking back to the cathedral with his friend Bishop Ahern, who gives the fascinating account of their conversation.

"When we got to the cardinal's residence he said to me, 'Let's you and I take a little walk.' It was quite late. We walked down 50th Street to where Hamburger Heaven was. The street was deserted. Terry Cooke said to me, 'I have something to tell you. Guess who the new Archbishop of New York is going to be?' I said, 'I don't have a notion.' He said, 'Me!' I said, 'Oh, Good Lord!' We stopped right outside of Hamburger Heaven and I threw my arms around him and slapped him on the back and said, 'You will be the best archbishop New York ever had.'

"He was crying. He really wept. Then he said, 'Nobody knows the situation better than I. I know the finances of the diocese and they're not good. I also know that all of the troops are jumpy, especially the priests. Everyone is in a very upset frame of mind and the guy who gets this job is going to catch all the flak that they have suppressed. It's going to be terrible, but that's what "Fiat Voluntas Tua" means.' He told me that he had told the delegate that he really felt someone else should have this job.

"The next morning I went down to his room for the announcement. When I found him getting dressed he was just radiant. He was happy. He had made his peace with the whole thing. It was a total contrast to the night before. He was filled with a beautiful confidence and serenity. He had a habit that I would kid him about; he would say, 'It's all going to work out.' I used to consider it a bit overly optimistic and I would josh him about it. He knew that it was a standing joke between us. So when I came into his room that morning he laughed and said, 'You know what, even this is going to work out all right.' He was a truly optimistic man."[24]

The reader will recall that this was the very attitude that he had learned from his father long ago. The optimism and faith, the courage and hope now came into full focus. Perhaps it is true that frequently in the course of human events, bishops, like other people in charge of things, are largely chosen because of the workings of human beings. No one should be surprised at that. But now and then, it may very well be that a bishop is chosen by the providence of God. This can only happen when that man has deeply written in his heart the words, "Thy Will Be Done!"

CHAPTER FIVE

THE NEW ARCHBISHOP

*I*n a certain sense Terence Cooke never saw himself as an archbishop or a cardinal. He saw himself as a parish priest who had been given these high offices to fulfill. No doubt he had pondered this message which Pope Paul VI wrote in a letter to all the priests of the Church, dated June 30, 1968:

> The priest is a man who does not live for himself but for others. He is a man of the community . . . from a lively consciousness of his vocation and his consecration as the instrument of Christ for the service of men, the priest derives the consciousness of another dimension of his personality, that of mysticism and asceticism . . . but the priest is not a solitary; he is a member of an organized body, of the universal church, of a diocese, and typically and superlatively of his parish . . . our thoughts go out to those many priests intent upon methodical efforts towards spiritual growth by the study of the Word of God, by faithful and rational application of liturgical renewal, by increased pastoral service of the humble and those hungering for social justice, by the education of peoples in the ways of peace and freedom, by ecumenical approaches to Christian brethren separated from us, by humble daily fulfillment of the duties assigned to them, and above all by a radiant love for Our Lord Jesus Christ, for Our Lady, for the church, and for all human beings. [1]

These words of Pope Paul VI expressed his own mind, his own idealism and his own expectations of priests. They were published only a few weeks after he appointed Terence Cooke as the new Archbishop of New York. On March 8th of that year the future cardinal had confidentially responded to the same Pope's request that he serve as archbishop: "I need not tell you, Your Holiness, of my feelings of unworthiness to fill this position of great responsibility. I ask your prayers, Most Holy Father, that I may have God's grace to meet the obligations which this appointment involves. To Your Holiness I pledge my loyalty, my humble prayers, and my support in your heavy burden in guiding the Church in these troubled times. I shall try by every resource at my disposal and with the guidance of the Holy Spirit to be a good shepherd to your flock in New York."[2]

Much has been made of the fact that the appointment of Terence Cooke as Archbishop of New York was a great surprise. The appointment of a relatively young man who had never served as a diocesan bishop and who had no national prominence at all did indeed make this appointment a surprise. But a surprise is not always a mystery. When one ponders the words of Paul VI quoted above and his expectations of the priesthood, and Terence Cooke's personal ideal which was lived out so enthusiastically as a priest and bishop, then one sees that the spirituality of the two men had much in common. In fact, their spiritualities converge.

This convergence is best illustrated by a comparison of the pope's words on the priesthood quoted above, and the handwritten notes found in the personal file of the young Father Cooke entitled, "The Perfection of a Priest."

> The priest must live in the world and not be contaminated by it. The most serious danger of the parish priest is worldliness. The priest must have a cloistered heart faithful to Christ. Each priest is a rock on which many souls will rest. Each priest is a fisher of men, a shepherd of the flock,

a laborer in the vineyard, a reaper in the fields. We are to be
the leaven of society, to be a delegate of God. We must then
be at the side of God to be a light to the world in reflecting
Christ. Christ has chosen me to be with him until I die. This
means close union with him and continual independence of
the world. Wherever Christ needs me I will go. I will be his
mediator, his instrument, ever seeking souls.

Tests of Perfection

1) How close am I to God?
2) Test my perfection to the obedience to the known will of
   God.
3) What is the generosity of my spirit of sacrifice?[3]

His First Goal: To Be a Totally Dedicated Priest and Bishop

It was perfectly obvious to anyone who knew the new
archbishop well that he intended to dedicate himself entirely and
without any exceptions to the role of being a shepherd of the flock
of Christ. Since he had been so involved with the work of Cardinal
Spellman during his last year, and had been "second in command"
to Archbishop John Maguire as administrator of the archdiocese
after the death of the old cardinal, Archbishop Terence Cooke had
little difficulty in taking over the reigns of the diocese. He immediately visited all the vicariates or sub-divisions of the archdiocese and was warmly received by all who met him. The comment
was often heard, "He hasn't changed at all. He is just like he
always was." People continued to find him the same courteous,
gentle man willing to serve the church and people as when he was
working in the CYO.

Perhaps the most difficult challenge that awaited him was
with the clergy and religious who in 1968 expected sweeping
changes to take place in the Church. The bright promise of

Vatican II was already beginning to fade a bit, since the expected changes in liturgy and customs did not produce anywhere in the Church the almost magical results which were expected. The easy answer to this perplexing lack of response appeared to be to make more changes and make them even faster. Archbishop Cooke was not afraid of change, but his instincts told him that the changes wanted would be too rapid and would cause the laity to lose their balance. He saw things very much from a "people" point of view, that is to say psychologically rather than sociologically. He often commented that people were disoriented by the rapid rate of change.

This insight as well as his close association with Cardinal Spellman, coupled with his own rather traditional piety, incited a degree of impatience among clergy and religious, especially during his first years as archbishop. Often this impatience came to a head at meetings of the Senate of Priests, which was established by Cardinal Spellman shortly before his death. Cardinal Cooke always attended the executive session but found the full session trying. He was often "put on the spot" for not moving faster with change. Clergy who worked in the inner city were swept up, understandably enough, in the social unrest and change of the late 1960's, especially after the assassination of Dr. Martin Luther King, Jr. Some of Terence Cooke's close friends from the past felt compelled to be constructively critical of him. Usually this was done with courtesy and even a familiarity which took the edge off criticism. Sadly, sometimes the criticism was severe and taxed the patience and charity of the cardinal. [4]

As a member of the Senate of Priests in those years, this author recalls feeling sorry for the cardinal after some of those meetings. He never denied the fact that he might be wrong, but he often appeared to be pleading for a little more patience and understanding from his friends. He also had to contend with personal friends who thought he was moving too fast or that only superficial changes were necessary.

His whole attitude toward this time of conflict was revealed in a very painful incident which occurred in the Senate of Priests in 1970. A young priest, a member of a religious community, bitterly attacked the cardinal on the floor of the senate for not moving fast enough and not giving enough leadership in social action. Among other things, he took it upon himself to represent all of the clergy when he said, "We are ashamed of you as our bishop." The cardinal never lost his composure, but responded to the young priest, telling him that he was doing the best he could, taking into consideration all the factors concerning this complex situation. Cardinal Cooke almost seemed to apologize for making the young man ashamed.

While many at the meeting that day were not in agreement with this priest, only a few people rose to the cardinal's defense. Others wished to avoid the appearance of currying favor. A few expressed admiration for the young man's forwardness. The significance of this priest's attack on the cardinal changed dramatically when he left the priesthood less than two weeks after the senate meeting. The archbishop never referred to the attack at future senate meetings, nor did he defend himself. I recall thinking to myself that a humble man is very vulnerable to unfair attacks.

Along with learning to deal with criticism and controversy, another change came into the life of Terence Cooke. From the time of his appointment, even when he was quite ill many years later, he rarely took any time off. The modest recreation which he had enjoyed as a priest and auxiliary bishop, thoroughly consistent with his state in life, would now be completely given up. As a young priest and chancery official he had occasionally enjoyed trips to concerts and the opera. This enjoyment would totally end now.

Once this author had commented to Archbishop Cooke that no one would be disedified if he made a rare appearance at Lincoln Center for some cultural event. He rejected this suggestion,

saying that people might take offense and would feel that he
should be working all the time. I pointed out jokingly to him that
he could be accused of being a workaholic. He seemed surprised
that I thought this would be a fault.

As a young priest Terence Cooke had enjoyed visiting the
seashore with priest friends who would take a house together.[5]
Once he became a bishop he relinquished his investment in the
modest house which had been purchased by a group of priests,
and began looking for a small place in the country. This little
retreat, which was called "Knock Moy" (after the village where
his father had grown up in Ireland), was an unpretentious dwelling
tucked away in the rolling hills of Connecticut. It was owned by his
sister and boasted only five bedrooms and one bath. Katherine
would occasionally accompany him and three other priest friends
to their quiet days off at Knock Moy. These days were spent
almost entirely in answering correspondence. Perhaps in the
evening the cardinal would enjoy preparing a meal. The four
friends celebrated the Eucharist together and often prayed together each day.

The three priests who were friends and companions at
Knock Moy were Monsignor William McMahon, Father William
Reisig and the late Father Richard Fallon. All enjoyed the quiet
and peaceful company of their old friend, Terence Cooke.[6] Although these were among the closest friends of the cardinal, none
of these priests ever received any special ecclesiastical consideration. The greatest recognition they did have was that Fathers
Fallon and Reisig were chosen to accompany the cardinal down
the aisle when he was installed as Archbishop of New York. The
clergy of the archdiocese were always well aware that his close
personal friends in the priesthood were devout and gentle men
who expected and received no signs of preferential treatment.

Terence Cooke, like most of the priests of his time, saw the
priesthood as a fraternity. He felt his first responsibility as archbishop was to support the priests and religious in their pastoral

work. His kindliness to priests, especially to those in difficulty, was proverbial. Perhaps nothing was more painful to him in his work as archbishop than assisting priests who wanted to leave the priesthood. He would find it personally incomprehensible that anyone could depart from the priesthood, and yet he gave every priest the opportunity to be his own person and to make up his own mind before God. One priest who received a dispensation from the priesthood wrote that he had been treated with the greatest kindness by the cardinal, and that during the process of his dispensation he was always received with respect and great personal concern for his future welfare.

The present author was in a position to be aware of the cardinal's attitude toward the priesthood and the painful question of men leaving the priesthood. He asked me to do everything possible to assist those who were in a crisis of vocation. He established the Office of Spiritual Development to assist priests in strengthening their vocation and to assist those who either felt that they should leave or concluded that they should return to the priesthood. Never once has anyone heard it said that Cardinal Cooke was unkind to a man leaving the priesthood. On the other hand, a number of men whose vocations were imperiled by difficult situations or the loss of morale during those difficult years found in him a faithful and loyal friend.

What the Priesthood Meant to Terence Cooke

Any good artist can tell you that a portrait must have a visual center, a focus where the viewer concentrates his vision and around which all other details are organized. Usually this focus is some portion of the face of the subject — often the eyes, as in Rembrandt's deeply moving studies of Christ, or the mouth, as in the Mona Lisa. A literary portrait is much the same. It must be apparent to any reader that the focus of the life of Terence Cooke, and consequently of this portrait, was the priesthood. He had thought of being a priest in very early adolescence and had prepared for this vocation every moment of his life until he was ordained. We have seen that even when he was a prelate with vast executive and financial responsibilities, he was in his own eyes simply a priest with special duties. No readers will ever understand Terence Cooke unless they are willing to focus their attention on what the priesthood of the Catholic Church meant to him.

According to the Catholic faith, the priesthood, like the Church itself, is a divine institution. This term fails to communicate everything in English that it should. In Latin it means something like, "set up and firmly established by God himself," such as the poles of the earth or the center of the universe. Few people, and not even all priests, have an adequate concept of what the tradition of the Church teaches about these two divine institutions — the Church and its priesthood. Cardinal Cooke summed up the theology of the priesthood succinctly in his sermon at the Mass of Chrism during Holy Week of 1977.

> The priesthood begins with a sacred anointing from on high, as a reminder that it comes from God and not from ourselves, and that it is a call to a life that will reflect the life of the Blessed Trinity in a wonderful and mysterious way. Today's Gospel tells us that Jesus stood up in the synagogue at Nazareth, where He had grown up, and proclaimed that the Lord had sent Him with a mission. He repeated the words of the prophet Isaiah, "The Spirit of the Lord is upon me; therefore He has anointed me. He has sent me to bring glad tidings to the poor, to proclaim liberty to the captives, recovery of sight to the blind and release to prisoners." Then Jesus told them that these words had been fulfilled in Him — the priesthood comes from God![7]

Of course, both the Church and the priesthood exist in time

and are subject to all the psychological, sociological and historical influences that shape the actual functioning of things in this world. The same can be said of the human family, a divine institution if you will, of nature rather that of revelation.

Terence Cooke was an orthodox believer deeply imbued with the old peasant faith of Ireland. His writings on the priesthood are firmly rooted in the concept that this institution came from apostolic times and patristic writings, but also from Tridentine theology, which defined the priesthood in sharp contrast with the ideas of the Protestant Reformation. The cardinal's personal piety saw the Catholic priest operating with the charism of the Good Shepherd, in much the same way that Pope John Paul II did in his first letter to priests of 1979.[8] The pope, while candidly reviewing the faults of priests and confessing them as his own, presented Christ the Good Shepherd, appointed by the Heavenly Father, as the practical model for the clergy of the Church.

For Terence Cooke, a priest was, first of all, a shepherd, a man responsible for others in the spiritual aspect of their lives, in which they could not function as they should without his help. This help — the thing that the priest had most to offer — was neither of his own making nor doing. This help was a collection of divine gifts: the sacraments, especially the Holy Eucharist; the Scriptures and the teaching of the Church. For the very reason that these gifts were not his own, the priest by definition had to be a humble man. His most important tools were unmerited gifts of grace, not of nature.

As anyone who is familiar with the countryside of Ireland or anywhere else knows, a shepherd works hard. He needs to be gentle and patient. He gets his hands dirty and receives modest rewards for his labors. Terence Cooke, who many say could have been a very successful man in the world of finance, was supremely satisfied to be a shepherd in the little parish of Saint Athanasius, where he was first assigned in the Bronx.

Some readers, even priests, may not agree with or be attracted by the idea of a priest as a shepherd. They may think it is exclusive, hierarchical or even antiquated. They may never even have been near a live sheep, much less a live shepherd, in their lives. They will not be able to fully appreciate Terence Cooke, despite all his gentle and attractive human qualities. He would have fallen short of their expectations, because although he was an agent of social action and change, a teacher, educator and leader, he saw himself first and foremost as a shepherd of souls. He saw Christ's parable of the Good Shepherd "who lays down his life for the sheep" as a direct challenge to the apostles and their successors, the bishops and the priests of the Church.

In Cardinal Cooke's mind, the role of the shepherd was totally consistent with the teaching of the Church that every Christian, and especially every ordained priest, must surrender his or her will and vital powers to live ever more fully the life of Christ, within and without. St. Paul's statement of the central theme of Christian spirituality — "I live no longer, but it is Christ who lives within me" — is at the heart of any truly valid discipleship. The Christian is called to try more and more to surrender to the life of Christ within himself or herself. To fulfill his vocation, the priest must relentlessly do this. From this imperative of the Christian vocation flows the rest of the spirituality of the priest.

The same Holy Week homily cited above reveals the conscious personal goals of Cardinal Cooke. Even the reader who does not share this mystical concept of the priesthood, even someone who rejects the message of the Gospel, will be forced to admit that these words reflect a self-concept which contains our most revealing psychological insight into the life of this man. This is all the more true when we realize the cardinal reiterated these ideas when he was dying.

Cardinal Cooke had received a terminal diagnosis on November 24, 1975. By Holy Week of 1977, when he penned the following words, the effects of metastasized cancer were already making themselves painfully apparent to him. He probably expected his death to occur in the next few years, if not sooner. Neither he nor his physician could foresee that he would live for six more years. These glowing words sum up how Terence Cooke saw himself and his vocation as a priest. His whole life, and especially his work as shepherd of the Church of New York, are concentrated in these words.

> From the day of his ordination, a priest can never forget that he has been called by God himself. The priest is called to be a SERVANT, giving up a family of his own, so that he can minister to those who need him more. The priest is called to be a VICTIM, ready to share the sufferings of his people and not hide from them, and even ready to bear their sufferings in their place if God asks him to do so. A priest is called to be a BROTHER, who shares the worries and fears and the frailty of the people around him, and who brings to them not any great strength and invulnerability of his own, but his joyful trust in the Father who loves him and in Jesus whose priesthood he shares. The priest is called to be a LISTENER, to learn prayerfully from the way in which God has worked in the lives of His people, and full of faith to carry that message to others. A priest is called to be a FRIEND, conscious of the need of justice and brotherly concern in our society, a friend to people who have few friends in their hour of need. The anointing that Jesus gives us is to help us bring Him into our world, not to carry us out of it. [9]

The above paragraph stands out among hundreds of documents which Cardinal Cooke wrote himself, or which others wrote for him and he amply edited. He repeats these same themes on the priesthood several times, suggesting that they are his own personal thoughts. One can see this concept of the priest — a servant, a victim, a brother, a listener, a friend — in the sermon at his installation as Archbishop of New York. The theme of victim and co-sufferer was to take greater prominence only later.

These five concepts of the priestly role will provide the outline for the remaining chapters of this spiritual portrait. The accomplishments and activities of Cardinal Cooke no doubt will eventually be the subject of an extensive historical biography. Such a work must be developed chronologically. In a spiritual portrait, however, that method might prove to be tedious and even inconsistent with our goal, which is to understand the motives and ideals of the subject. It seems wiser to analyze the cardinal's fifteen years of service from the different aspects of his priestly role as he saw it; as brother, friend, servant, listener, and finally, in the last weeks, as victim.

Terence Cooke Named a Cardinal of the Church

He was Cardinal Cooke for so many years that people forget he was for a short time Archbishop Cooke. It was inevitable, however, that he would be made a cardinal as Archbishop of New York. It was no surprise, then, when he was informed in the spring of 1969 that he would be created a cardinal at the next consistory. Five hundred guests accompanied him to Rome for the occasion. Mr. John Mulcahey, a friend of Cardinal Cooke, paid for family members and priest classmates to go with him to Rome. [10] Terence Cooke received the cardinal's red biretta from Pope Paul VI on April 28th. On his way home he stopped in Ireland with his priest friends and family to pay a visit to the churches at Knock Moy and New Castle where his mother and father had been baptized.

His sister, Katherine, recalls that her brother was less enthusiastic about being a cardinal than he was when he became a priest, and later a bishop. [11] Sacramentally, these two roles meant a great deal to him, whereas the title "cardinal" was largely honorary. Being a cardinal, however, meant receiving certain new responsibilities. It led to appointments to pontifical committees and carried a certain amount of prestige, which could be useful in accomplishing some good purpose. Elevating a man to the cardinalate also means that he becomes an elector of the pope. Terence Cooke used his right as cardinal in the election of two popes, John Paul I and John Paul II. He expressed to this author his personal satisfaction at the election of the first Polish pope a few days after he returned from the conclave and papal installation. However, being a priest and bishop meant much more to Terence Cooke than being a cardinal, because in these roles he was able to perform special apostolic tasks that are reserved to these two holy orders.

Cardinal Cooke decided not to have a large reception on his return to New York. There had already been a reception when he was installed archbishop a year earlier, and he felt that he did not want either to incur the expense or cause the inconvenience that another gathering would have occasioned. Consequently, he decided on a unique plan for his reception. He was welcomed back to New York City at a Mass on May 7th, and then he received visitors on the steps of the Cathedral.

In the first contingent of visitors, of course, were the governor, mayor and other official dignitaries. The new cardinal stood on the steps well into the night, receiving all who wished to congratulate him and promise their prayers. It was indeed a very proletarian reception on the sidewalk. The receiving line was so long that priests in the cardinal's residence and the Cathedral rectory were assigned turns of half-hour duty to stand with the cardinal as he received his guests. He himself stood there for many hours. Although tired and approaching exhaustion, he obviously enjoyed this opportunity to greet so many, both friends and strangers.

This unusual reception — open to all who wished to come — was symbolically the most fitting way for him to become a cardinal. Those who knew him realized that his only enjoyment of this rank was the joy that it gave to those who could tell their friends and relatives that they had met "the cardinal." Many times, this rank cost him a great deal of inconvenience.

For example, the day after the solemn beatification of Kateri Tekakwitha in Saint Peter's Basilica on June 22, 1980, a Mass was offered by the various prelates who attended the ceremonies. This Mass was of special importance to the Native Americans who had sacrificed to make the long journey to Rome for the occasion. It was a sweltering hot, Roman summer day. The Mass was held at the North American College. Understandably, after the Mass, the clergy in attendance were anxious to get out of their ceremonial robes and escape to some cooler place. One of the prelates said to Cardinal Cooke, "Let's get out of here quickly." He gave no response. [12]

Cardinal Cooke spent the rest of the afternoon in his cardinal's robes visiting the Native Americans who had come for the Mass. Each one wanted to have his picture taken with the cardinal. Tucked away on many reservations in the United States are photographs of Native American couples beaming as they stood with the cardinal archbishop of New York. It was their one and only chance to have their picture taken with the cardinal, and they did not want to miss it. Little did anyone realize that afternoon that Cardinal Cooke was only three years away from death, and in the sweltering heat was feeling quite exhausted.

Another aspect of the cardinal's concern for others emerges from an interview with Father Jerome Vereb[13] of the Passionist Community, which is responsible for staffing the Church of Saints John and Paul, the titular Church of Cardinal Cooke in Rome. The cardinal was very fond of this church and never went to Rome without visiting it. He loved to ask Father Norbert Dorsey, then general councilor of the Passionist order, now auxiliary bishop of Miami to take visitors around and explain the many interesting historical details in the church. This was typical of the cardinal, who never tired of making guests feel important and showing them things of interest.

Father Vereb recalls that when Pope John Paul II narrowly escaped death at the hands of an assassin, two American women were wounded at the same time. [14] Cardinal Cooke went to Rome immediately after the Pope was shot and asked to see the women. Apparently, they were not being cared for as well as they might have been. He visited with Mrs. Ann Odre for some time and talked to her in a hospital near the North American College, where he was staying. He was so ill that he could not make the short trip back up the hill that afternoon, but had to call for a taxi. In order to avoid calling attention to the fact that he was so ill, he explained that he needed a taxi because Monsignor Lawrence Kenney was with him and had a bad cold.

Cardinal Cooke underwrote the cost of Mrs. Odre's transportation back to the United States, and followed up her return to Buffalo and her recovery. He also saw to it that Mrs. Rose Hall, the other wounded woman, was flown from Germany to New York, where she received medical treatment at Lenox Hill Hospital from Doctor Kevin Cahill, Cardinal Cooke's personal physician. Father Vereb had the opportunity of reassuring the Pope after his own recovery that these two women had been cared for by Cardinal Cooke. This was typical of the cardinal's concern for ordinary people who became involved in world events and tended to be lost in the shuffle.

A Prince Among Men

Cardinals have traditionally been referred to as the "Princes of the Church." This title, which hearkens back to the aristocratic ways of the past, is seldom used today. Cardinal Cooke would never have thought of himself as a prince. He saw himself as someone who was there to be a brother to all. There was, however, one aspect of being a prince that appealed to Cardinal Cooke.

The medieval adage, "noblesse oblige," means that someone who holds noble rank is obliged to live up to it. Cardinal Cooke welcomed the obligations that fell to him as a prince of the Church, and he fulfilled them nobly. It even caused him to be magnanimous with his critics and his enemies, like the bitter young priest in the senate. He could show the magnanimity of a good prince even to his destructive critics. Some saw this forgiving and meek spirit as a weakness, but weakness masquerading as greatness of heart will soon complain and become bitter. Although he never thought of himself as a prince for one minute, endless numbers of people, especially ordinary people, thought of him as a prince. He treated them with genuine nobility, dignity and humility. It cannot be denied that, in the eyes of many, Terence Cooke was a prince among men.

CHAPTER SIX

A BROTHER TO ALL HE MET

The concept of brotherly love and concern for others, borrowed from the analogy of sibling relationships, has a long history in Christianity. The close ties of brothers and sisters and the mutual concern they are expected to show towards each other come to their most powerful expression in the Gospel. In the life of Christ, the Son of God shows himself to be the brother of all human beings and calls them to share the life of God which he possesses, and which he extends to them by adoption.

The saints of the Church stressed this same fraternal idea, and struggled earnestly by charity and good works to be brothers and sisters to all whom they met, especially those in need. In modern times the growing possibility of international cooperation and the reaction to the bizarre racism of the Nazis has fostered the idea of universal brotherhood, an idea which in the west has been supported by all major religious bodies. The establishment of the United Nations, the growth of the ecumenical movement and the conciliatory tone of the Second Vatican Council converge to make brotherhood both a human and Christian ideal.

This ideal of brotherhood was unreservedly accepted by Terence Cooke and explicitly expressed several times at his installation Mass. For example, the new Archbishop of New York said, "I thank Almighty God for the opportunity to spend my life in service to the laity, religious and priests of New York; to the men and women in our armed forces and the splendid chaplains who care for them; to all who are brothers in Christ; to our dear friends of the Jewish faith; to all who believe in God and, so far as they permit me, to those who do not — for we are all God's children."[1]

Personally, the word "brother" called forth a strong emotional response from Terence Cooke because he was very close to his own brother and sister. They had done things together and cared for each other all of their lives. Family ties meant so much to the cardinal that his sister-in-law, Peggy Cooke, assures us that he went to all the graduations and family events even when he was busy as archbishop and burdened by illness.[2] Parents at a public high school graduation in Yonkers were once startled to find that sitting amongst them was the cardinal archbishop of New York, who as Uncle Terry always managed to get to such functions.

The Death of a Martyred Brother

Cardinal Cooke knew that to be a brother meant to accept the responsibility of helping another, of putting yourself out for your brother or sister. If you were really serious about being a brother and you believed in the fatherhood of God, then you needed to extend yourself to those who are very different, those who don't even know you or perhaps never even thought of you. Cardinal Cooke believed in this ideal of brotherhood and was able to put it into effect in a most dramatic way on the day of his installation.

This writer recalls that day very well. When the installation of the new archbishop was over, I went up to Harlem to visit a Black family I knew. It was an unusually warm April afternoon and the windows were wide open. Strange sounds came up from the street, and then one of the boys in the family broke in with the news, "Dr. King was shot! They killed him!"[3] The family would not let me leave the apartment until the shock was over and the streets of Harlem were filled with mourning people. They did this because they feared that in the immediate shock I might be the target of some disturbed person's rage. At that time Archbishop Cooke had left the reception given in his honor at the Waldorf-Astoria Hotel and had gone to pray with the Greek Orthodox metropolitan, Archbishop Iakovos, at the latter's residence. Their prayer that day was for the soul of Martin Luther King and for racial justice and peace.

Terence Cooke went on to Harlem that very evening to pray with the mourning people. Almost the first public act of the new archbishop was to attend the funeral of the martyred civil rights leader in Atlanta. In the first public statement he made as archbishop, he said, "On the day of my installation as Archbishop of New York, so filled with brotherly friendship, I was deeply shocked and saddened at the tragic news of the death of Reverend Martin Luther King. He died in the cause of racial justice and peace, the cause for which we all must work and pray unceasingly. His visions and ideals will live on in the hearts of his countrymen."[4] The archbishop ended his statement by requesting that prayers be offered in all churches for the repose of the soul of Dr. King and for the cause of racial justice. He also requested that wherever possible, appropriate memorial services be held and churches remain open for prayer.

The following Saturday, before leaving for the funeral of Dr. King in Atlanta, Archbishop Cooke attended a memorial service in Saint Charles Borromeo Church in Harlem. He said to the mourners gathered in that venerable church, "We lament the loss of the man who sought justice, the loss of a beloved leader, and we lament the shattering moment in which insanity outran the protective love with which we would have surrounded our Dr. King."[5] The Catholic people of Harlem responded with great warmth to this first act of their new shepherd as they shared tears together that sorrowful night.

Archbishop Cooke wished to establish some kind of memorial to Dr. Martin Luther King. He chose an activity which was very close to his own heart — a day camp. At Saint Joseph's Seminary he established the Dunwoodie Day Camp, which annually served over seven thousand children from economically depressed areas of the city. Sad to say, it is now defunct. Later he led representatives of fourteen religious groups in starting "Project Equality," an ecumenical group of clergy and business people which attempted to remove racial discrimination from New York City commercial firms.

Less dramatically but far more effectively, he turned his attention to New York Catholic Charities, which was the largest voluntary welfare organization in the United States. During the years of his administration Catholic Charities strove to serve increasing numbers of needy persons, especially members of different minority groups. This was done while the city was in a fiscal crisis and the resources of Catholic Charities were diminishing because of the decline in religious vocations.

Cardinal Cooke and the Struggle for Racial Equality

During the first years of Archbishop Cooke's administration the civil rights movement gained momentum. As this movement inevitably became more confrontational and at times more expressive of the pent-up rage of decades of injustice, gentle voices like the cardinal's were drowned out. The late 1960's and the early 1970's were times of confrontation and controversy. Terence Cooke was a man of conciliation with a strong belief that most people will do the right thing if they can be brought to see what it is.

As the atmosphere calmed down in the late 1970's, a compelling fact began to emerge. Cardinal Cooke had done everything possible to keep the parochial schools open in the inner city. These elementary and secondary schools provide the best opportunity for African-American and Hispanic children who live below the poverty level to get a good education. The cardinal believed that education was the best way out of the economic oppression which was the legacy of racial prejudice and ultimately of slavery.

In New York City the simple fact was that the majority of African-American and Hispanic students who obtained a regents diploma opening the door to a good college education came from Catholic schools, regardless of their religious denomination. No single person is more responsible for this than Cardinal Cooke, whose determination and economic skill in beginning the inter-parish finance commission kept these schools open. [6]

At the time of his death, the Black community hailed Cardinal Cooke as a friend and leader. "Cardinal Cooke knew the streets of Harlem. He supported us. He put the church's resources in the poorer neighborhoods where they were needed. He made a difference in Harlem. All the difference." [7]

In a later chapter we shall briefly review Cardinal Cooke's works of charity, which have been substantially directed to many New Yorkers who are of African-American origin. Here we must focus simply on his brotherly concern, which was expressed in so many ways including his work with Catholic Charities.

Cardinal Cooke nominated the first Black auxiliary bishop of New York, Bishop Emerson J. Moore. Only a few days before his death, one of his very last letters was addressed to Bishop Moore and through him to the Black community. The dying cardinal recalled the triumphant visit of Pope John Paul II to Harlem and the Bronx. It was the expressed wish of the Pope to visit this historic Black community and through his visit to extend greetings to all Black Americans.

The cardinal also recalled the privilege of initially working on

the cause of canonization of Pierre Toussaint, a devout Haitian
layman who had generously looked after the poor in New York at
the end of the eighteenth century. He wrote warmly of the
generosity of Black Catholics in supporting schools and in works
of justice and charity. Recalling the many happy liturgies he had
celebrated in Harlem and in Black parishes elsewhere, the cardinal thanked the people for sharing in his suffering. Recalling the
civil rights days in a most touching way, he ended his letter by
asking God's blessing on the Black community as "we join hearts
and hands and voices on our journey to heaven."[8]

Cardinal Cooke and the Hispanic Community

As we have mentioned, Cardinal Cooke had been involved
with the Hispanic community in New York since his days as a
young volunteer in Casita Maria. In the whirlwind of activity
during his first months as archbishop, he found time to visit
Puerto Rico and to go to the Eucharistic Congress in Bogota. The
New York Spanish-speaking community is an exuberant mixture
of Puerto Ricans, Dominicans and Cubans, with people from
every country in Central America and most countries in South
America. It is a deeply religious community which the Church of
New York has made great efforts to serve. Beginning with the
efforts of Cardinal Spellman, which Cardinal Cooke expanded,
over a hundred parishes of the archdiocese have Spanish Masses
as well as Spanish-language pastoral programs.

Cardinal Cooke nominated the first Hispanic auxiliary
bishop, Bishop Francisco Garmendia, who is a Basque. He recognized the talents of the late Monsignor Raul del Valle and several
other Spanish-speaking priests by appointing them to various
posts. The cardinal also supported the appointment of Bishop
David Arias, OAR, who had directed the Spanish Cursillo for a
decade, as auxiliary bishop of Newark. Cardinal Cooke especially

encouraged members of the Hispanic community to enter the permanent diaconate, and he initiated a program to encourage vocations to the priesthood and religious life in both the Hispanic and African-American communities.

Those who had the opportunity to attend the annual San Juan fiesta knew that the cardinal entered into the spirit of this great Puerto Rican festival with gusto and obvious satisfaction. When various other celebrations of different Hispanic groups were held, the cardinal would be there with his smile and his enthusiastic response to the warmth of the Spanish-speaking people. His command of Spanish was limited and his accent came through, but the people responded enthusiastically to his attempts to speak to them in their mother tongue.

During the period of retreat before his death, the cardinal wrote to Deacon Luis Fontanez, "I received your beautiful letter which you sent me on behalf of the Hispanic community of the Archdiocese of New York and I was deeply touched by it. You have expressed in such a tender and loving way what it means to be the people of God, the Church united in joy and in suffering with Our Savior, Jesus, and with each other in the paschal journey to eternal life. I am especially grateful for your words which gave me consolation beyond telling that I have been a pastor to my Hispanic brothers and sisters."[9]

Two weeks later he wrote to the Hispanic community which held a prayer vigil in Saint Paul's Church in East Harlem, "I thank the Lord for the many and unique gifts which you bring to a society in need of spiritual and family-centered values as I pledge my prayers and love for your continued commitment to God, your Church, your country and your rich and beautiful heritage."[10]

Cardinal Cooke's efforts on behalf of the Hispanic community were very well recognized by its leaders and members. In addition to the wonderful tribute in *El Diario* mentioned earlier, these words also sum up the feelings of this colorful community toward the shepherd of the Church of New York.

The Hispanic community is grateful to God for the gift of Cardinal Cooke's life and leadership, as well as His Eminence's vigilance in defending the dignity and sacredness of all human life. His Eminence believed sincerely Jesus' words, "Blessed are the poor," and through his actions showed God's special concern for those who suffer.

In him, we Hispanics have always seen a true pastor and friend and we have valued his pastoral concern for our rights and dignity as sons and daughters of God.

We join our fellow Catholics, and all people of good will, in prayer that God will receive His good and faithful servant into his eternal reward. [11]

Cardinal Cooke at the Ethnic Crossroads

New York is often called the crossroads of the world. If this seems presumptuous to non-New Yorkers, as well it may be, the city is certainly one of the ethnic crossroads of the human race. Innumerable ethnic groups make up the swell of humanity around the megalopolis. Gradually, as the older ethnic groups are absorbed into the general American culture, new groups come along to take their place and continue to give the city and its surroundings a uniquely cosmopolitan atmosphere. It is important for any leader in New York to be attentive to the identities, customs, histories and accomplishments of all of these groups. This is particularly true for the shepherds of the two huge Catholic communities in the city, one centered in Manhattan and the other in Brooklyn. Both Cardinal Cooke and his contemporary, Bishop Francis Mugavero, were outstanding for their efforts in this delicate area.

One noticed something unusual about Cardinal Cooke's relationship with these various ethnic communities. He obviously enjoyed the qualities of each ethnic group and valued the distinctions that diverse national cultures brought to New York. Whether it was the hauntingly beautiful liturgy of the Eastern Churches, or the exuberance of the Celts, or the emotional enthusiasm of the Italians, or the unequivocal spirituality of the Poles and Slavs, he personally entered into the encounter with every group. He was particularly aware of the needs of recent immigrants who often were refugees from political or even religious persecution. Chinese, Korean, Vietnamese and other Asian refugees found a sympathetic hearing for their needs. In the reception room of his office or that of the vicar general, one found clergy from Africa, Eastern Europe, Central and South America and Asia asking for help where they knew they could find it.

He was concerned about the Holy Land and the Near East. He raised funds for the pilgrimage guest house, Notre Dame in Jerusalem, where pilgrims found not only a fine place to stay but also a center of identity for Catholic residents of Jerusalem. Anyone close to Cardinal Cooke knew that he or she had to be prepared for an appeal for some kind of help for needy people from almost anywhere. When he traveled as Military Vicar or head of Catholic Relief Services or Catholic Near East Welfare Association, the cardinal not only obtained help for those in need but sympathized with people he met and generously assisted them out of his own meager resources. It was no surprise to those who knew his generosity that when the cardinal's last will and testament was read, he left only seven thousand dollars, and gave all of it — all he possessed — to the archdiocese. Like a loving brother, he had given away most of what he himself had a right to.

A True Man of God and a True Brother

The same fraternal spirit was characteristic of Terence Cooke's relations with members of other religious groups. He gave a signal of his openness to ecumenism when he preached at the Episcopal Cathedral of Saint John the Divine within two months of his installation as archbishop. He visited a number of Orthodox, Protestant and Jewish houses of worship during his years as archbishop. He established an ecumenical commission of the archdiocese under Monsignor James Rigney, rector of Saint Patrick's Cathedral, and included a special committee within that commission for Catholic-Jewish relations.

Perhaps his closest ecumenical relationship was with Archbishop Iakovos, metropolitan of the Greek Orthodox Church in North and South America. So close were they that Cardinal Cooke was invited to preach at the twentieth anniversary of the enthronement of Archbishop Iakovos as primate of North and South America. When the cardinal died, Archbishop Iakovos rendered this tribute to his ecumenical pioneering brother, "Christian humanity and love and humility could not have had a more eloquent exponent than Cardinal Cooke. Through his concern for the cause of unity, justice at home and peace abroad he endeared himself to millions of people throughout the world. I mourn his death as a personal bereavement, for I lose a fellow bishop, a loving shepherd, a valiant Christian soldier, a true man of God and a true brother."[12]

Another close relationship Cardinal Cooke had was with Father John Andrew, rector of Saint Thomas Episcopal Church, a few steps away from Saint Patrick's Cathedral. Father Andrew loves to tell how the cardinal referred to him as "his co-pastor on Fifth Avenue." When Father Andrew was interviewed[13] by Pastor Weber on the Feast of the Assumption in 1989, he recalled that "there was never a great ceremony in the Cathedral that His Eminence did not invite me. Once when there was an ordination of bishops — one of whom I knew rather well — the cardinal had taken his place in the sanctuary and was just greeting the people. He forgot momentarily that the microphone was on and leaned over to say to his vicar general, 'I forgot to invite Father John.' "

Theirs was a genuine friendship. "Cardinal Cooke was always very respectful," said Father Andrew. This is evident because the cardinal always referred to him as 'Father John,' whether in public or in private. As a term of endearment, Father John referred to himself as 'your Anglican son.' Before any public announcement concerning the cardinal's terminal illness was made, Father John was told privately. According to Father John, he was the only non-Catholic to be mentioned in the funeral wishes of the cardinal. Cardinal Cooke wanted Father John to be with his body when it was waked in the Cathedral. This 'Anglican son' so honored his dying friend's request.

A story that Father Andrew told is typical of the character of Terence Cooke. "There was an evening one January when my Boy's Choir was invited to sing at an ecumenical gathering at the Holy Family Church. Agostino Cardinal Casaroli was there to deliver the Holy Father's message to the United Nations. When the event was over Cardinal Cooke asked me, 'Father John, how are you getting back?' I replied, 'Well, Your Eminence, I'm going to get a cab.' 'No, no, don't do that,' he said, 'why don't you travel back with me?' I said, 'I've got my curates with me, two or three of them. I doubt if there is room in your car.'

"The cardinal continued, 'It's quite obvious, Father John, that you haven't taken kids to the beach in some time.' So he made one of the curates sit to the back of the seat, the next curate sit forward, and he continued to stagger the rest of us in the back seat of his car. It was typical of him. When we arrived at his residence we all got out. 'You get right back in there,' the cardinal insisted, 'and my secretary will take you to Saint Thomas.' It never occurred to Cardinal Cooke to have an ounce of starch at all."

Many religious leaders in New York found in Cardinal Cooke a friend and an ally in numerous good causes. He was particularly compassionate to the situation of the Armenian Orthodox and Catholic communities. He made a special effort to welcome the Armenian community to Saint Patrick's Cathedral with the Armenian apostolic Archbishop Manoogian on the anniversary of the Armenian Holocaust.

There is no place in the world where interfaith relations are more important for the Jewish community than in New York City. Not only does New York City have the largest Jewish community in the world outside of Israel, but for years it was simply the largest Jewish community anywhere. New York life has been colored and enriched in many ways by the Jewish immigration at the turn of the century. While relationships have not always been smooth, there are very few New Yorkers who do not have friendships that cross the Jewish-Christian lines. This was certainly true of Terence Cooke all of his life. Such distinguished members of the Jewish community as the real estate entrepreneurs, the Rudin brothers, the financier Charles Silver, the opera stars Robert Merrill and Richard Tucker, and the comedian Phil Silvers were all close friends of the cardinal.

At the time of Archbishop Cooke's appointment, Rabbi Marc Tanenbaum noted that the Jewish community was very pleased because of his reputation in interfaith affairs. During his years as archbishop, representatives of the clergy from the three main branches of Judaism were always in attendance at important occasions in the Cathedral, including the papal visits. Cardinal Cooke arranged for this author to accompany the rabbis to a place of honor in the front of the Cathedral before the procession, so that they would not be expected to be led in by the cross, which is a specifically Christian symbol. The Jewish delegation always appreciated this act of tact and courtesy.

The depth of his good will was reflected at the end of Cardinal Cooke's life. At the installation of his successor, Archbishop John O'Connor, Rabbi Israel Moshowitz turned to me and whispered, "This is how things should have been through the centuries." Rabbi Tanenbaum, commenting on the life of Cardinal Cooke at the time of his death, made the following observations:

On his designation as Archbishop of New York, the American Jewish Committee sponsored a luncheon in his honor, attended by prominent Catholic and Jewish leaders. In his maiden address on Catholic-Jewish relations, Cooke spoke of his commitment to "heightened respect, sympathy and affection" between Catholics and Jews. He went on to repudiate anti-Semitism in these words, "In these years following the Second Vatican Council, we Roman Catholics are more than ever convinced that anti-Semitism should never find a basis in the Catholic religion and must never find a place in any Catholic's life . . . Conscious of our common heritage of salvation in the covenant between God and Abraham and his descendants, we pledge ourselves to continue fostering stronger and more extensive bonds of mutual respect, concern and cooperation."[14]

Rabbi Tanenbaum points out that in many ways Cardinal Cooke had implemented that goal, which he stated at the beginning of his work as archbishop. At a press conference in 1980 concerning the Indo-Chinese refugee crisis, the cardinal said, "Our generation witnessed the savagery of the Nazi Holocaust, which led to the destruction of millions of Jewish lives. To our eternal shame, most of the world stood by while human beings were being destroyed. We are now trying to learn our moral lessons from that tragedy, and that is why we Christians and Jews together are joining hands to stand against the evil which is afflicting these poor Vietnamese refugees."[15]

So popular was Cardinal Cooke in the Jewish community that it was suggested that the memorial prayer cards for his cause of canonization carry a Psalm along with a Christian prayer. The reason is that a number of Jewish people were interested in the cause and wanted to participate in it in some appropriate way.

Brother in Spirit and in Blood

With all of his appreciation of different national and ethnic groups, Cardinal Cooke had a special love for the people he came from. As it did for thousands of first generation Irish-Americans, the word "home" meant Ireland to him when he was growing up, because that is how his family referred to Ireland. Like many people in different ethnic groups, some Irishmen are convinced that God made them first, but Cardinal Cooke was modest about being Irish. Nevertheless, he loved to visit Ireland, especially the villages of Knock Moy and New Castle, near Athenry, County Galway, where his parents had come from. Many relatives and friends recall with deep affection his visits to them and his very simple ways.

Standing in front of the mural of Saint Colman that Cardinal Cooke had given to the Cathedral of Galway, a reporter, Willie Fahey, recalled how he knew the cardinal when he worked in New York. Willie mentioned that the cardinal always asked about his family and how things were in Ireland. The late Tomas Cardinal O Fiaich, primate of Ireland, and several other Irish bishops have enthusiastically supported the possibility of a cause for Cardinal Cooke.

Only a few days before his death, Cardinal Cooke published a letter about the Irish situation which he had been working on for some time. It is the most personally revealing of all his letters and it conveys his feelings about his Irish heritage better than anything someone else might write.

> Dear Brothers and Sisters of the Irish-American
> Community:
>
> At this grace-filled time of my life, I greet you in the name of
> the Lord Jesus, in the peace which He offers to us, and in
> the love of freedom and the common heritage which unites

us. I offer to each one of you and your families my special love and affection.

In my years as a priest and bishop, God has given me the grace and the strength to serve His people of many beautiful national and ethnic groups. I thank God for this privilege and for the richness of the diversity of our Community of faith and love. I pray for fidelity to His sacred call, even in this time of serious illness.

I thank God especially that I have been able, with His help, to serve the people from which I myself have come. We, who are daughters and sons of Ireland, are descendants of a race which strives for goodness, truth and beauty and which has also known oppression, religious persecution, injustice and denial of human rights.

I am intensely proud of Ireland, our beloved Ireland, the small Nation which, despite centuries of suffering, "has never surrendered her soul." I rejoice in the tradition of faith and love, of learning, culture and freedom which we have received from the generations of her people. I pray that we will always remain faithful to the rich heritage which has been handed on to us. [16]

Cardinal Cooke felt like a brother to what we call in New York "the friendly nephews and nieces of Saint Patrick." These are people of many oppressed national groups who feel some affinity because of the common struggle they had all experienced and the common hope they had found in the United States of America. Perhaps only someone whose intimate family members have found in America a place of refuge and opportunity can fully appreciate such feelings. Cardinal Cooke expresses what the sons and daughters of many who came past the Statue of Liberty feel in their hearts, regardless of their place of origin.

Like you and so many sons and daughters of Ireland, I am profoundly grateful for the hope and for the freedom and opportunity which our beloved Nation, the United States of America, has offered to us, to our families, to those who have gone before us and to all who will come after us. When repression and starvation had all but crushed the spirits of our ancestors, they found here a welcome, a home, a place to worship God, to work and to be educated and to raise their families in freedom and in peace. May the Lord our God continue to bless our land and preserve it as a haven for the poor and the oppressed.

I offer to you, my brothers and sisters of the Irish-American Community, my heartfelt appreciation for all you have been to our nation and to our Church. Your contributions are ever so many — in education, in government, in public service, in the defense of peace and freedom, in the dedicated service of your sons and daughters who have entered the Priesthood and the Religious Life, in the close-knit and loving families in which moral and spiritual values are lived and handed on. For all this — and for so much more — I thank God with you and for you. [17]

Cardinal Cooke ended his letter with a passionate appeal for justice in Northern Ireland. He had already spoken about the immense injustice suffered by Catholics in the six counties, and had published a statement, "The Quest for Peace in the North of Ireland," the preceding February. In all his statements, public and private, Cardinal Cooke had taken a strong stance against the use of violence and terrorist tactics in this struggle. He deplored violence on both sides.

This strong position against violent means brought Cardinal Cooke to one of the most painful decisions of his life, only six months before he wrote his deathbed letter. The incident was so painful that he discussed it with this author at our final visit when he was already confined to bed a few weeks before his death.

A Family Heart

For those who are unfamiliar with New York, it is important to realize that one of the city's great events of the year is the Saint Patrick's Day parade. This parade, which started out as a civil rights demonstration in the nineteenth century, has become a social occasion for hundreds of thousands of New Yorkers whose ancestors would not know a shamrock from a shillelagh. Citizens of many ethnic groups and religions enjoy the lively folk music and good cheer generated by the offspring of Erin. For a race that loves symbolism, especially religious symbolism, the high point of the day — the moment when the parade really begins — is when the grand marshal of the parade stops the line of march in front of Saint Patrick's Cathedral, and on behalf of all the marchers ceremoniously greets the cardinal archbishop, and in the old world custom, kisses his episcopal ring.

In 1983, the committee in charge of choosing a grand marshal chose Michael Flannery. Mr. Flannery had been a leader in the struggle for freedom from British rule in the North of Ireland, and had been a supporter of Noraid, an organization alleged to be linked with groups in Northern Ireland that are said to be responsible for violence and terror. Cardinal Cooke let it be known that he could not condone the choice of Mr. Flannery as grand marshal, and felt obliged to disengage himself and the archdiocese from any act that might be misconstrued as support for violence.

The parade committee decided not to back down, and so Saint Patrick's Day dawned on a stand-off. Even the cardinal's closest aides did not know what he was going to do, especially since Mr. and Mrs. Flannery attended the Saint Patrick's Day Mass offered that morning in the Cathedral. When the cardinal explained his position at the Mass, the only one to stand and applaud him was Michael Flannery. [18] Some thought that the cardinal would weaken and accept Mr. Flannery's greeting. Others, including Flannery, thought that the cardinal would not attend the parade at all. [19] The parade began and still no one knew what the cardinal would do. After much prayer he had decided on a very Irish solution to a very Irish dilemma. He came late.

As the marshal passed the Cathedral, there was no sign of the cardinal or his representatives on the steps. This seemed to be the answer. After a few minutes, however, the cardinal emerged from behind the Cathedral doors and appeared on the steps, but then the unthinkable happened. The Archbishop of New York was booed by a crowd of people assembled near the steps. This so deeply disturbed him that he was still puzzled by it when I spoke to him shortly before his death. He said, "I never thought that Irish people would boo the archbishop." I observed that this group of a few hundred had been gathered there to do just that. We could have found five thousand Irish who would have cheered the cardinal's action that day. The cardinal looked at me very seriously and said, "We must not be upset at them." He continued, "It was my fault. I did not make my position clear to them. They did not understand me. It was my own fault."[20]

Unless you are Irish-American, and despite my name I partly am, it is almost impossible to appreciate the pain of this incident and the depth of forgiveness it required. This forgiveness was not feigned nor did it begin with Cardinal Cooke's final illness. He had learned to be forgiving from his gentle father, Michael, who had brought his faith with him from Ireland long ago.

Michael Flannery agreed to be interviewed for this book. When Pastor Weber spoke with him, he recalled that the cardinal met with him on the morning of the parade before the Mass. When Mr. Flannery arrived at the Cathedral, he was requested to see the cardinal, who was waiting for him in his little office just off the sanctuary. Mr. Flannery recalled that the cardinal treated him very graciously and very kindly, and was not hostile in any way. Although much of what they talked about in those few minutes before the Mass remains confidential, it was obvious that Cardinal Cooke and Michael Flannery agreed to disagree.

There were reports throughout the press that the cardinal had passed Mr. Flannery and his wife by at the distribution of Holy Communion. That was untrue. Michael Flannery denied any reports that there had been unpleasantness between the cardinal and himself. He did say, "The cardinal was the type of man that grieved over things that did not go as smoothly as they should have gone. He was not hostile. One of my admirations of him was that he was tremendously kind to the poor. He was an advocate of theirs in every way. He was a very holy man."[21]

When asked what he thought about the possibility of a cause of canonization, and whether he thought the cardinal could be a saint, Mr. Flannery answered, "I'd say that he certainly should be. He lived a holy life. He was never in the limelight or seeking it. It wasn't his way of doing things. Holy people don't go in for publicity and all that sort of thing. He lived a holy life quite concerned about the poor of this city. That is a very saintly trait. He was a shepherd in every sense of the word and he worried about his sheep."[22] When the funeral Mass of Cardinal Cooke was celebrated, Michael Flannery was there.

It would be unfortunate and contrary to the personality and spirit of Cardinal Cooke to end this account of a very painful episode without something to lighten the story. After all, it is an Irish story, and the children of Erin learned long ago that humor can lighten the worst of situations, even wakes and funerals. This story is provided by Monsignor Charles McDonagh, who was the cardinal's secretary for seven years and who himself became the butt of the story. (It was Monsignor McDonagh who fulfilled the cardinal's final wish, namely, to accompany his sister, Katherine, to Galway and to offer Mass in the churches that his parents had come from. The cardinal wished to provide an opportunity for his family to be part of the observance of his funeral, so that they might not feel they were left out.) When people questioned Cardinal Cooke about his reaction to the incident on the Cathedral steps, he apparently did not share his real feelings about that occasion. It happened that Monsignor McDonagh walked out of the Cathedral a few steps ahead of the cardinal on Saint Patrick's Day. When the cardinal was asked about this event, with a glint of humor and teasing in his eyes, he would say, "They weren't booing at me. They were really booing at Charlie."[23]

Peace Be With You

The recognition that all human beings are brothers and sisters has its origin in various world religions. It was taught with the greatest clarity and universality by the founder of Christianity. In Matthew's Gospel, Our Lord Jesus Christ called for forgiveness of one's enemies, referring to them as brothers, and he forgave his own enemies from the cross. He calls us to love our enemies, to do good to those who hate us. This command has sometimes placed the disciples of Christ into conflict, especially when there was injustice and tyranny and even murder. The need to defend oneself, and even more important, to defend the innocent and helpless, has led to some very serious soul searching among those who sought to follow Christ.

At a time when rulers frequently went to war for reasons of greed and vanity, Saint Augustine limited the possibility of a just war to self-defense and defense of the innocent. This theory, based on the Gospels, has probably prevented more wars in history than any other single human document outside the Gospels themselves. Christ's teaching in the Gospel, and Saint Augustine's application of it to the just war, guided Cardinal Cooke and his commitment to world peace while he was the Military Vicar, bishop of all Catholic military personnel and their families.

It must be obvious to the reader, as it was to anyone who knew Terence Cooke, that he was a most peaceful man by nature. He did not even like an argument. His entire personality made him an arbitrator, a person capable of bringing together opposite sides. He was, in a word, a "peacemaker." The only qualities that suited him for the job of Military Vicar were a respect for legitimate authority and an innate belief that people in charge are usually trying to do the best they can. Sometimes this belief served him well, and sometimes it made him vulnerable to those who sought to take advantage of him.

He also felt a special responsibility to the young men and women in the military because they were in danger and far from home. He showed special concern for military wives and children stationed on bases, because he felt that they needed to feel the support of the great family of the Church and to know that it was there to help them.

The irony of such a gentle peacemaker being the bishop of the military was heightened by the fact that he grew up during the Second World War, which may have fulfilled Augustine's requirements for a just war better than any other conflict in modern times. Many Christians had come to view the war in Europe, and later the wars in Korea and Vietnam, as attempts to contain the armed imposition of Leninist, Stalinist and Maoist ideas and the total control of the peoples of the East. This is especially true after the so-called "cultural revolution" in Maoist China. All of these conflicts were accompanied by severe and deadly persecution of Christians and usually of all other believers, especially Buddhists.

The events in Russia, with glasnost in the 1980's leading to the dismantling of Stalinist policies, and in China, with the unprecedented surge of popular aspirations for democratic government in 1989, give ample testimony that there were hundreds of millions of voiceless people in Eastern Europe and Asia who have been willing to risk their lives in resistance to the violent imposition of an ideology that they never believed in. Cardinal Cooke, although a man of peace, was deeply concerned about these millions of people who had been permitted no voice at all in the determination of their lives.

Cardinal Cooke never believed that war was a solution but a catastrophe to be avoided. It is necessary for us to document this because of criticisms of him by those who objected to his being the Military Vicar which was a matter of Church policy at the time. [24] There is also criticism because of his close association with Cardinal Spellman, who had been Military Vicar during World War II and the most difficult days of the cold war. The following quotations from Cardinal Cooke's sermons to the armed forces, as well as his pastoral message on peace of May 19, 1972 (appendix II), will provide surprises for some of the cardinal's critics. These statements were not secret. They were given in public and often quoted in the press. They reflect an attitude that is clearly opposed to war and strongly in favor of peacemaking.

Cardinal Cooke saw himself as a brother to the men and women of the armed forces who were stationed overseas, especially in the very dangerous conflict in Vietnam. In his first talk given to American troops in Vietnam on Christmas Day in 1968, he told the following story of a military family placed in temporary quarters until permanent quarters could be found for them. "The youngest member of the family, a boy about five years old, was playing out in front one day when a neighbor came by and said, 'Isn't it too bad that your family doesn't have a home?' The little boy thought about that for a moment and replied, 'We have a home all right, we just don't have a house to put it in yet.' "

The cardinal went on to make a comparison between this family and the Holy Family. He ended his first sermon by saying, "Each year that it has been my privilege — and it is a privilege — to travel across the world to be with you at Christmastime, I think of home. I think of your homes and the homes of your loved ones back across the sea. I know that you think of home too, more than any other time of the year. It is my hope and prayer that you will be home soon, certainly for next Christmas and for many Christmases after that."[25]

He not only exhorted the military personnel to do their job

with justice, compassion and peace, but he also recognized the fact that military personnel are themselves not in favor of war. He underscored this in another talk given on his Christmas visit in 1968 to Vietnam. It is important to recall that his audience was well aware that service people were the objects of criticism by those who opposed the war.

> There are critics today who scoff at the idea that our military forces are interested in peace, but you are more deeply interested in peace than any group I know or with whom I have been in contact . . . Today, we again celebrate the birthday of the Prince of Peace and pray together before his altar that peace may quickly come to a world weary of conflict. Above all, we pray for inner peace, the peace of the soul. That was the peace experienced by the Holy Family in spite of their surroundings of hostility. That is the peace that is our heritage as followers of the One who came to speak "peace to the nations." May this peace be yours. [26]

In another talk at the time, the cardinal cited Cardinal Spellman, who had apparently addressed similar words to American troops in previous years. Speaking of American troops, Cardinal Spellman had said, "They seek the victory of convincing the enemy to come to the conference table ready to work out a just and honorable solution. Victory in their eyes does not mean the wholesale slaughter or crushing of their enemies, nor does it mean the conquest of North Vietnam. The victory of Vietnam means nothing else than victory for the sake of genuine peace in Vietnam. A peace with justice after victory, justice for all countries and all people." [27]

Peace did not come in Vietnam, as Cardinal Cooke and everyone else hoped it would come. The war dragged on, and casualties mounted on all sides. Because of his own doubts about the conduct of the Vietnam conflict, Cardinal Cooke decided that he would not return to Vietnam at Christmas in 1971. As much as he was concerned about the troops, he did not wish to appear to be supporting the continuation of the war. He went instead to the Shepherds' Fields in Bethlehem and visited troops in the Near East. At the shrine which marks the general vicinity of Jesus' birth, the cardinal said, "Let us work, then, for justice in the world, so that the nations of the earth will be moved to draw back from ominous arms races and unbalanced concentration on the tools of war, from the terrifying proliferation of nuclear weapons and from senseless quarrels and insane hatreds. Let us turn our united efforts instead to true human development throughout our world and to the betterment of all our brothers. Let us pray on this night, Christmas Eve, that all the nations of the earth may turn away from the ever present sounds of conflict and hear the angel's clear invitation to peace through love of God and neighbor."[28]

By May of the following year, Cardinal Cooke's tone had become much more urgent. In his peace statement, he said, "The recent developments in Vietnam, the escalation of military activity both by North Vietnam and our own nation have placed in harsh perspective a conflict over which so many of us have agonized for so long. Just when the conflict seemed to be on the verge of ending, hostilities flared anew and our hopes for a quick solution had been placed in jeopardy. Therefore, I am moved to speak again not just for an end of this terrible war, but for the prevention of future wars and for peace in the world."[29]

In this talk Cardinal Cooke recommended the United Nations and acknowledged this international organization as having the moral influence to arbitrate conflicts if supported by all parties to an agreement. A number of other people at the time also suggested calling an international conference of scholars, scientists and world leaders to work out a program by which war could be prevented. The cardinal reiterated the statement of Pope Paul VI to the United Nations seven years before, "War never again!"[30]

Cardinal Cooke's concern about the proliferation of nuclear weapons was not something new. Over and over again, religious leaders throughout the world had called for nuclear disarmament. In the mid-1970's, a movement began in the United States calling for unilateral disarmament by our government. This movement had its origins in the frustration of many at the proliferation of nuclear weapons.

It goes beyond the scope of this book to discuss the advisability or feasibility of such a proposal. It is necessary, however, to mention that this proposal put Cardinal Cooke in a difficult position. If it were in fact immoral for a good Christian to serve in the military forces of the United States because of the possession of nuclear weapons, it would have been necessary for him to counsel the military chaplains to discontinue their service. The Church had already defended the right of individual Christians to take the route of conscientious objection in order to bring home the importance of world peace. But that was not the issue. The issue was whether anyone could serve in the military and be morally justified while the nuclear stockpile continued to grow.

Cardinal Cooke issued a statement that, in summary, maintained "that since the United States gave evidence of working seriously towards world peace there could be a temporary tolerance of the possession of nuclear weapons until there was an agreement on all sides to gradually relinquish these weapons."[31] The eruption of a popular desire for democracy and peace in many Eastern nations in the late 1980's was accompanied by severe criticism of the communist governments of these nations by their own citizens and even by their own public officials. From this it is easy to conclude that a unilateral destruction of nuclear weapons by the United States during these decades might have precipitated a Third World War. In the late 1980's even the leadership of the Soviet bloc countries has been forced to admit that their former leaders were not justified in their pursuit of world domination.

As we have mentioned before, Cardinal Cooke took the criticism of his statement calmly. He simply shrugged his shoulders and said, "They don't understand me." It was apparently his belief that any attempt to impose his views on clergy who disagreed with him would have been construed as stifling dissent. It may also be that he himself was so frustrated by the continued development of the nuclear arsenal that he honestly did not know what other position to take. His own statement, issued on December 7, 1981, could never be reasonably understood as a moral defense of the possession of nuclear weapons, except as a deterrent to hostile forces which also had these weapons. A man of peace remains peaceful even when he is accused of being in favor of war.

A Brother to the Least and Forgotten

In going through the personal effects of Cardinal Cooke, this author was shocked one day to come across a photograph in his prayer book. It was one of the most distasteful and repellent sights I had ever seen in my life. The photograph showed a child who was perhaps eleven or twelve years old, terribly disfigured by a rare facial disease. Apparently this child was suffering from something similar to the disease that was the subject of the play and film *The Elephant Man*. The pitiful child in this picture was reading a book and was well dressed. It took a certain amount of composure even to look at the picture, because this child's sufferings were so intense and the distortions were so tragic and pervasive. Why, I asked myself, did Terence Cooke carry such a picture in his prayer book? No doubt he must have looked at it frequently.

There are in the world at all times people whom the rest of us never see or think about — the severely retarded and handicapped, or the physically deformed, like this child. Cardinal

Cooke thought of these people every day. He prayed for them and did many things for them. Through Catholic Charities of the Archdiocese of New York, he was responsible for a number of facilities for chronically ill people. So concerned was he about these people that after his death the archdiocese opened the Cardinal Cooke Residence for the Chronically Ill.

Cardinal Cooke not only visited the forgotten people of the world, he cared about them, thought about them and did as much as he could for them. His final pastoral letter for Respect Life Month was read at all Masses in the archdiocese and the military vicariate the weekend after his death. It clearly communicates his deep convictions not only against abortion, but also for human life. It shows his profound concern for the forgotten people of the human race.

The cardinal wrote,

> The gift of life, God's special gift, is no less beautiful when it is accompanied by illness or weakness, hunger or poverty, mental or physical handicaps, loneliness or old age. Indeed, at these times, human life gains extra splendor as it requires our special care, concern and reverence. It is in and through the weakest of human vessels that the Lord continues to reveal the power of His love . . . At this grace-filled time of my life, as I experience suffering in union with Jesus Our Lord and Redeemer, I offer gratitude to almighty God for giving me the opportunity to continue my apostolate on behalf of life . . . We can never yield to indifference or claim helplessness when innocent human life is threatened or when human rights are denied. [32]

We have seen in this chapter how Terence Cooke, the little brother of a struggling immigrant family, came to see himself as brother to every human being. He had his critics and even a few enemies, but he never responded to them in kind. There were people who misunderstood him and even mocked him. He accepted all of this as part of his own destiny in his attempt to follow the Gospel. He never became bitter, cynical or self-centered. In his long years of illness, Cardinal Cooke focused his attention not on his own pains but on the needs of others. No one was excluded from his concern, but the ill and handicapped received special attention. When he traveled abroad as Military Vicar, the cardinal spent as much time as he could visiting the hospitalized.[33] At any ecclesiastical function, the cardinal sought out those in wheelchairs and gave them his blessing. This author recalls the first time he came up to Trinity Retreat. One of his first question was, "Who's the little lady in the wheelchair?" referring to our receptionist, Karen. He went to greet her first.

The picture of that pitiful child in the cardinal's prayerbook — a child whom probably very few human beings have ever seen, a child who may even at this time be sequestered away — his concern even for this child shows that he was indeed a loving brother to every human being. What causes a person to maintain such an attitude throughout an entire lifetime? For the Christian it is a strong, personal and continuous identification with Jesus Christ. This identification was the very foundation of the life and faith of Terence Cooke.

Cooke Family (1925), Margaret and Michael,
his parents, Joseph and Katherine, his brother
and sister, and Terence in the middle.

On graduation from
Cathedral College
(1940).

Going off to
Dunwoodie
(Sept. 14, 1940).

Deacons Terence Cooke
and William Reisig at
St. Joseph's Seminary
(March 7, 1945).

Ordination to the priesthood by Cardinal Spellman (Dec. 1, 1945).

Episcopal ordination of Bishop Moran and Bishop Cooke by Cardinal Spellman
(Dec. 18, 1965).

Photo by W. J. Fahy

Pictured (from left to right) sister-in-law, Mrs. Joseph Cooke, his brother, Joseph,
his aunt, Mary Gannon, the newly ordained bishop, his uncle, James Gannon,
and his sister, Katherine.

Archbishop John T. McGuire, Apostolic Administrator, receives Bishop Cooke's credentials prior to his installation as archbishop (Apr. 4, 1968). Note he is not yet vested and is symbolically dressed in travelling clothes.

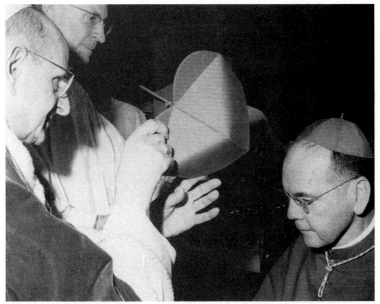

Cardinal Cooke receives the red hat from Pope Paul VI (Apr. 30, 1969).

Cardinal Karol Wojtyla is greeted by Cardinal Cooke and Msgr. Arthur Rojek at LaGuardia Airport (Sept. 9, 1976).

Cardinal Cooke preaches at Sabbath Services (Nov. 1976).

Cardinal Cooke and Archbishop Iakovos of the Greek Orthodox Archdiocese receive Archbishop Michael Ramsey in St. Patrick's Cathedral (Mar. 12, 1970).

Cardinal Cooke explaining Blessed Kateri Tekakwitha to students at the doors of the Cathedral.

Cardinal Cooke congratulating Marist Brother Joseph Stephans on sixty years of Teaching (June 1971). Looking on are (from left) Bishop Joseph Flannelly, Msgr. Edward Connors and Msgr. Joseph O'Keefe, now Bishop of Syracuse.

Sr. Margaret Mary, RSHM, 84, of Marymount, Tarrytown, greets cardinal on Recognition Day for retired religious. Sister Janet Baxendale looks on (May 23, 1982).

With prisoners (Dec. 1980).

With serviceman on crutches.

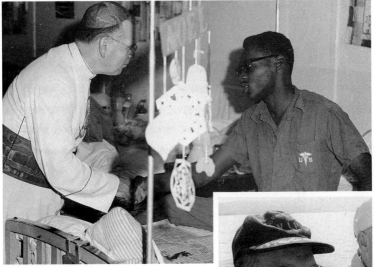

Visiting a Veterans' Hospital.

A moment of relaxation.

Showing personal interest in the work of Catholic Charities.

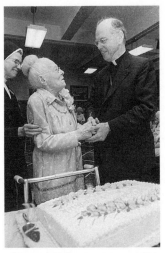

With Sister Edmund, O.Carm. congratulating a lady on
her 101st birthday. For him, life was no less beautiful
at one or one-hundred.

Visiting Mrs. Catherine Holmes at Mary Manning Walsh Home with
Sister Bernadette Mary, O.Carm. (1967).

At the Youth Reception for Pope John Paul II in Madison Square Garden
(Oct. 3, 1979).

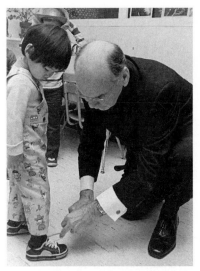

Bending to the task.

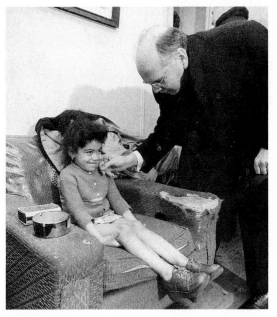

Visiting a poor family whose heat had been turned off
during an especially cold winter. He got the heat turned
back on (Feb. 10, 1977).

With his father on a visit to Knock Moy, County Galway, Ireland.

In his last public appearance, Cardinal Cooke greets a youngster in Project Hands, a Catholic Charities program for special children who are hearing impaired.

John Cardinal O'Connor blesses the tomb of Cardinal Cooke while Katherine, the late cardinal's sister, looks on.

In a thoughtful mood in the relaxed atmosphere of his own room.

CHAPTER SEVEN

A PRIEST SHOULD BE A FRIEND

*C*ardinal Cooke had stated in his homily for the Chrism Mass of 1977 that a priest was called "to be a friend conscious of the need for justice and brotherly concern in our society, a friend to people who have few friends in their hour of need."[1] Terence Cooke himself had many friends on all sides and in many degrees of friendship, ranging from friendly associations with community leaders to the closest personal friendships from seminary days. He probably never once in his life experienced the painful lack of a friend, a feeling common enough to so many people. Consequently, it is remarkable that he should have been so aware and so sensitive to those who needed a friend. When he could, he chose to be that friend.

Jesus had said to his disciples, "No longer do I call you servants . . . but I have called you friends" (John 15:15). "Greater love has no man than this, that a man lay down his life for his friends" (John 15:13). There is no doubt that both of these texts found their fulfillment in eminent ways in the life of Terence Cooke. It would be impossible to survey all his friendships and acts of kindness done to others, but at least a comprehensive summary must be made. These acts of kindness and mercy extend from personal friends in need to works of charity for many people who depended upon him as Archbishop of New York, but who in fact never even met him.

Not Servants, But Friends

A good place to begin this consideration is with those who are not called "servants," but "friends." Two examples stand out very clearly; Maura O'Kelly, the faithful housekeeper of the cardinal's residence for twenty-seven years, and Margaret Wallace, who served as his personal lay secretary during his years as archbishop. Neither of these ladies ever thought of the cardinal as anything but a close, personal friend. He was concerned about their welfare, their families and their needs. Maura gives the following touching account of what happened to her shortly after she began her employment at the cardinal's residence, unsettled in the strange world of America.

"When I first met Cardinal Cooke he was a monsignor. He was very, very gentle and very, very kind. I had a lot of problems when I came here from Ireland. For some reason or other Cardinal Spellman detected something was wrong. He spoke to me one day and said, 'Maura, if you have any problems, and I do know something is wrong, the best and nicest person you could speak to is Monsignor Cooke.' The cardinal spoke to him and later I spoke to Monsignor Cooke myself concerning my problems. He asked me what was bothering me and I told him. It was a funny feeling. After I spoke with him I felt a weight lifted from me. I always remember he gave me a beautiful rosary and said that it had touched a relic of the true Cross. We were always fantastic friends. He was like a father to me."[2]

"I never heard him raise his voice," Maura recalled, "or say a harsh word to anybody. He respected even the beggars who came to the door as gentlemen. I remember the day he became bishop. There was great excitement here. We had a wonderful reception at the Waldorf to which he invited my whole family . . . He was always a very spiritual person. He was always praying and in the chapel."[3] When asked if she remembered the day he became the Archbishop of New York, Maura said, "Indeed! I used to say after Cardinal Spellman died that we ought to be looking for different jobs. So he looked at me, only a few days before it was announced, and said, 'No, no, no Maura. You stay here. Don't you worry about anything.'

"When I came in the next morning I will always remember it. The cook, Mary Hines, said to me when I walked in about twenty after seven, 'Did you hear the news?' 'What news?' I said. 'Bishop Cooke is the new Archbishop of New York.' We couldn't believe it. We all went crazy. I ran right up to him. He was elated too. I kissed and hugged him. I couldn't believe it. He kept on saying in a very kind and gentle way, 'Isn't it wonderful, Maura?' He was excited himself, but very, very gentle. My father came over for the installation from Ireland.

"He never changed when he became archbishop. He was nice to everybody. When he went to Ireland he would always see my mother or telephone her. He never changed one bit . . . He was a walking saint. He was very spiritual, a very kind man. He would always explain things to you in a simple tone. When his family were coming, the cardinal would say to me, 'My people are coming, simple people. Now set the table, but don't do anything too fancy to embarrass them.' He would always share a slice of bread with anybody. He was what a priest was expected to be."[4]

His private secretary, Margaret Wallace, was extremely devoted to him. She also reiterated the statement that she had never seen him lose his temper or get annoyed in any way. When asked whether she thought that Cardinal Cooke might be a saint, she answered, "I thought he always was a saint. I think it is good that you are opening his possible cause of canonization."[5]

A Friend from the Other Team

Of the many friendships Cardinal Cooke enjoyed, those with persons who were very different from himself often were the most engaging. An example of this is his friendship with Mr. Murray Riese, a well-known Jewish business man in New York City. Cardinal Cooke had played stickball in the streets of the Bronx with Murray as a youngster. Years later they met again when Mr. Riese was a successful restauranteur and his old stickball companion was Cardinal Spellman's secretary. They rekindled their friendship and eventually Murray Riese became the host of Cardinal Cooke's annual Christmas party for the elderly. Mr. Riese wanted to do something for people at Christmas and the cardinal suggested a party for senior citizens to be held annually in various restaurants. It became one of the social events of the season, not for the powerful and wealthy but for the elderly. Mr. Riese recalls that Cardinal Cooke was "the most godly and saintly person I ever met. He was a miracle himself. It was no accident that he was here in this world."

Cardinal Cooke wanted to be a friend to everyone he met regardless of race, color or creed. The quality of friendship — wanting to be a friend to all he met — was noted by Mr. Thomas Cuite, a well-known political leader in the city. Friendship is an almost forgotten art in a highly competitive and consumer-oriented society. These two men of the world, one a Jewish business man and the other an Irish politician were intimately drawn to Cardinal Cooke because of his instant ability to be a true and lasting friend. They both helped him in his work for others. Yet, they both felt that he had helped them much more.

A Friend in Need

One of the best ways to become a friend of Cardinal Cooke was to have some need. Many sought to take advantage of him as Archbishop of New York. There are people in the world and in the Church who will use the position of someone else; usually those with power, prestige, and, in most cases, wealth, in order to advance their own schemes and motives. Most people generally have a pressing need. It was to them that the cardinal became a friend. Often he identified a need that had gone undetected so long that those closest to the situation accepted the need as it existed.

A touching story was related to us by Sister Aloysius McBride when she first met Father Cooke. The meeting happened years before he was Archbishop of New York. It took place when Terence Cooke was simply a priest without any power or influence. The story, however, gives us a glimpse of how he lived his life as a friend, whether a priest or a cardinal.

In her reflective way, Sister told us of her first meeting with the cardinal. "When I first met Father Cooke, it was in 1952. Gifts, including a piano and a sum of money were being presented to our institution. I was the director and it seemed important to me to make an impression on our benefactors, but a few things went wrong. The major embarrassment came when the public address system caused so much static that the executive from the company presenting the gift could not be heard. Father Cooke had come as a friend of a priest who was attending officially from Catholic Charities. I had never met him before and his presence increased my embarrassment. He sat quietly through all the confusion and then as he left, he touched my hand in a comforting way and said to me, 'You need a new mike. I'll see that you get one.' The remark was made in such a way that I felt he understood and experienced all that I was feeling. The new mike was not important at that moment, but that someone really understood and took time to express it mattered very much. Within a few days I received a brief personal note with a personal check — a substantial one. The note read something like, 'I promised you a new mike. Here is the first payment.' This was the beginning of his influence in my life."[6] Sister Aloysius concluded, "It was for me a revelation of greatness that set him apart."

A Friend to Those Who Have Few Friends

His own personal gifts of friendship did not absolve Cardinal
Cooke from the much larger responsibility of caring for hundreds
of thousands of needy, aged, infirm, destitute and even imprisoned people in New York City. These were people he did not
personally know but considered his friends. During his time as
archbishop, New York went through a period of social change so
profound that in retrospect the whole time appears to have been
one long upheaval. Attempts to care for the poor and needy were
often stymied in the public sector because of the serious financial
crisis that brought the city to the edge of bankruptcy. The
situation became catastrophic one summer because of repeated
incidents of arson; entire neighborhoods were wiped out by
landlords seeking in a dangerous and illicit way to recover some of
their investments by insurance claims and tax write-offs. As real
estate values sky-rocketed and vast fortunes were made overnight, whole neighborhoods of middle-class and working poor
people were destroyed. In 1977, the situation was so bad that
Cardinal Cooke challenged the candidates for public office with
this statement, "As the time of the mayoral election draws
closer, the people of New York need to know that their prospec-
tive leaders are aware of the whole complex range of problems
and that they are ready to come to grips with them, so that
Election Day 1977 will not be an exercise in futility."[7]
    It was not sufficient for the archbishop to call public officials
to task. It was necessary for him to work with them for the
improvement of services — or at least for their continuation — in
the chaos caused by financial disaster. It was also necessary for
him to keep Catholic Charities functioning at the highest level
possible. Cardinal Cooke had inherited from Cardinal Spellman
the largest local, private charitable institution in the United
States, perhaps in the world. During his administration, Catholic
Charities annually assisted an estimated eight hundred thousand

people of all faiths and races. This was done through 205 charitable and health-related corporations. Assistance could range from simple consultation and referral to total care for years.

It is not unusual in New York City to meet young people who have lived their entire lives under the care of Catholic Charities, starting with their birth in the Foundling Hospital and going through graduation from high school, and even beyond. It would be beyond the scope of this portrait to list all that Cardinal Cooke did as archbishop for Catholic Charities and for community welfare. His own background as a social worker and his years of experience in the youth apostolate of Catholic Charities prepared him well for this task. Not long after he became archbishop, he appointed his own secretary and friend of many years, Monsignor James J. Murray, to head Catholic Charities.

A list of the accomplishments of Catholic Charities could be tedious in a biography.[8] However, there are certain highlights that need mentioning. In 1970, after a comprehensive and painstaking review, the cardinal organized a Catholic Charities annual appeal to expand educational services for children in the archdiocese. This proved to be very successful to all concerned. It was now possible to launch such endeavors as special education programs, educational television, volunteer teachers corps and a basic adult education program.

The cardinal's commitment was to helping the poor escape from poverty and its effect, especially lack of education, miserable housing and inadequate health care. This led to the creation of the new Catholic Charities department of social development in 1976, which was followed by the appointment of a commission on social development to serve the department in an advisory and policy-making capacity. This department served to mobilize "people power" so that those in need could exert an appropriate influence on local, state and federal government decisions affecting the quality of their lives.

All his life Cardinal Cooke had had a special love for the

elderly and the aged. It was one of the traditions of his own family and ethnic background. In fact, Ireland numbers second in the world for its percentage of elderly people. During his time as archbishop, construction was completed on nine Catholic-Charities-affiliated nursing homes, including the 520-bed Kateri Residence in Manhattan, 360-bed Mary Manning Walsh Home in Manhattan, the 320-bed Ferncliff Nursing Home in Rhinebeck, the 300-bed Carmel Richmond Nursing Home on Staten Island, the 203-bed Jeanne Jugan Residence in the Bronx, the new wing of the 200-bed Providence Rest in the Bronx, the 200-bed Saint Cabrini Nursing Home in Dobbs Ferry, the 100-bed Saint Teresa's Nursing Home in Middletown as well as a 200-bed nursing home adjacent to Saint Joseph's Hospital in Yonkers.

Through community services for the aging, Catholic Charities developed 136 parish-based senior citizen programs for the social, nutritional and recreational needs of the elderly within their own neighborhoods. Cardinal Cooke appointed a special archdiocesan task force to conduct a study on the particular problems of the aging in areas of safety, housing, physical and mental health, social services, loneliness and abandonment.

Cardinal Cooke also initiated three new Catholic Charities programs for the imprisoned, the handicapped and the disadvantaged. He opened an office of the handicapped to coordinate and expand Catholic Charities community services for the disabled, the physically and mentally handicapped and a correctional apostolate which assists male and female parolees and released prison inmates at home in finding job placement, counseling and vocational guidance. Monsignor Eugene Clark recalls that Cardinal Cooke showed very special concern for the ill and handicapped in prison. [9]

The cardinal was also very interested in the housing problem caused by the vast migrations right within the city. He initiated the Archdiocesan Housing Development Program. The cardinal also encouraged priests and laity in their own neighborhoods to work for appropriate housing. Some of the largest housing efforts, including the Southeast Bronx rehabilitation program, were carried on by clergy, religious and laity with the encouragement of the archdiocese.

The problems in child care became especially acute during the years of Cardinal Cooke for two reasons; first, there was a growing belief in social work that dependent and neglected children should no longer be cared for in institutional settings, but rather in foster care; second, the decline in the number of religious brothers and sisters created a crisis in the many child care agencies run by Catholic Charities. The astonishing fact is that when Cardinal Cooke became Archbishop of New York, Catholic Charities cared for over sixty percent of all dependent and neglected children in New York City. Many are not aware of this remarkable service. It became necessary to develop a large foster care program and to try to preserve the institutional programs, which were still needed.

Cardinal Cooke liked to remind people that he was the guardian and father of about 5000 children in his role as head of Catholic Charities. Monsignor Clark said, "The cardinal took that responsibility as a pointedly personal one and always spoke in those terms. Whenever he went to the New York Foundling Hospital or other child-care institutions he would relate to the children in an exceptionally friendly way and become completely attentive to them. At times the cardinal would lead them in singing or tell a story or two. He always had their complete attention."[10] The cover art of this biography captures this aspect of his personality. It is revealing. As Archbishop of New York, Cardinal Cooke saw himself most comfortably as a father to the poor and orphaned.

During Cardinal Cooke's years as archbishop, well over two hundred thousand dependent, neglected, abused and court-remanded children obtained non-institutional care under Catholic-Charities-affiliated child care agencies. Currently, their population is composed mainly of older adolescents, many of whom are classified as delinquents or persons in need of supervision. A large percentage of these teenagers have serious emotional, educational and behavioral problems. Seventy-five percent are Black or Hispanic children and over twenty percent are non-Catholic. During the cardinal's time, Catholic Charities established more than 150 community based homes and residences.

Cardinal Cooke also encouraged privately-run programs which were related to the Catholic Church. The most prominent of these is Covenant House, begun by Father Bruce Ritter, OFM Conv., in the late 1960's. The cardinal made a substantial donation to the beginning of Father Ritter's work in the Times Square district, and continued to be supportive of this vital outreach. The Covenant House program has now spread to many cities in the United States and in other countries. It takes care of thousands of homeless teenagers who would otherwise be prey to prostitution and drug addiction.

In a similar way, the archdiocese indirectly encouraged the Day Top Village program run by Monsignor William O'Brien. Day Top Village provides residential treatment for hundreds of addicted teenagers and young adults over an extended period of time. It has proved to be one of the most effective drug rehabilitation programs in the United States.

The health-care program of the archdiocese was vastly increased under the care of Cardinal Cooke. Fourteen general and special hospitals were coordinated under the Department of Health and Hospitals of Catholic Charities, including the new Calvary Hospital for terminally ill cancer patients. Cardinal Cooke also encouraged the Catholic affiliation with the New York Medical College in Westchester County, a unique example of cooperation between the Church and the private sector in providing medical education.

In all of these endeavors it has been said of Cardinal Cooke that his "bottom line" was people. He did not see people in large sociological groups or as statistics. The cardinal was deeply aware of the personal and individual needs of the people in Catholic Charities programs. Because he was an executive member of the board of so many institutions, it was difficult for him to be directly involved in each of the over 200 agencies. When it was possible for him to visit one of the Catholic Charities offices, however, he always showed a personal interest in the work. He would speak to as many of the people under care as possible and would always compliment and encourage the staff. As his vicar general, Bishop Joseph O'Keefe, said so well, "His agenda was people."[11]

A Friend to the Young

When Cardinal Cooke became Archbishop of New York, he inherited one of the largest privately financed school systems in the world. The archdiocese supervised almost four hundred elementary schools and high schools. Inflation and other problems led to the consolidation of schools and reduced their numbers by the time of his death to 336. Spiraling costs, demographic changes, and the decline in the number of religious all contributed to a drop in enrollment which distressed Cardinal Cooke very much. The story is told that one day someone mentioned the word "retrenchment" at a meeting. In one of his few apparent acknowledgments of annoyance, the cardinal stopped the meeting and said somewhat humorously, "Never, never mention that word in my presence again."[12]

Despite that resolution it has been necessary for the archdiocese to retrench, although because of Cardinal Cooke's efforts it reduced its services at a slower rate than most other systems in the country. In order to achieve this, the cardinal had undertaken a major scientific study of Catholic schools in the archdiocese. He had attempted to get state aid through two acts which were unfortunately declared unconstitutional by the Supreme Court. He countered by encouraging a comprehensive program of Catholic released-time education and catechetics for non-parochial school children. Guidelines for elementary and secondary schools and CCD religion programs were published. A catechetical institute for training religious educators was established in affiliation with Saint Joseph's Seminary in Yonkers.

Perhaps the most important thing that Cardinal Cooke did for Catholic education was to establish the Inter-Parish Finance Commission. This commission dispersed funds received from affluent parishes to those parishes that were in financial need, especially where the maintenance of schools was endangered. [13] During his years as archbishop, $41 million was dispensed through this commission. The cardinal also established the Inner-City Scholarship Fund to raise money for the support of inner-city Catholic schools, where disadvantaged minority students were able to receive the religious education they so desperately wanted. This program assists children of all races and creeds. Many non-Catholic benefactors have contributed substantively to this fund over the years. Monsignor Clark remembers that Cardinal Cooke was at first reluctant to allow another fund raising dinner. He did not want to impose on the same generous people who were already burdened by many public functions. He was finally convinced on the grounds that a wide spectrum of people would find this kind of fund raiser attractive. The fund became very successful when a number of women volunteers took buses of other interested women up to Harlem and the Bronx and they witnessed the remarkable accomplishments of the Catholic school system in the inner city. [14] It is not inappropriate to comment that these non-Catholic donors have been so generous largely because of the personal regard they had for Cardinal Cooke and now have for his successor, Cardinal O'Connor.

Cardinal Cooke was not satisfied simply with preserving the Catholic schools; he constantly improved their quality. He was the guiding spirit behind the establishment of the Instructional Television Center, which, when it opened, was the largest microwave system in the United States. Telecasts would reach almost all of the Catholic schools in the archdiocese. This educational programming enhanced teacher presentation and the breadth of curriculum in many ways. Studies over the past few years demonstrate that in all subject areas, archdiocesan student generally achieve above-average scores on tests designed by Science Research Associates, [15] an independent testing service.

Beyond these statistics is the picture of a man overburdened by responsibility and struggling against diminishing physical health. Cardinal Cooke enjoyed the professional assistance of a large number of carefully chosen educators, led by very competent secretaries of education and school superintendents, including his own close associate, then Monsignor Joseph O'Keefe, now bishop of Syracuse; however, his own personal involvement in maintaining quality education was essential. One only had to go with him to a Catholic school graduation or event to see that Cardinal Cooke was enormously enthusiastic and deeply involved with the welfare of the students. In his archives are innumerable talks given at graduations, each one of them addressing the students' own personal needs. He had a remarkable ability to stand in front of a thousand students whom he had never met and speak to them as if they knew him.

Attached to the new chancery office that Cardinal Cooke erected at Fifty-fifth Street and First Avenue is Cathedral Girls High School. This school largely services children of minority groups. It was a special favorite of the cardinal, and he inaugurated its school band. How proud he was of that band and how involved he was in all the school activities. Little did the students realize that their archbishop's special interest in them was a reflection of his interest in every school in the archdiocese. It just happened that they were the closest school at hand, and they received a special share of his concern because he had time to show it to them. The students at Cathedral still know that they were special to him, but they probably don't realize that his special concern extended to all students of the archdiocese whether they attended a Catholic school or not.

Good Intentions

It is an old Irish proverb, quoted by many other nationalities, that the road to hell is paved with good intentions. Cardinal Cooke had for all needy people in the archdiocese only the best of intentions, but he did not stop there. In every conceivable way, beyond any reasonable expectation and despite limitations, the cardinal strove to make the services of the archdiocese to the young and to the needy the best possible ones he could offer. [16] It must never be forgotten that this was done in the midst of a cultural revolution and a fiscal crisis. It was also done at a time when vocations and values were on the decline.

Cardinal Cooke was always an optimist. He was fond of saying, "There are no obstacles, only challenges." When one considers the awesome obstacles that stood in his way, one can see that his buoyant optimism was tested to the nth degree. Why was he able to go on? Why did nothing deter him? Why did he always look on the bright side of things?

Deep within his heart he was convinced that by the grace of God, goodness will win out. He was also personally convinced that everything he was able to do for the poor, the weak, the sick, the imprisoned, the handicapped and the young, he did for Jesus Christ. It made no difference to him if they knew him. It was important that he served them. It made no difference whether any one thanked him; many did not. It was only important to him that he had been able to lay down his life for his friends.

CHAPTER EIGHT

THE SERVANT OF GOD'S PEOPLE

*I*n the homily which provided the outline for the second part of our spiritual portrait, Cardinal Cooke states that the priest is called to be "a servant, giving up a family of his own so that he may minister to those who need him more."[1] Christ had said to his apostles, "I am among you as One who serves" (St. Luke 22:27). He had performed the task of a servant in washing the feet of the apostles. He had also admonished them to serve each other and to take on the role of a servant. In papal documents the pope is traditionally referred to as "servus servorum Dei," the servant of the servants of God. The work of a servant is often tedious, unseen, even unrecognized, and in the case of a faithful servant done at personal sacrifice.

The Role of the Archbishop of New York

Earlier in this portrait it was mentioned that during the lifetime of Patrick Cardinal Hayes[2] the role of Archbishop of New York had begun to change. In the nineteenth century, the task of archbishop had been a confrontational and daring role calling for leadership, as the Church quickly expanded during the immigration years in the face of anti-Catholic prejudice. Some feisty men like Hughes[3] and Corrigan[4] had taken up the challenge and made their mark on history. After the large immigrations had established the Church, however, the role of archbishop had become one of presiding over and providing for a Church that almost automatically grew on its own.

Terence Cooke was such a servant who had inherited the care of the entire household. He never forgot how to be a good servant. Monsignor Florence D. Cohalan, the distinguished historian of the archdiocese, remarked that Cardinal Cooke did his very best work when he was the second man to Cardinal Spellman.[5] Those who worked in the archdiocesan structure at the time that Cardinal Spellman was growing old realized that much of the smooth operation of the archdiocese was due to Terence Cooke. He worked quietly and ably with Archbishop John Maguire to delicately assure that things went on as smoothly as possible when Cardinal Spellman was growing old.

Terence Cooke had all kinds of techniques that he would employ to get things done. For instance, he knew that Cardinal Spellman did not like to leave issues undecided. The young chancellor would wait until he got into the elevator with the old cardinal and then present the problem. He would receive an answer before they reached their offices on the third floor.[6] Cardinal Cooke liked to joke about this technique. We would disagree respectfully with the assessment of Monsignor Cohalan about Terence Cooke's best years, because he brought the same skills he had used with Cardinal Spellman into his own work as archbishop.

The Cardinal and the Media

Cardinal Cooke was a splendid engineer when it came to ecclesiastical structures, but he was not what the historian would call a leader of large and impressive proportions. He did not tower over the archdiocese by some personal charism. He also did not engage the media well,[7] and charism is often a media by-product. In fact, the media-makers often misused him, perhaps because he would tell them so little.

The American media are programmed for noise and glitz, with little sensitivity to moral or spiritual values. The media tend to abuse even those who take them on and engage in dialogue with them. They will patronize and belittle a quiet servant like Terence Cooke. What could the media know or understand about a servant who spent so much of his time and energy making sure that things ran smoothly, and who was mostly interested in providing for the spiritual and physical needs of ordinary people? To the media, Terence Cooke was just another public servant. It was only in the weeks before his death that the media began to treat the cardinal as a servant of God.

The Servant of the People of God

Cardinal Cooke, who saw himself as an "administrative revisionist,"[8] made it very clear that every administrative decision must be based on pastoral considerations. In fiscal, organizational, educational and even personnel decisions, the good of the people of the Archdiocese of New York had to be the final deciding norm. The cardinal considered this the central internal theme of his administration. Early on he launched a campaign to establish a parish council in all parishes wherever possible. A parish council is designed to involve the widest possible range of parishioners in parish planning and the pastoral apostolate, and to draw on their ideas and energy. Obviously, a good deal of cooperation on the part of clergy and laity is necessary for this undertaking, in addition to planning and training. For this reason the cardinal began an office for the orderly establishment of parish councils. To do this work he chose Monsignor Henry Mansell, later to become chancellor of the archdiocese. These councils have become a major source of strength in the Church of New York at a time when other resources have been declining.

Cardinal Cooke's well known fiscal abilities were put to work very quickly by the United States Catholic Conference. He was made chairman of the bishops' committee to devise a uniform system for reporting finances in all dioceses throughout the country. Under his chairmanship, a volume of norms and guides was published. In 1973 the New York archdiocese became the first diocese in the United States to publish a total financial disclosure. It set a benchmark for this kind of reporting by dioceses around the country.

In order to provide for better administrative function in the archdiocese and to save money, Cardinal Cooke initiated a consolidation of all archdiocesan administrative facilities. A twenty-story building was erected at First Avenue and Fifty-fifth Street, in a much less expensive area and away from the congestion around Saint Patrick's Cathedral, where the offices had formally been located. This new building included Cathedral Girls High School, Catholic Charities, the Department of Education and central administration. This building was completed in 1974 under the direction of then-Monsignor William McCormick, now Bishop McCormick and the national director of the Society for the Propagation of the Faith.

Under the cardinal's watchful eye, a permanent diaconate program was established in the New York archdiocese with an expanding training program. Many dioceses throughout the country have recognized the importance of permanent deacons as part of the pastoral apostolate of the Church. In New York this revival of an earlier ministry has been particularly important in serving the needs of minority groups and of outlying parishes.

Cardinal Spellman had established a Senate of Priests in 1967, the year of his death. Cardinal Cooke attended monthly the meetings of either the full senate or of the senate's executive committee. In conjunction with the senate, he established a due process system through which lay persons, religious or priests who feel they have not received equitable treatment from an archdiocesan institution may seek redress. The cardinal also established a personnel board to review the placement of priests, consult with them and make recommendations on assignments to the archbishop.

The cardinal directed the opening of special archdiocesan offices for the care of particular ethnic groups. Both the Office of Black Ministry and the Spanish-speaking apostolate focus on the concerns of these large segments of the archdiocese. He began an Office for the Italian apostolate to care primarily for recent immigrants from Italy. The cardinal showed himself to be especially interested in the needs of smaller immigrant groups, like Albanians, Vietnamese, and other recently arrived minorities.

Cardinal Cooke initiated an Office for World Justice and Peace. He established the Center for Spiritual Development, which conducts the largest adult education program in the United States focused on the spiritual growth and education of laity and religious. It also provides for training for clergy, religious and laity as spiritual directors. He provided for the spiritual needs of the clergy by establishing Trinity Retreat in Larchmont, which is one of two retreat houses in the United States exclusively for the clergy.

During these years, Cardinal Cooke served on the executive committee of the National Conference of Catholic Bishops. He was chairman of the NCCB Committee for Pro-Life Activities, which we will discuss in the next chapter. The President of the United States appointed him to several important national committees, including the Task Force on Foreign Aid and the Task Force on Violence. Fortunately, as his friend Monsignor Joseph Murphy has pointed out, he loved to go to meetings.[9] They were his recreation. In the last year of his life, despite illness, the cardinal participated in over two hundred meetings.

As One Who Serves

In his sermon at the Chrism Mass in 1977, when Cardinal Cooke spoke about the priest as a servant, he observed that a priest is called to give up his own family to serve the needs of others. It is important to recognize that although Cardinal Cooke was involved in numerous activities, it would conceivably have been possible for a man with a family to do the same thing. Admittedly, that family could have complained about being neglected. There are many public figures in the United States who are busy and involved, and yet are parents of families. Cardinal Cooke's remarkable apostolate had another dimension, however, that is, he saw himself as a personal servant to all who were in need.

In the cardinal's immense archives there are approximately one hundred fifty thousand letters written while he was Archbishop of New York. About half of these letters are expressions of his gratitude for help given to other people, especially the poor. He signed almost all of these letters himself. Cardinal Cooke had to beg for money to keep so many programs going. He was always grateful to those who had been generous to him and to the Church of New York, and solicitous for their well-being.[10] This caused him to be deeply involved in the personal concerns of thousands of people.

Those who knew the cardinal well realize that like many dedicated bishops and priests, he could not possibly have done justice to a family. He spoke very personally and from his own heart when he said that "the priest as a servant must give up his own family." One can speculate what kind of a father he would have been to his own children. From what he did for other people's children, it is safe to conclude that he would have been loving, patient and concerned like his own father. He was such a good spiritual father to so many, there is no doubt he would have made a very fine father of a family.

Cardinal Cooke always saw himself as a servant. It was his obsession to wish to make those whom he met happy, and to make them accept themselves. It was his apostolic intent to bring all whom he met closer to God through a relationship with Jesus Christ.

In this regard Cardinal Cooke had learned his lessons well as a schoolboy. He had been taught by the sisters at Saint Benedict's to be a generous and gracious disciple of Christ, filled with cheerfulness and a willingness to be helpful.

A touching detail about his dedication and love for others was revealed when we did the interviews for this portrait. One of Terence Cooke's teachers in the early grades of grammar school, Sister Anthony, O.P.,[11] is now retired at the Dominican Motherhouse in Blauvelt, New York. Sister Anthony regularly sent to the cardinal notes and clippings of his picture from the newspapers. Naturally, pictures and articles appeared many times, and Sister Anthony, being retired, had the time to send her illustrious former student dozens of them. When she was interviewed, Sister Anthony came armed with two scrapbooks filled with 150 personal letters from Cardinal Cooke. Many of these letters contained some handwritten note of family interest, as well as warm greetings. It is astonishing that a man with so many responsibilities and so many demands made upon him could find the time to acknowledge each note from his grammar school teacher.

The reader is asked to ponder this little detail after reading through the long list of the cardinal's accomplishments. The world would not recognize the importance of those scrapbooks of Sister Anthony's, but they might provide a better insight into the kind of man we are considering more than all the titles he had or great things he accomplished.

Cardinal Cooke took his busy life very lightly. He did not feel sorry for himself or consider himself overburdened. In fact, there was a mysterious center of joy and optimism in his life during all of these endeavors. He could say quite honestly to the housekeeper Maura O'Kelly, "I don't have bad moods."

On one occasion Cardinal Cooke was speaking to the musician's union and delighted them by revealing that when he was young he had played the violin. After discussing some of the things he had to do as archbishop, he explained to the members that although he cherished the union card they had given him, he no longer played. Referring to his responsibilities as archbishop, the cardinal gave this excuse for deserting the musical ranks — "It really doesn't leave me much time to practice."[12]

CHAPTER NINE

SPEAK, LORD,
YOUR SERVANT LISTENS

*L*istening to others is an art that is particularly important for those who wish to be helpers in this world. Cardinal Cooke described a priest as a listener. He believed a priest needs "to listen, to learn prayerfully from the way that God has worked in the lives of his people, full of faith to carry that message to others."[1]

Cardinal Cooke was preeminently a listener. This quality annoyed some and assisted many, even those who were annoyed when he listened to other people. It is obvious from his life and from the statement just quoted that the first one he listened to was God. He was open to God's speaking to him through others, even others who disagreed with him. Cardinal Cooke was convinced that God could speak through others even when, to some degree, they were wrong. He believed that one could learn not only from the intelligent observations of others, but even from their mistakes. He was willing to listen not only to the prophet and the saintly person, but also to the poor sinner and the person who was desperate.

Each one of the people he listened to evoked from him a response based on faith, a response that he hoped was inspired by God. One understands Terence Cooke only when one is able to recognize this complex way of thinking that came so naturally to him. Even if he was speaking with someone who was severely critical of him or with an enemy of religion, he was convinced that this person might be able to highlight some message from God which was already in divine revelation.

The personal quality that most assisted Terence Cooke as Archbishop of New York was his ability to listen. He did not necessarily commit himself to doing what his listeners wanted, but he tried to give them a hearing. As we have said, it was a time of immense turmoil in the Church. Terence Cooke's goal as archbishop was to do all he could to limit the damage this turmoil was doing to the Church, and at the same time to bring the disparate elements of the Church together. The following quotation, taken from his sermon at his installation as archbishop on April 4, 1968, reveals a great deal about his goals and expectations.

> I know that some of our people have been troubled by the recent efforts toward renewal in the church. They feel tempest-tossed and threatened by the process of change they have experienced. Others are disturbed because worthwhile changes seem to come too slowly, and they wonder if renewal and reform will ever be achieved. I hope that all of us will continue to realize that we are *one* people, one family of God; and I hope that in spite of different views and feelings, we shall maintain the unity of love. In a day when we are on the verge of healing ancient wounds that have divided us from others, in a day when ecumenism is in its springtime, surely God calls us to be a shining example of unity among ourselves, with much patience, with much forbearance, with deep and persevering love for one another. Love never divides people; it unites them, and love is the priceless heritage which Christ left to His church. [2]

It is obvious from this quotation that Terence Cooke intended to listen to people on the right and on the left, if we may use these inadequate spatial analogies. It did not mean, as some have construed it to mean, that he was going to be "led around by the nose." Those who expected him to be a carbon copy of Cardinal Spellman — to use a cynical phrase which made the rounds at that time, "a transplanted soul" — were sorely disappointed. The times in which Cardinal Cooke served were very different from those of Cardinal Spellman. Terence Cooke surprised many by being very much his own man. In no way did he surprise them more than by his ability to listen.

This ability was probably a natural trait. Frequently at a meeting Cardinal Cooke spoke last. By speaking quietly — and after everyone else had spoken — he was able to sum up the situation and present an adequate solution. A number of people have described tedious meetings at which Cardinal Cooke said practically nothing and then, at the end, quietly proposed what seemed to most a satisfactory solution.

In this chapter we will take up several important issues in the life of Terence Cooke that illustrate his ability to listen. Among these issues are the encyclical *Humanae Vitae* of Pope Paul VI; the pastoral care of homosexually-oriented people; the question of renewal in the Church, especially the role of women; and finally, the issue of pro-life activities and the abortion controversy. These are among the most challenging issues that the cardinal faced as Archbishop of New York.

The Way He Thought

Before we consider these important issues, it may be helpful to point out that Cardinal Cooke was not an abstract thinker. He was not a theologian or a philosopher. In fact, he probably felt uncomfortable speculating about theological issues because he had not had the privilege of advanced theological training. The cardinal did enjoy a good religious discussion now and then, but generally tended to embrace new ideas only if they were in accord with the accepted Catholic tradition. His intelligence was focused more on practical areas than on any speculative pursuits. When confronted with a theological dilemma, he almost always used the principle that virtue lies in the middle. With a twinkle in his eye, he would often use analogies drawn from baseball when he was speaking with would-be innovators. He would say, "Keep your eye on the ball," or, "Get it over the plate."[3]

On the other hand, when Cardinal Cooke was presented with a new idea, especially by a recognized theologian, he did not reject it so long as it was not obviously inconsistent with the Catholic faith. What he did do was act much like the behavioral scientist. While the person was presenting his idea, Cardinal Cooke would be examining the speaker or writer for these qualities — reverence for God, respect for the Church and tradition, sympathetic understanding of the needs of others, and an ability to relate to the genuine and heart-felt religious sentiments of the ordinary person. If the speaker or writer, no matter how brilliant or even how traditional, showed disrespect for God or irreverence for religion or insensitivity to other people's needs, chances were that he was not going to be taken seriously by Terence Cooke.

Strident voices on the far left and on the far right of the Church did not impress the cardinal, according to Monsignor James Wilders, a close friend for many years. It was Cardinal Cooke's goal to try to bring people together; Monsignor Wilders describes him as a quintessential centralist. This is not always the best of positions. It was not the position of some of the prophets of Israel, who were willing to go against the culture of their times. Those who knew Cardinal Cooke well might speculate that he would have been more sympathetic to the traditionalism of Saint Peter than to the innovations of Saint Paul in the conflict over kosher foods. In the long run he probably would have found some way to bring everyone together. But if the Holy Spirit had been on the other side and Cardinal Cooke had been the first of the apostles, Catholics would still be eating sandwiches made with tuna fish instead of ham.

Nevertheless Cardinal Cooke agreed eminently with Saint Paul's description of charity as kind and patient, not dealing perversely and not rejoicing at wickedness, but rejoicing at the truth. When he became archbishop there were many strident voices in the Church. Some of these have calmed down, others have become even stronger. As we have seen, it was his goal to try to listen to all these voices and to hear what God might be saying through them, even if those who were speaking did not accept what he believed to be God's Word. He always respected the possibility that God was speaking through the individual, no matter how confused that person might be. The cardinal also believed that the best thing to do was to offer people alternative opportunities in a situation which had limited their choices. In a very perceptive observation, Monsignor Michael Wrenn called Cardinal Cooke "the Master of Alternatives."[4] Often, Cardinal Cooke responded to situations created by the confusion of the post-conciliar period by going to great lengths to set up alternatives to what was in vogue.

Humanae Vitae

One of the most painful issues to confront the Catholic Church since the Second Vatican Council was the question of the moral acceptability of artificial contraception. Like a great many other priests Terence Cooke was caught between "a rock and a hard place." He was a traditional Catholic with no apologies. He had always accepted the Church's teaching that artificial forms of family planning were morally unacceptable even when there was a good reason to limit the number of children in a family or to avoid pregnancy at a particular time. The Church has always made serious demands on its members concerning chastity. In light of Sacred Scripture, it did not seem to Cardinal Cooke or to most of the clergy at that time that the teaching on avoiding artificial contraception was excessive or impractical. Almost all agreed, though, that it was difficult.

As the average number of children in a family declined and the life style of the western industrialized nations became more affluent and consumer-oriented, not to say indulgent, the problems of Catholic couples interested in following the teachings of the Church became more acute. The so-called "sexual revolution" (really a shift in cultural mores leading to a general weakening of moral values) affected all areas of life and culture. A growing voice was heard in the Church in favor of adjusting traditional teaching on this matter. Many will recall that as the time for a promised papal statement on artificial contraception drew near, there was real confusion among the clergy and laity. Some informed persons, including theologians, seemed convinced that a change in papal teaching was about to occur. Others were just as certain that no change would come.

Priests such as Cardinal Cooke who were sympathetic to the problems of couples found themselves between "the rock" of traditional teaching and "the hard place" of wanting to help relieve the distress of a great number of couples, young and middle-aged, who found the application of Church teaching in the practical order very difficult. It was a dilemma that many saw reflected in the long delay of Pope Paul VI in publishing the encyclical *Humanae Vitae.* This official pastoral statement, which has serious binding force on the faithful, maintained the traditional teaching that the use of artificial contraception was forbidden. It also reflected considerable sympathy.

One of the first bishops in the entire Church to respond was Archbishop Cooke. Archbishop Theodore E. McCarrick, then rector of the Catholic University in Puerto Rico, was with Terence Cooke at the time the encyclical was published. Archbishop McCarrick told us that "once *Humanae Vitae* came out the press immediately started to go after him for a statement. He struggled to come out with the right words. We decided that there should be a cablegram to the Holy Father in which he would express his adherence to the teaching. Then, there would be another statement for the archdiocese and the press. There was no question in his mind that he was going to be opposed on *Humanae Vitae.*"[5]

In his statement to Pope Paul VI, Archbishop Cooke wrote,

> "Thou art Peter. Where Peter is there is the Church." United with you in your paternal care to safeguard the holiness of marriage and the human family. Assure you of our prayerful pastoral efforts in fulfilling this urgent responsibility.
>
> Your devoted Son,
✠ Terence Cooke [6]

There is no doubt that Terence Cooke realized that his statement would be unfavorably received in many quarters. Those who were not enthusiastic about the statement might see his response as a self-serving one. On the contrary, it was the thing to do. The cardinal's response was totally consistent with the person we have come to know in this portrait. "The Holy See was surprised at the strength and the promptness of his adherence," Archbishop McCarrick recalls.

Cardinal Cooke and Courage

In the late 1960's and early 1970's the homosexual population of the United States began to become vocal and to make its demands heard. Many people, even in New York City, were surprised by the large number of people who identified themselves as homosexuals and by their complaints about how they were being treated. Many people were aware of this mistreatment, which can be cruel and destructive. Cardinal Cooke was among those who began to think of the needs of this group, which included many members of the Church and people of vastly contrasting opinions.

Since the cardinal would support and be guided by Church doctrine, it may be helpful to summarize the traditionally accepted teaching at the beginning of this account. The Catholic Church teaches that homosexual tendencies are not in themselves sinful, but genital homosexual behavior is morally forbidden. It also teaches that the virtue of modesty requires that a person with homosexual tendencies avoid behavior that is likely to lead to genital homosexual acts. The Church teaches that everyone is obliged to avoid giving scandal, that is, to avoid leading another person into sinful behavior or into an acceptance of behavior that leads to sin. Pope John Paul II reiterated this teaching to the Catholic bishops of the United States in Chicago as recently as 1979. The Congregation of the Doctrine of Faith also issued a document on the subject on October 1, 1986.[7]

In the 1970's the homosexual movement in the United States began demanding civil rights. Obviously some of these demands were quite justified, such as protection from violence, public insults and discrimination. Members of the homosexual segment of society began to see themselves as a sexual minority group; they demanded a right to decent employment and housing. Some demanded that their life style be accepted as normative behavior on the same level as married life. The message had been given in the 1960's that sex was for fun. This message came largely from the heterosexual community, and often led to a gradual abandonment of marriage and a decline in family life. The homosexual movement was doing little more than saying: "If sex is for fun, then it's fun for us too."

In New York the homosexual community reflected a wide range of opinions, from those with militant points of view who advocated that homosexual "couples" should be allowed to adopt children, to those who had lived active homosexual lives but were convinced that this form of behavior was an illness and even immoral. In a city with a homosexual population numbering in the hundreds of thousands, the pastoral problems presented by the homosexual community could not be ignored.

Several times the cardinal discussed with this writer the pastoral care of homosexuals, because he was interested in different views drawn from psychiatry and psychology on this issue. Together we consulted various moral theologians to see what seemed to be the best course of action from a pastoral point of view. It was clear from traditional theology and from the recent teachings of the popes that there could be no compromise on the immorality of homosexual acts.[8] It was also clear, however, that everyone has a right to be accepted as a person. Moreover, every Christian has a right and responsibility to participate in the life of the Church, even if he or she does not live up to its teachings.

Late in the 1960's a group of Catholics who identified themselves as having a homosexual orientation had founded an organization called "Dignity." From their literature, especially the magazine *Insight,* it seemed obvious that this group did not actively support the traditional Catholic teaching on the moral necessity of avoiding homosexual acts. It was not so much that such behavior was explicitly encouraged, but the publications of this group did not clearly offer a chaste life as the single acceptable alternative. Some of the early publications of this movement were often irreverent and disrespectful in tone, and openly defiant of the Church. One is grateful to say that gradually the strident tone of these publications has diminished over the years.

Cardinal Cooke suggested that a few representatives of the archdiocese might make informal contact with the leaders of Dignity to discern if there was any possibility of their accepting the traditional teaching of the Church. This author attended these meetings along with the recognized leadership of Dignity. It was clearly indicated that there was no possibility of a meeting of minds.

Cardinal Cooke then asked me to explore the possibility of initiating an organization for Catholics with homosexual tendencies who were explicitly determined to be guided by the teaching of the Church. I was able to obtain the assistance of Father John Harvey, OSFS, a theologian who had for thirty years worked with homosexually-oriented people, assisting them to live chaste lives. The cardinal was so impressed by this wise and largely unrecognized apostle that he asked Father Harvey to come from Washington, D.C. to New York to start such a group. The first members chose the name "Courage" for their group. This organization has now spread to several cities and is gradually making an impact with its challenging message for those who are willing to take the Church's teaching seriously. It was the pastoral insight of Cardinal Cooke that gave homosexually-oriented Catholics the alternative.[9]

The following scene reveals the compassionate and yet careful thinking of Cardinal Cooke. In the same conversation in which he asked me to find someone to start a group like Courage, he said as we walked along Long Island Sound, "I don't want to hurt anyone who is struggling with homosexuality. I don't want to unnecessarily hurt anyone at all, but I don't think we should be so accepting of this problem that a male grammar school teacher may invite his fourth grade class to his wedding with another man."[10] For this precise reason Cardinal Cooke was willing to risk serious criticism especially from the media by opposing the Gay Civil Rights Bill. While not opposed to civil rights he believed that these bills as presented gave mass approval to the gay life style. The cardinal who admitted to finding homosexual attractions incomprehensible said that he had known some fine people who struggled with this problem. Being familiar with the behavioral sciences, the cardinal was aware that society and the

Church as part of society must do everything possible to encourage children toward a heterosexual orientation. This is particularly true at a time when there are many dysfunctional families, causing a rise in the number of youngsters who have ambivalent or poorly formed sexual identities.

The cardinal's position on homosexuality and the Dignity movement has been vindicated in very recent years by the growth of a twelve-step organization called "Sexaholics Anonymous."[11] Although the organization is not exclusively dedicated to assisting people with homosexual tendencies, large numbers of the members of Sexaholics Anonymous are in fact people who are attempting to overcome homosexual behavior by leading a chaste life. This movement, perhaps more than any other single development in this issue, points out that the cardinal was wise and justified in his unwillingness to accept Dignity and in establishing an organization for homosexually-oriented persons which upheld Catholic moral teaching.

Some have asked why Cardinal Cooke tolerated a Mass for Dignity at a Catholic church in Manhattan. The archdiocese never gave permission for such a Mass, and it was held as part of the regular Mass schedule of Saint Francis Xavier Church. The chancery attempted several times to have the religious community in charge of the parish discontinue any publicity given to this Mass as a liturgy for homosexually-oriented people.[12] To my knowledge this request was not honored.

I am frequently asked, "Why didn't the cardinal put his foot down and cancel the Mass?" The answer is found in his own words quoted a few paragraphs above, "I don't want to hurt anyone who is struggling with homosexuality. I don't want to unnecessarily hurt anyone at all." Before criticizing the cardinal for weakness, it might be well to recall that Church authorities have tolerated all kinds of human behavior over the centuries. In fact, so did Our Lord Jesus Christ tolerate human weakness. He said to the apostles, "How long shall I put up with you?" (Mark

9:19), referring to their lack of faith. To Peter, He said, "Satan demanded to have you, that he might sift you like wheat, but I have prayed for you" (Luke 22:31). At times most of us must tolerate inconsistencies in our own lives which we do not approve of, but which we cannot at first overcome.

Cardinal Cooke held it as a pastoral principle that he had to try to listen with faith and compassion, even to those who were not at the moment prepared to follow all of the commandments or to lead a chaste life. He knew very well, on the other hand, that the Church cannot condone behavior that is against the moral teachings of Christianity or would cause grave scandal. Yet it cannot turn its back on the sinner. Those who are not ready at this moment to overcome the sinful and scandalous behavior of alcoholism or of chronic bad temper do not expect the Church to conduct a weekly Mass for them. Neither Cardinal Cooke nor any one else working within the administration at that time thought that there should be a Mass for any group of poor sinners unless they were already on the road to repentance and reform.

The archdiocese would certainly sponsor a Mass for the Matt Talbot Circle of AA, or for Courage, or for Catholics belonging to Sexaholics Anonymous. The Church should not offer a Mass for active alcoholics, nor for those who actively support homosexual behavior. The real question is, if one is confronted with the existence of such a liturgy and serious attempts to discontinue it are not successful, does one do more harm than good by forcefully suppressing it? If one is as gentle and kindly as Terence Cooke, one will probably seek to offer some options to those who participate in it. This is precisely what the cardinal did.

Since the death of Cardinal Cooke, at the initiative of the Holy See, public Masses sponsored by Dignity have been discontinued. There should be no doubt in anyone's mind that if such an initiative had been given at that time, it would have been acted on immediately by Cardinal Cooke. The reader must decide for himself or herself whether his gentleness in dealing with this issue was a fault or a virtue. One suspects that the cardinal asked himself the same question. From what we know about his ability to listen to others and his devotion to the truth, it is difficult to doubt the sincerity of his answer.

Changes in the Church

Cardinal Cooke was not only a centrist, he was also a gradualist. Because of his training as a social worker, the cardinal recognized that rapid change was often disturbing to people and therefore counterproductive. Because of his training in the behavioral sciences, he recognized that one of the most difficult changes of all is change in religious expression and religious symbolism. Religious symbols have profound emotional and psychological roots in the personality and experience of an individual. To fail to take these roots into account is to sow the seeds of serious religious discord. It is also counterproductive, because people often resist change when it is proposed too rapidly. As a result, needed changes are not made.

Many people criticized Cardinal Cooke for not going "fast enough." Indeed, as we have seen in the previous chapter, many innovations and changes took place during his years as archbishop. Inevitably, these changes were gradual. Those who were impatient were often quite critical of the cardinal. It could be said by anyone objectively examining the Archdiocese of New York that when changes were made, especially in regard to religious symbols and public ceremonies, they were made with an eye both to dignity and to respect for Catholic tradition. Esoteric and flamboyant symbolism was never the order of the day in the archdiocese. Cardinal Cooke himself was personally and deeply uncomfortable with any approach to the sacred liturgy which lacked reverence. On the other hand, as we have pointed out, he might annoy the liturgical expert by his impulse to involve people as closely and spontaneously as possible in liturgical worship.

The Role of Women in the Church

One of the most sensitive issues in all of the changes taking place in the Church is one that reflects a change in the whole culture of western civilization. This is the new role of women. It is well to recall that among the most important people in Cardinal Cooke's life were several women, including his mother, Margaret; his Aunt Mary; his sister, Katherine; the Dominican Sisters who taught him and other religious women who worked closely with him; and the women who assisted him in the chancery and in his residence. He especially had a tremendous love and respect for religious sisters. The dedication and humility called for by religious life was something which was innately attractive to him.

As changes came in the Church, Cardinal Cooke welcomed the opportunity to put women in places of importance in the government of the archdiocese. Being a gradualist, he moved more slowly in this area than some would have liked. Being a traditionalist, he gave no support at all to movements for the ordination of women, especially since the Holy See had indicated that this question was not open for discussion. On the other hand, his sympathetic and open personality made him acutely aware that women needed much more recognition in the Church. For this reason, and despite the opposition of numbers of men and women of a more conservative stamp, women took as much of a role as possible in the liturgical services at Saint Patrick's Cathedral.

Cardinal Cooke particularly enjoyed three movements in the Church in which women had an equal role with men. These were the Cursillo, the Christian Family Movement, and the Charismatic Renewal. He recognized all three of these movements as powerful and spontaneous invitations to spiritual growth. He supported each one and welcomed them to Saint Patrick's. He participated in their diocesan functions and enjoyed himself thoroughly.

A small personal vignette may be revealing about one side of his personality. Although Cardinal Cooke was a very warm and expressive man, he did not like to be kissed, especially by strangers or people he scarcely knew. His innate appreciation of the dignity of the clergy, and especially of the office of bishop, made him shy away from the contemporary custom of kissing total strangers at the drop of a hat. Several times I remember accompanying him to charismatic meetings or programs of the Christian Family Movement. He would look at me wryly as we walked in the door and say, "Now, Benedict, we will get some souls out of purgatory." I knew that he meant that we would be offering up the many kisses we would receive as a prayer for the holy souls.

I recall Cardinal Cooke leaving a huge charismatic meeting, trying to wipe the lipstick of the enthusiastic children of the Holy Spirit from his cheeks. He was very amused when I remarked that it blended so nicely with the color of his cardinal's robes. Although he did not appreciate being kissed in public, the cardinal would never in any way resist this impulse of others, for fear of hurting their feelings or making them feel as though they were inferior to him. Perhaps even this might be considered an example of heroic virtue.

The Struggle for Life

One of the most serious issues to confront Cardinal Cooke and one that occupied his attention to the very end was the struggle for life. His entire attitude toward human beings and their intrinsic value — the great and the small, the healthy and the sick, the young and the old, the wanted and the unwanted — caused him to be deeply distressed by the legalization of abortion in the United States. So intensely did he believe that abortion was one of the worst moral evils in our society, and the worst form of

child abuse, that he proposed to the American bishops an entire
program for pro-life activities and was made chairman of the
Bishops' Committee on Pro-Life Activities.

Because of certain historical facts and treacherous actions
by some public officials, Cardinal Cooke's support for the pro-life
cause and his opposition to pro-abortion legislation have occasionally been called into question. It is necessary, then, even in this
spiritual portrait, to take a more intense look at this issue and
particularly to try to understand how it affected the spiritual life of
the cardinal. Monsignor James J. Murray, who once served as
Cardinal Cooke's secretary and was subsequently appointed to
his present post as director of Catholic Charities, provided us
with much of this information. [13] He recalls that as early as
mid-1960, then-Bishop Cooke and Archbishop John Maguire assisted Cardinal Spellman in opposition to pro-abortion legislation
in New York. When Terence Cooke became archbishop he made
every conceivable effort to halt abortion in New York State and on
a national level. These were two distinct battles and are best
discussed separately.

The Struggle in New York

During the year after Terence Cooke was named cardinal, a
tremendous battle raged in the New York State legislature over
abortion. This battle placed Cardinal Cooke in a dilemma, because he was opposed to any action that even looked like an
attempt to directly influence a legislator. He believed that an
informed electorate should influence the legislature. He was not
the slightest bit bashful, however, in trying to inform that electorate about pertinent issues concerning morality. But the cardinal
was not at all comfortable with the idea of politicians being
controlled by religious leaders. He felt that that was a style that
belonged to an earlier day, when anti-Catholic prejudice was

strong and as a result there were semi-official, pro-Catholic political leaders.

In the New York State Catholic Conference, Cardinal Cooke joined all the bishops of the state in clear opposition to the pro-abortion legislation that was proposed. From his personal advisors this author has learned that the cardinal believed there was enough opposition in the legislature to defeat the pro-abortion bill in the spring of 1970. Then an unprecedented act of treachery took place. A rumor was circulated in the legislature on the morning of April 10, 1970 that "a deal" had been worked out between Governor Nelson Rockefeller and Cardinal Cooke. In this purported deal, according to the rumor, the cardinal had agreed to soft-pedal opposition to the abortion issue in return for the passage of the Mandated Services Law for Private and Parochial Schools. An informed and reliable witness has told us of speaking to a right-to-life picket who was told outside the legislature that morning by an unknown person that the cardinal did not want pickets there that day.

This lie spread through the legislature that morning, and several members who saw the bill as a political hot potato were relieved to be able to go along with it. The bill passed because of this act of treachery, 31 to 26. The cardinal was deeply distressed both by the passage of the bill and the lie that was reported about him. Several advisors urged the cardinal to expose this lie directly, but that was not his way of doing things. The next day the New York State bishops, led by Cardinal Cooke, attacked the new law as they had attacked previous legislation and appealed for its veto. This was done almost as a matter of form because the governor himself was a strong supporter of the law and of abortion in general. The bishops wrote,

> It is difficult to express our shock and distress over this event particularly since it seems destined, God forbid, to lower respect for all human life — the aged, the sick, the

unwanted. We cannot forget that this Bill was endorsed by
many because it would help parents rid themselves of unwanted children.

The Law of New York may be changed, but that does not
change the Law of God. Abortion is a heinous crime and
remains a crime against man's nature even though it may no
longer be a crime against man's law in New York.

We believe life, all life, is God's gift. We urge our people to
rededicate themselves to its protection in the face of the
present attacks against the aged, the neglected, the unwanted, the abandoned and the unborn. [14]

Shortly afterward an important dinner was held at the
Waldorf-Astoria Hotel to which Cardinal Cooke was invited, and
at which Nelson Rockefeller was one of the honored guests.
Cardinal Cooke refused to attend the dinner, but two other
priests, Monsignor Patrick Ahern and Monsignor Gustav
Schultheiss, represented the archdiocese and walked out when
the governor came in.

On June 29th Cardinal Cooke called for a boycott of the
abortion law and the state bishops again attacked the law, calling
it a tragic chapter in our history. The following December Cardinal Cooke issued a pastoral letter on abortion which was read at
all Masses.

Once more we denounce this outrage against humanity.
Together with all the bishops of the world we hold and teach
that "abortion is an unspeakable crime." We urge you, our
fellow Catholics — and through you all men of good will —
not to be deceived because a civil law permits abortion.
God's law comes first, and God's law says: "Thou shalt not
kill." No civil law can ever displace God's Commandment.

We plead with you to recognize the terrible consequence of
legalized abortion. Once innocent life at any stage is placed

at the mercy of others, a vicious principle has been legalized. Thereafter, a simple majority may decide that life is to be denied to the defective, the aged, the incorrigible, and granted only to the strong, the beautiful and the intelligent. The day may come when lawmakers could set standards which people must meet if they are to remain alive. Already one standard has been set; who can say what others will come next? For, once respect for human life has been undermined, the murderous possibilities are limitless.

We urge you, as strongly as we can, to oppose and reject abortion. Lest anyone take our words lightly, we must also remind you that the Church invokes a severe sanction against any Catholic who raises his unfeeling hand to destroy this most defenseless of all human beings — the unborn baby. The Church disowns by immediate excommunication any Catholic who deliberately procures an abortion or helps someone else to do so. [15]

In April, the cardinal announced the establishment of "Birthright," a program which offered an alternative to abortion. Through this archdiocesan-sponsored organization many young mothers have been helped who decided to keep their babies. He also announced a large scale, informational advertising campaign to make Birthright known to pregnant women and girls who were considering abortion. He also offered any assistance to women in need including medical care, counseling and help after the birth of the child. Through Birthright and several other Catholic sponsored agencies, thousands of needy young women have been assisted over the years.

It is not unusual in New York for an unwed mother with her child to be cared for even up to two years after delivery. Many mothers who have chosen to have their babies adopted have received total care through services which are either part of Catholic Charities or are under Catholic sponsorship in the archdiocese. Hundreds of lay Catholics and religious concerned to do something about abortion have given substantively of time and energy to work for the programs in order to save the lives of the unborn.

The abortion battle was just beginning. The New York State legislature passed a repeal of the abortion law of 1970. Governor Rockefeller offered a compromise bill which would reduce the number of weeks during which an abortion could be legally performed. Of course, the bishops had no choice but to reject this proposal and to state their unalterable opposition to the taking of human life at any time. This was done in a document of May 5, 1972. On May 13th Governor Rockefeller vetoed the repeal of the abortion law of 1970. Cardinal Cooke on the same day expressed great sorrow and regret at the governor's veto.

Monsignor Clark gives us a full account of an incident that reveals how Cardinal Cooke handled conflict. As the Al Smith Dinner approached, an annual fund-raiser hosted by the Archbishop of New York, the cardinal was in a quandary. The Governor of New York was usually invited to be one of the speakers. Because Governor Rockefeller had vetoed the pro-life bills the cardinal believed he could not in good conscience invite him to speak. However, he did not want to withdraw his invitation to attend the dinner. Monsignor Clark was sent on a delicate mission to inform Governor Rockefeller that they were stream-lining the dinner and he would not be invited to speak. The governor responded by suggesting that he knew the stream-lining had a very important purpose. The governor was so sure that Cardinal Cooke would relent that he brought a speech with him the night of the dinner. The cardinal did not change his mind. [16]

In the days immediately preceding the veto an extremely interesting event took place which again shows a certain amount of political deception. President Richard M. Nixon had heard about the opposition of the New York archdiocese to abortion. He wrote a letter to the cardinal and indicated that this letter could be published to underscore his opposition to abortion. This letter was delivered by express mail directly from the office of Mr. Patrick Buchanan, a presidential aide, late on a Friday afternoon. It was decided to release this letter on Monday. An advance copy would be given to the *Daily News,* which indeed carried the letter. The *Daily News* sent a photographer to the cardinal's residence to take a photograph of the presidential letter, since the archdiocesan officials would not let the original out of their hands. We quote from the following letter which appeared in the *Daily News.*

Dear Cardinal Cooke:

I read in the *Daily News* that the Archdiocese of New York, under your leadership, has initiated a campaign to bring about repeal of the state's liberalized abortion laws. Though this is a matter for state decision outside Federal jurisdiction, I would personally like to associate myself with the convictions you deeply feel and eloquently express.

The unrestricted abortion policies now recommended by some of Americans, and the liberalized abortion policies in effect in some sections of this country seem to me impossible to reconcile with either our religious traditions or our Western heritage. One of the foundation stones of our society and civilization is a profound belief that human life, all human life is a precious commodity — not to be taken without the gravest of causes. Yet, in this great and good country of ours, in recent years, the right to life of literally hundreds of thousands of unborn children has been destroyed — legally — but in my judgment without anything approaching adequate justification.

Your decision, and that of tens of thousands of Catholics, Protestants, Jews, and men and women of no particular faith, to act in the public forum as defenders of the right to life of the unborn, is truly a noble endeavor. In this calling, you and they have my admiration, sympathy and support.

Richard Nixon [17]

According to all reports, this letter was very upsetting to Governor Rockefeller. It was also upsetting to Mr. John Ehrlichman and Mr. John Haldeman, Nixon staffers, to such an extent that some of the national news magazines and newspapers reported that these men denied that the president actually signed the letter. They claimed that the letter was released without the president's knowledge. This later turned out to be untrue. Thus, some conscious distortion of facts had again gone into the attempt to block the opposition to abortion.

In August of that year Cardinal Cooke was invited to speak at the first annual American Health Congress in Chicago. He spoke to a large group of representatives of hospitals and health-care agencies throughout the country. Cardinal Cooke again condemned abortion as well as other medical procedures, such as euthanasia, which encroach upon the sacredness of human life. In his talk he quoted the famous Protestant missionary Albert Schweitzer, who said, "If a man loses his reverence for any part of life he will lose his reverence for all of life."[18] He also stated, "the philosophical principles behind the euthanasia movement are utilitarian and materialistic and they run contrary to the Judeo-Christian tradition which respects the sacredness and dignity of all human life."[19]

On January 22, 1973, the Supreme Court of the United States legalized abortion by a substantive judicial decision. Cardinal Cooke joined bishops and religious leaders throughout the country in condemning this decision of the high court. Twice in 1973 Cardinal Cooke issued statements attacking abortion. On January 14, 1974 he urged the passage of an anti-abortion amendment to the constitution of the United States. It was in March of that year that the cardinal was made chairman of the Ad Hoc Committee on Pro-Life Activities of the National Conference of Catholic Bishops. Along with Bishop Francis Mugavero of Brooklyn in November of 1976, he supported a detailed plan for the passage of a pro-life amendment. The cardinal also appealed to the Board of Education to keep five schools open for pregnant high school girls. In the meantime, Birthright and other programs under the sponsorship of the archdiocese continued to grow.

In his statement in January 1983, on the tenth anniversary of the Supreme Court decision to legalize abortion, Cardinal Cooke wrote,

> The decisions of the Supreme Court on January 22, 1973 have been a national tragedy. They have made it legally impossible for the government at the local, state and federal level to fulfill one of its fundamental duties — the protection of the most dependent and defenseless members of our society, the innocent unborn. No longer is the unborn child considered a person according to the Fourteenth Amendment. He or she is now not entitled to constitutional protection. A woman's right to privacy has legal precedence over the right to life of the unborn.
>
> Abortion is much more than a Catholic issue; it is a concern of millions of other Americans as well. Not only is it a matter of personal morality; it deals with the most fundamental of human and civil rights — the very right to life. When an abortion takes place, the life of an unborn human being is ended. The fact that society allows this, much less supports it by law and sometimes — as in New York State — even pays for it with public monies, is a serious obstacle to the safeguarding of human dignity and the rights of each and every individual. [20]

The National Pro-Life Struggle

While the battle raged in New York State, Cardinal Cooke became the leading Catholic bishop in the entire country in the struggle against abortion. It is important to realize that in the early 1970's many of those who would become outspoken opponents of abortion for religious reasons were still confused. This confusion is very well described in the evangelical publication *Christianity Today*.

> Few anticipated the complete victory that Roe v. Wade gave pro-abortionists in 1973 . . . *Christianity Today* greeted Roe v. Wade with a fire storm of criticism . . . But *CT* was ahead of many evangelicals. In its news report on Roe v. Wade, it quoted the prominent Southern Baptist pastor W.A. Criswell: "I have always felt that it was only after a child was born and had life separate from its mother that it became an individual person, and it has always, therefore, seemed to me that what is best for the mother and for the future should be allowed." (He has since repudiated this position.) It would be years before such a statement from an evangelical leader would be unthinkable. According to Brown, an editorial writer for *CT*, evangelicals simply could not imagine themselves lining up with Roman Catholics, nor could they imagine that the Supreme Court of their beloved nation (which they thought of as Protestant) would support a cause directly opposed to Christian values . . . An editorial in the *Christian Century* proclaimed that "this is a beautifully accurate balancing of individual vs. social rights . . . It is a decision both pro-abortionists and anti-abortionists can live with."[21]

Unfortunately, most of the so-called mainstream Christian denominations in the United States did not oppose abortion and have not even yet taken a stand against it. At that time there was even a Catholic priest in Congress, Father Robert F. Drinan, S.J., who forcefully defended the use of public funds for abortion and attacked the Hyde amendment which would have prohibited paying for abortions with tax money.[22]

Monsignor James T. McHugh, now bishop of Camden, New Jersey, worked closely and intensely with Cardinal Cooke after his appointment as chairman of the Bishops' Committee for Pro-

Life Activities. He asserts that it was Cardinal Cooke who initially recognized that a comprehensive pastoral plan for Catholic pro-life activities was needed. The cardinal and Bishop McHugh were responsible for the formulation of that plan and for the education program that it sponsored. Bishop McHugh says, "Cardinal Cooke worked closely on the draft of the plan. He indicated the idea to all the staff and stayed on top of it until it was finally approved by the bishops in 1975. The cardinal was convinced that a detailed plan of action was necessary to guide and direct the long-range effort. During the NCCB Administrative Committee meeting he deftly managed the debate and assured adoption of the pastoral plan by the conference. He always asked me to tell him if I needed any assistance or financial help, and he would get it."[23]

From the years when he was working with Cardinal Cooke, Bishop McHugh recalls the following unusual and almost unprecedented incident in the life of the cardinal: he got angry!

Bishop McHugh reports that Cardinal Cooke was at a press conference on Pro-Life Activities when some of the reporters began to bait him, saying that it seemed to them that he was getting very close to directly influencing political activities. They suggested that he had crossed the line of separation between Church and state. Without answering their questions, Cardinal Cooke said, "Have I crossed the line? Look at this." Then he reached into his briefcase and brought out several scurrilous ads that had been sponsored by a local chapter of Planned Parenthood. These ads directly attacked the Church and irreverently misused the name of the Blessed Virgin Mary. Cardinal Cooke said, "Did I cross the line? Look at this. Look at this. What do you think about this?" They were all struck to silence. Without uttering another word, the cardinal stood up and left the room.[24]

Bishop McHugh maintains that there was no person in the United States who was more effective in the work of establishing a Catholic pro-life movement than Cardinal Cooke. He holds that the cardinal, throughout his years as chairman of the Bishops' Committee on Pro-Life Activities, was the leading Catholic opponent of abortion in the United States. Even when other Christians were confused or doubtful or silent about this issue, Cardinal Cooke was the explicit and outspoken defender of the unborn among all the principal leaders in the United States.

A Special Splendor

Little did Cardinal Cooke realize when he established the first week of October as "Pro-Life Week" in 1972 that his last public statement as Archbishop of New York would be on the occasion of the pro-life observance in the Archdiocese of New York and the Military Vicariate. This statement was in fact published and read at all Masses in the archdiocese and the vicariate on the Sunday after Cardinal Cooke's death. This pastoral letter has been quoted thousands of times and is probably the most forceful document that Cardinal Cooke ever wrote. The fact that it was written by a man who was in the last stages of his own physical life and who used his dying energy to make this statement has proven to be immensely moving to those who read it. The following sentiments stand out as revealing what this terrible controversy had taught the cardinal in his own soul.

It is at times when life is threatened, such as times of serious illness, that the Lord gives us special grace to appreciate the gift of life more deeply as an irreplaceable blessing which only God can give and which God must guide at every step from the beginning of human life, from conception until death and at every moment between, it is Our Lord God who gives us life, and we, who are his creatures, should cry out with joy and thanksgiving for this precious gift. We are made in God's image and likeness and this fact gives a unique dimension to the "gift of life." We have even more reason to be grateful. It is tragic that at our time, concepts which are disastrous to the well being of God's human family; abortion, euthanasia and infanticide are falsely presented as useful and even respectable solutions to human, family and social problems.

. . . From the depths of my being, I urge you to reject this anti-life, anti-child, anti-human view of life and to oppose with all your strength the deadly technologies of life destruction which daily result in planned death of the innocent and the helpless. [25]

Cardinal Cooke ended this pastoral letter with these moving words: "At this grace-filled time of my life, as I experience suffering in union with Jesus, Our Lord and Redeemer, I offer gratitude to almighty God for giving me the opportunity to continue my apostolate on behalf of life."[26]

This statement reveals what this long and painful controversy had cost Cardinal Cooke and what he had gained from it. This statement will probably outlive all the rest of his words. Cardinal Cooke was uncomfortable in any position where he had to accuse others of serious wrongdoing. He had an innate respect for authority, especially for the authority of the civil government. He liked to agree with people and not disagree with them. The painful controversy for the pro-life cause and against abortion had added a certain deep pathos to the spirituality of Cardinal Cooke. It had opened up to him an insight into the value of human life which few of his contemporaries could share. It explains the frightening picture of the deformed child that I discovered in the back of his prayerbook.

"The gift of life, God's special gift, is no less beautiful when it is accompanied by illness or weakness, hunger or poverty, mental or physical handicaps, loneliness or old age. Indeed, at these times, human life gains extra splendor as it requires our special care, concern and reverence. It is in and through the weakest of human vessels that the Lord continues to reveal the power of his love."[27]

A Change of Style?

In an interview with the *New York Sunday News* on Sunday, December 20, 1981, the staff writer, Mr. Frank Lombardi, writes the following about Cardinal Cooke, "Despite twelve years of having his ring kissed in reverential obeisance and being addressed as 'Your Eminence,' Terence Cardinal Cooke can still be best described as 'a kind man from the Bronx.' To most New Yorkers, the 59-year-old prelate comes across as a gentle man with a shy, toothy smile even in the full regalia of a prince of the Church. The bespectacled Cooke looks and acts as unassuming as a choirboy."[28]

In spite of his shy and unassuming manner, Cardinal Cooke had been forced to become more directly involved with legislative procedures. He never broke his resolution about avoiding direct influence on individual legislators; however, he realized that he had to be a bit more direct than he had been in the past.

After asking several incisive questions, Mr. Lombardi continued, "You testified last month before Congress on the issue of abortion. It could be construed as a lobbying activity. Is this a change of style or an intensifying of attitude?" Cardinal Cooke replied, "I hope it's an intensifying. We've been consistent. I have been chairman of the Pro-Life Committee since 1976. I was in Washington for the hearings in 1976 and there have not been hearings since then. We were fulfilling our responsibility to give this testimony.

"There is no doubt that abortion is a very tragic situation. When you think of the millions of unborn children destroyed this is very, very sad. Talk about a violent society, there is nothing more violent than an abortion. Yet my heart goes out to anyone who suffers an abortion too. They need our understanding and prayers. We also have to provide for alternatives to abortion."

Mr. Lombardi then asked the cardinal another question which revealed some change in the cardinal's attitude: "You also seem to be getting more involved in Albany where last year you helped spur Welfare increases." The cardinal replied, "We were involved because Welfare assistance hadn't been adjusted over seven or eight years and poor families couldn't survive on that. I think we all have to be involved. We all have to express our concern and do that privately and publicly. We tried to do it in a manner that is gentle but firm.

"Let there be no doubt about where we should stand by and see any of our brothers and sisters abused and mistreated and do nothing about it. No matter what the sacrifice is, no matter what the cost is we are going to be right there and concerned." As Bishop O'Keefe summed it up so well, "His agenda was simple. It was people."[29]

His Critics

Like any person in the public eye, Terence Cooke had many critics. He was criticized for being too liberal by some and frequently for being too conservative by others. Many thought that he was too tolerant of the point of view that was opposite their own. Because he was a centrist, his goal was to pull people of even fairly divergent views toward the middle by fostering tolerance and by offering alternatives. His efforts were sometimes misunderstood; he was criticized in many articles appearing in Catholic publications for being either too progressive or too conservative. One of the problems that a convinced listener faces is that some of the people he listens to will criticize him for listening to the people on the other side. Terence Cooke was not a listener by constitution. He was a listener by conviction. At times it was possible to observe this. If he was put in a situation where he felt that he was going to be severely challenged or pushed beyond the level of his own competence, he could lose his composure. This happened occasionally in the public meetings with the clergy. He would not be abrupt or discourteous, but he would talk rather than listen. This phenomenon was observable in his first few years as archbishop. It leads the observer to realize that listening was not second nature to him. He was in fact a man of very clear ideas and obvious abilities for leadership. He had to learn to restrain himself and to wait till his critics and advisors had their say.

There is every reason to suspect from his own personal writings and from his conversation that Cardinal Cooke listened from spiritual and religious motives. From his prayer life he was deeply convinced that God spoke through others, even his adversaries. Discourtesy, hostility and confrontation only prevented people from speaking; therefore they were not to be used.

A very revealing incident took place at lunch with a prominent public official. This official, although a Catholic, allowed himself to be put in a compromising position on the question of the legality of abortion. Cardinal Cooke was evidently distressed by this position and let it be known in public. When the official and his wife came to the cardinal's residence for lunch, the cardinal said to him, "Before we begin I want you to know that I disagree with your opinion on the legality of abortion. Now let's have lunch."[30]

"If Today You Hear His Voice"

When Cardinal Cooke said that the priest must be a listener, he meant mostly that the priest should listen to God. Like any orthodox Catholic, he was convinced that God speaks to us first of all through the Scriptures, then through the magisterium of the Church, and then through the legitimate authority of the Church at the present time. He was also quite humbly and simply convinced that God spoke to him through everyone that he met and through all the circumstances of life.

On being named Archbishop of New York, Terence Cooke reflected, "I felt there was no doubt that I had been called to be a priest by God while I was still in high school. I became even more convinced when I went to college. Today I am even more and more convinced."[31] It is one of the profound teachings of the masters of spiritual life that those seeking for perfection must be willing to listen to God's voice, wherever and whenever they hear it; in whatever circumstances, however painful and disconcerting, and no matter what its message is. In the classic on the spiritual life, *The Imitation of Christ*, we read, "If your heart were pure every creature would be to you a mirror of God and a book of holy doctrine."[32]

In his own personal life Terence Cooke was profoundly convinced that God spoke to him and to all of us at all times. He was also convinced that prayer is the way that we come to recognize and make part of our own thinking what God is saying to us. Speaking to priests in 1971 at the annual clergy conference, the cardinal said, "It seems to me that many of our present frustrations in the priestly ministry come from the neglect of regular prayer. We cannot be men of faith unless we persevere in our prayer life.

"A priest who is a man of faith and prayer is able to be truly a man of service because he has a vision of God and of his kingdom. Prayer is among other things the motivation, the contemplation of that vision. Our priestly prayer is both the exercise of our faith and the nourishment of our faith. Therefore, every priest must make the daily effort to persevere in faith and love, in private prayer, liturgical worship and pastoral service. It will continue to be a daily struggle to achieve a balanced integrity in private prayer, liturgical worship and pastoral service. But without that balance our priestly lives will suffer and we will not enjoy the abundant spiritual life that is our heritage."[33]

Like any person making progress in the spiritual life, Terence Cooke came to rely more and more on prayer as God's speaking to him rather than his speaking to God. He became more and more a listener.

It is legitimate to speculate that an added motivation for this listening was to be found in his serious illness. The decline of the body and the gradual relinquishing of our physical powers can be seen in a very positive way as God calling us beyond this transitory and earthly life. For the believer, serious illness can be the summons of God, reminding the individual to seek not the passing things of the flesh but the eternal things of the spirit.

Terence Cooke was totally prepared by his background, family experience and education to hear the voice of God speaking to him in his illness. This indeed was the meaning of his selection of the motto "Thy Will Be Done." He reveals a great deal about his spiritual life and his practice of listening to God when he tells us why he selected his episcopal motto. In an interview he gave on May 7, 1969 we read, "When I was asked, as all new bishops are, to choose a motto, I selected from the Lord's Prayer the phrase, 'Thy Will Be Done.' Those words are very much in my mind and heart today. I think I feel them more deeply than ever before.

"Today and tomorrow and for whatever time God chooses that I remain Archbishop of New York, I must devote all my efforts to doing God's will by being a good bishop, serving my fellow men. If God's will is to be done, we must have the will to chart a course of action that is independent of all fears. If our Heavenly Father's will is to be done on earth, then we must achieve above all and ever more fully the consciousness that we are our brother's keeper and that our brother is every man. 'Thy Will Be Done' — a motto, a design for life, a prayer, a noble hope. I pray today that God will strengthen me to be a good instrument of understanding, love and peace to my fellow men. I pledge today that I will work each day of my life to accomplish God's message of goodwill for all the members of the human family."[34]

CHAPTER TEN

TO LIVE AND DIE WITH GOD

Although he kept his impending death a strict secret, the cardinal allowed this awesome fact to shape his thinking about what his own life meant. A year after he received his terminal diagnosis, when Cardinal Cooke addressed the priests at the Chrism Mass during Holy Week, he spoke these words which are most revealing in light of what was to happen to him. "The priest is called to be a victim, ready to share the sufferings of his people and not hide from them, and even ready to bear their sufferings in their place if God asks him to do so."[1]

The ancient concept of a person being a victim in the place of someone else is one that modern psychology associates with a severe form of pathology called "psychic masochism." The person who is afflicted with this disorder is believed to attain satisfaction from suffering and even to experience a certain form of mild paranoid grandiosity at being able to suffer for another.

Obviously, the desire to be a psychic victim is a highly pathological trait. Unfortunately, one cannot be around the religious world very long before one encounters those who derive considerable personal satisfaction from being victimized. In fact, one can even find these self-appointed victims where few or no religious values are evident, as in the case of a mother who controls her child by appearing to be a victim or the husband who suffers in order to control his wife. In most cases these victims are obviously depressed people. They tend to exhibit their pains and sufferings in public for others to see. They complain about their sufferings and make others feel guilty because they are in pain. Frequently they are angry and judgmental.

Such a psychological profile hardly fits the subject of this spiritual portrait. Terence Cooke was constantly and almost irrepressibly optimistic. He abhorred suffering in public. Even his closest relatives and associates did not know that he was terminally ill. During his long illness the cardinal never appeared depressed. In fact, his close friend, Bishop Ahern, commented that he "had never even seen the cardinal yawn during the long years of illness."[2]

When Cardinal Cooke's terminal condition was finally revealed at the end of August in 1983, it was clear that only a few individuals knew of his long struggle. Most people assumed that he had been ill for only a few weeks. Careful investigation among his closest friends revealed that only two or three people besides his physicians knew that he had been terminally ill for nine and a half years. Moreover, the cardinal always followed his physician's orders carefully and accepted pain medication so long as he would not be deprived of the use of his mental faculties.

The question remains then, why did he see himself as a victim and offer this as an ideal for others? The answer is to be found in the most profound depths of Christian teaching and spiritual theology. Those unwilling to look into these depths will find Terence Cooke forever an enigma. If they are honest they will find his Master an enigma as well.

Amoris Victima

As early as the prophecy of Isaiah, the Messiah was seen as one who carried the sins of others. "He has borne our griefs . . .

and with his stripes we are healed" (Isaiah 53:4-5). Speaking of His own death, Jesus indicated that he "would lay down his life for his friends" (John 15:13). In an obvious allusion to his impending passion and death He said, "When I am lifted up from the earth, I will draw all men to myself" (John 12:32).

No one recognized this aspect of Christ's message more clearly than Saint Paul, who in numerous passages describes Our Lord's suffering and death as a victim to "take away the sins of the world." To cite but one text, in Philippians 2:5-8 we read, "Have this mind among yourselves, which is yours in Christ Jesus, who, though he was in the form of God, did not count equality with God a thing to be grasped, but emptied himself, taking the form of a servant, being born in the likeness of men. And being found in human form he humbled himself and became obedient unto death, even death on a cross."

The idea that the disciple of Christ should expect to suffer should not be a surprise to anyone. Was it not Our Lord who said, "If anyone will come after me, he must take up his cross daily and follow me" (Luke 9:23)? Yet many contemporary Christians pay little attention to this aspect of discipleship. Some even demean it.

Starting with such post-apostolic fathers as Saint Ignatius of Antioch, the ancient Church took up the teaching of Saint Paul and made the voluntary endurance of one's own suffering and the endurance of suffering in order to help others a keystone of Christian spirituality. Down through the ages such giants of the spiritual life as Augustine, Francis of Assisi, Teresa, John of the Cross, Ignatius of Loyola and John Henry Newman had made the endurance of pain and sorrow with and for Christ an integral part of their teaching and example to others. Even in our own times such outstanding Christian writers as Abbot Marmion and Archbishop Goodier (both cited in the notes of Cardinal Cooke), Edith Stein, Simone Weil, Maximilian Kolbe, Padre Pio and many others have reiterated the traditional Christian teaching about the importance of suffering in the place of others and in union with Christ Jesus.

Among living Christians of great renown one need only mention Pope John Paul II, Brother Roger of Taizé, Jean Vanier and especially Mother Teresa of Calcutta to see that the powerful idea of taking up the sufferings of others and enduring discomfort and pain for them is still a viable Christian ideal. These outstanding Christians of past and present are cited here because a superficial religiosity based on the shifting sands of pop psychology continues to disparage the concept of accepting suffering with others and for them as a prayer of patience and love in union with the Crucified One.

Perhaps one may respond that it is not the notion of suffering for another but the word "victim" that is offensive. Admittedly this word lends itself to psychological misuse, as we have already indicated. Others find it offensive because this idea has been widely abused to keep the poor in subjection. Nevertheless, the very idea of Christ as the "amoris victima," the victim of love, was the most powerful expression of faith for the Catholic immigrants who came to the American shores. Almost every Irish home had hanging over the fireplace or dinner table an old oleograph of the Sacred Heart of Jesus with His wounded hands extended in a gesture of loving affection toward the individual.

In the Cooke home, as in millions of Catholic homes of devout ethnic groups, the idea of uniting one's personal struggles and illnesses with the suffering of the Crucified as a prayer for the salvation of the human race was a central act of devotion. It was included in such prayers as the Morning Offering, which most devout Catholics said, uniting their day with Christ crucified. It was probably the most common prayer after the simple intercession for what one needed. This way of thinking and praying was the foundation stone of the prayer life of Terence Cooke before and during his illness. It remained with him to the hour of death.

To Live and Die with God

Another key idea in the spirituality of Terence Cooke was that of abandonment to divine providence or the acceptance of the divine will. This was clearly indicated in his choice of an episcopal motto, *"Thy Will Be Done."* Many classical writers see it as a sign of progress in the spiritual life if, more and more, we put our own will and desires behind us and accept what life brings as the will of God. This is not to be confused with quietism, where the person simply does nothing but accept life as it comes. The doctrine of acceptance of the divine will means that the individual constantly struggles to find God in whatever happens. The masters of the spiritual life call for very active acceptance of the divine will. This requires that the individual strive to do the best with whatever happens, and accept the vicissitudes of life and even the injustices which arise from human malice as part of the road to holiness.

This doctrine is very powerfully explained in a spiritual classic, *Abandonment to Divine Providence,* by Jean-Pierre de Caussade.[3] Cardinal Cooke often discussed the basic ideas of de Caussade's book with me. This classic work was the focus of a retreat that I had given to him in 1973. Accepting the vicissitudes of life as Christ had done was the perfect way to unite oneself with the sacrifice of Christ on the cross. The message of the suffering of Christ is one that is extended to every Christian in the world. Christ saved us because He accepted all mishaps, pains and sufferings of this life without taking advantage of his divine power. As Paul says, "He emptied himself, taking on the form of a servant." To understand this is to understand why Christ constantly said that He did the "will of the Father and not His own will."[4] Surely it was the will of Christ to remain with His Church and not to die when the apostles were so unprepared to take His place. It must also have been part of the human will of Terence Cardinal Cooke to remain with the Church of New York at this

time and to carry out the mandate he had been given. He felt that
he had a great deal to do. In imitation of Christ he accepted the fact
that he had to die. He did not think that God was calling him to
something special, but rather that the Lord expected him to endure
what everyone else must endure in life, even terminal illness.

In writing his final letter to the chaplains of the Military
Vicariate, Cardinal Cooke clearly made the acceptance of illness a
part of his spiritual life. "At this grace-filled time of my life, I am
grateful for the prayers and sacrifices you have offered for me in
my illness and for your willingness to help me to accept God's Will
in union with Christ for the good of the Church. I rejoice that
through, with and of the Eucharistic Christ, I am able to serve
God's People in the Military Vicariate in sickness as I have in
health. I offer my suffering and my prayers for you and for all
whom you serve so faithfully."[5]

He wrote in very much the same vein to Pope John Paul II on
August 25, 1983, the day after he received his terminal diagnosis:

> I thank Our Heavenly Father for the gift of the Priesthood
> and also for the opportunity of carrying out my pastoral
> responsibilities as Archbishop of New York and Military
> Vicar. Knowing that all things are possible with God, and
> that He uses the weak instruments of the world to confound
> the strong, I have tried to serve and to nourish His People
> by Word and Sacrament and by special works of charity
> towards the sick, the poor, the young, the old and the
> troubled . . . I have attempted to walk in the way of the Lord
> Jesus, guided by the Holy Spirit, ever mindful that we stand
> in the presence of the heavenly Father.
>
> For the past eight years, I have received medical treatment
> for a lymphoma condition. Thank God, this illness did not
> prevent me from fulfilling my responsibilities . . . Now, in
> addition to the controlled lymphoma, an acute leukemia has
> developed.

Since I now suffer from limitations, I write to Your Holiness, knowing that the pastoral care of the people of the Archdiocese of New York and the Military Vicariate will be provided for by my collaborators with your encouragement.

I wish to assure Your Holiness of my complete acceptance of God's will — "Fiat Voluntas Tua" — in His will is my peace. I have offered my prayers for and sufferings in union with Jesus Christ for Your Holiness and for all God's people, especially those in the Archdiocese of New York and the Military Vicariate.

United with Your Holiness in mind and heart and praying always for the intercession of Our Lady, Mother of God and Mother of the Church, I am,

> Devotedly and faithfully yours in Christ,
> ✠ Terence Cardinal Cooke
> Archbishop of New York [6]

His Way of the Cross

To understand the long road of Cardinal Cooke's illness, suffering and death, it is necessary to go back sixteen years, about a year before his consecration as a bishop. For the exact date and specific details we must rely on Bishop Patrick Ahern, who was then Cardinal Spellman's secretary. He was living with Monsignor Cooke in the cardinal's residence.

As chancellor, Monsignor Cooke had been requested to represent Cardinal Spellman at the funeral of Archbishop Joseph Francis Rummel of New Orleans. Monsignor Cooke had mentioned to Bishop Ahern that he felt a little lump on his jaw a day or two before he was to leave for the funeral. When it did not go away, the bishop was alarmed and suggested that someone else go to New Orleans. Monsignor Cooke agreed and went to see Doctor William F. Robbett. A few weeks later Terence

Cooke was operated on. When Sister Anthony Marie, the administrator of Saint Vincent's Hospital, called Cardinal Spellman, Bishop Ahern assumed from the tone of her voice that something was wrong.

That evening when Bishop Ahern went to see his friend he tried to be jovial. Bishop Ahern recalled that the future Archbishop of New York was as casual as he could be, but he appeared to be deeply affected and his eyes were slightly wet. Bishop Ahern recalled, "Terry was trying to put up a brave front, but he wasn't doing much better than I was. He said, 'You know, I'm going to have to take radiation.' So I said, 'Ah, that's only because you're the chancellor and very important to them.' He said, 'Absolutely!' Each of us was kind of lying to the other. Then I recall he said, 'The problem is, Aunt Mary is going to be very upset. So would you be sure in telling Aunt Mary to explain it gently.' I remember going home and feeling extremely sad. I was sad to tears."[7]

It was on this very evening, as reported earlier, that Bishop Ahern confided the bad news to Monsignor Vincent Kenney, who responded that their friend was not going to die because he had much to do and was a saint.

Bishop Ahern reported that Monsignor Cooke came home and did not miss a day in the chancery. He went down from the office at a certain hour to have his radiation therapy. He worked as though there were nothing wrong with him. During the years from 1964 until 1975, Terence Cooke became a bishop, an archbishop and a cardinal; there was no recurrence of cancer.

In his single visit with Cardinal Cooke after the announcement of the cardinal's terminal illness, Bishop Ahern asked him how he managed to do what he had done especially in the years since he had received the terminal diagnosis. In response to the comment that he must have been in pain, the cardinal said, "Yes, I was." The bishop asked, "How were you able to do it?" Cardinal Cooke smiled and said, "God helped me to do it, and if I had not done it and had let everybody know what I had, I would have been a lame duck as an archbishop. I would never have been able to get done the things that I knew had to get done."[8]

Throughout his years of illness Cardinal Cooke was motivated by his lifelong determination to accept God's Will. He was probably less aware that another factor was in operation — his courage. Monsignor Clark who was director of communication for the archdiocese for several years gives us the following powerful insight. The cardinal had let Monsignor Clark know he was going for surgery around the mouth on two or three occasions because he was concerned the story might get into the newspapers. "He would be back in 24 hours at his desk with the savage burn marks just visible on his lips and inside his mouth and without a word of complaint. He must have been in acute pain given the area of his surgery and he literally ignored the whole matter and carried on as if nothing had happened. He was not only very courageous but had a great deal of style personally."[9] It is worth noting that while courage is a moral virtue it is also a gift of the Holy Spirit. The virtue helps us to do what is difficult, the gift enables us to do what is impossible. As the account of the cardinal's final illness unfolds it might be well to keep this distinction in mind and try to judge if we are observing both dynamisms, virtue and gift, at work in the cardinal's life.

We receive another insight into the cardinal's reaction to his first bout with cancer from his personal physician, Dr. William Robbett. "The cardinal took everything in a spirit of optimism. No matter what the information was, even the worst, he never allowed it to get him down emotionally or keep him from going ahead with his plans. He accepted everything as it was — no questions asked, no doubts, no hesitation. That almost spells out one of the striking characteristics of his personality."[10]

Dr. Robbett also remembered that Cardinal Spellman had spoken with the highest praise of Monsignor Cooke. "There was a miserable job to be done, namely to organize the archives of the

Cathedral and of the chancery. It was a thankless job and no one
wanted it. Monsignor Cooke volunteered to do the job in his free
time. Cardinal Spellman told me that Father Cooke was spending
hours beyond belief in getting those archives in order. It was
probably the most unrewarding work ever. This shows you the
kind of person Cardinal Cooke was. He was totally devoted and
dedicated to any job that he undertook."[11]

Dr. Robbett recalled that during the operation he became
suspicious that other cancerous tissue was present. He removed
the entire submandibular gland.[12] In the middle of the operation a
note arrived in the operating room from Cardinal Spellman. He
requested that Dr. Robbett "announce to everyone in the operating room that no information concerning this surgery should be
discussed with anyone outside the operating room. Everything
was to be held in the strictest of confidentiality."[13] Dr. Robbett
recalled that he gave Monsignor Cooke the diagnosis at the time
of the surgery as a "reticulum cell sarcoma," which is a malignant
tumor. From all indications, after a thorough examination, there
was no other sign of cancer cells actively present in Terence
Cooke's body.[14]

In a recent letter Dr. Robbett adds to his earlier testimony.
"The tissue removed was examined by several pathologists.
There were some diversity of opinion as to the type of cancer cell
present in the tumor. However, there was no doubt of it being
malignant.

"Several cancer specialists were consulted concerning the
disease present in the tissue removed from Monsignor Cooke's
left upper neck. It was a consensus of opinion that with this type
of malignant tumor, treated with surgery and radiation, the life
expectancy was less than five years.

"In 1982, the cardinal said in his usual quiet and gentle
manner, 'Well, it is eighteen years since the operation. That is
certainly many years beyond what was predicted. It is just
another sign that God has been very good to me.'

"However, he knew that his disease at that time was very extensive and his time was limited. As he was leaving the office, he stopped and said, 'It is more than two decades that we have had a quiet and confidential relationship as patient and physician — and as friends.' He was undoubtedly expressing his gratitude, in his own unique way, as he did with everyone he knew."[15]

Dr. Robbett saw Cardinal Cooke regularly over the intervening years. In 1974 the cardinal had gone to Africa and was quite ill when he returned. He apparently contracted malaria while in the Republic of Chad. Arriving back in New York exhausted, the cardinal saw his physician, who looked into his mouth and noted that on the left side of his hard and soft palate there was a mass of tissue. He operated on Cardinal Cooke at Manhattan Eye, Ear and Throat Hospital for the removal of the tissue. This was the first time that Cardinal Cooke went to the hospital under an assumed name. He was referred to as "Father James Gannon."

Early in 1975 Dr. Robbett initiated care of Cardinal Cooke, now known as Father Gannon, at Memorial Sloan-Kettering Hospital in New York City. The results of a total body scan showed that the cancerous tumor was diffused throughout the body. The cardinal's abdomen had an almost complete diffusion of cancer cells. His vital abdominal organs were saturated with cancer.[16] The cardinal was immediately put under the care of a chemotherapist. For the next few years there was a continuous effort to balance chemotherapy so as not to damage the healthy blood cells. It was a delicate balance, and the cardinal continued in this type of care until his death in 1983.

The following paragraph will give us a clearer idea of the implications of the cardinal's condition. Dr. Robbett reports, "From 1975 on he had a diffused disease throughout his body. Not only that, but one that imposed a tremendous strain on the system from the disease as well as from the treatment and its adverse effects. I see patients under similar circumstances and they complain, rightly so, about how awful they feel. Chemotherapy is a pretty bad treatment. Cardinal Cooke never once complained about his treatment."[17]

For a number of years Cardinal Cooke had been a friend and patient of Doctor Kevin Cahill, well known in New York as a specialist in infectious diseases. Through Dr. Cahill, Doctor Thomas Fahey became involved as soon as a clear diagnosis of lymphoma was established. Dr. Fahey is on the staff of Memorial Sloan-Kettering Hospital, where Cardinal Cooke was quietly and secretly treated for the rest of his earthly life. Dr. Fahey involved the services of Doctor Joseph Buchenal, one of the earliest leaders in the treatment of lymphoma and related cancers.

A simple but effective chemotherapy regime was worked out. According to Dr. Fahey, most of the administration and evaluation of Cardinal Cooke's treatment during those years was done by Dr. Cahill, and the results were passed on to him. The drug used in this early stage was chlorambucil. In the course of time, this drug became less effective. As his disease began to transform itself by a process similar to that of leukemia, the cardinal began to develop an alarmingly low white blood count. His medication was then changed to prednisone, which caused his appearance to change. He became bloated and looked healthy. This medication was effective in controlling his blood condition for a number of years.

About a year and a half before he died, Cardinal Cooke began to have acute medical problems, according to Dr. Fahey. He required frequent blood transfusions, which were given either in Dr. Cahill's office or in the cardinal's residence. Dr. Fahey reports,

> It always amazed me, since I knew what his blood count was and what kind of things were happening to him physiologically, that he was able to keep any kind of schedule at all. He rarely missed any scheduled function. It was an amazing

thing to witness. . . . The cardinal wanted us to fully understand that when we felt that the disease would interfere with his functioning as Archbishop of New York, we must tell him. This the cardinal would reiterate a number of times over the years. The cardinal told us it would not be correct for him to continue as archbishop if he was impaired mentally in any way by the things that were happening to him, or he would not be able to physically manage. . . . As long as he could hang in there, that would be better for everybody. It was not until a very serious infection developed that required him to cancel some of his appointments in the summer of 1983 that it was revealed to the world how seriously ill Cardinal Cooke was. [18]

Dr. Fahey goes on to describe the meeting in which he had to tell the cardinal very bluntly that he could be managed much better if he were in the hospital.

Cardinal Cooke questioned us (myself and Dr. Cahill) very carefully about whether or not there were any other alternatives. Part of his questioning was that he wanted to understand for himself how much that kind of intensive treatment in the hospital really would effect his outcome and prognosis. When the cardinal understood we could not give him any definite answers whether he was going to be better by doing this or that his life span would be increased, he came to the decision that he did not wish to be hospitalized. I thought it was a very tough decision because we spelled out all the problems that this would incur because of the need to treat him very intensely with continued intravenous drugs and antibiotics. Essentially we would have to establish a hospital room at his residence on Madison Avenue. His wish was to remain at home. He also did not want any kind of treatment that was for treatment's sake alone. The cardinal was prepared to let nature take its course. He wanted to know exactly what to expect from his disease. He faced it all very courageously . . . A crisis developed when Dr. Cahill was called away to Rome. The infection that the cardinal had became more acute. He did suffer. There was a tremendous amount of suffering during the last month of his life — pain, discomfort, weakness and fever . . . The cardinal developed a perirectal abscess which is one of the most painful things you can have. It essentially does not get cured if you do not have white cells that are effective in taking care of the bacteria. [19]

Dr. Fahey mentions that once the news broke, all kinds of gratuitous medical advice poured in both to the chancery and to the doctors involved. Because of this, two disinterested hematologists who had not been involved in the case previously saw the cardinal in consultation. Everyone who saw the cardinal agreed that Dr. Cahill and Dr. Fahey were following the best possible procedures. According to Dr. Fahey the precise name of the cardinal's final terminal illness was aleukemic leukemia. Commenting on his entire relationship with Cardinal Cooke, Dr. Fahey made the following statement,

Once he had made all the decisions necessary it was like a burden was lifted from his shoulders. He no longer had to hide. He offered his sufferings up for other people with similar conditions. The most amazing thing to me was that the cardinal just had a saintly approach to everything in life. God's providence was going to take care of everything ultimately. He was probably the best person I ever met. [20]

A significant event took place during the cardinal's final illness. A physician who was unrelated to the case had written a news column and commented on Cardinal Cooke's illness. He claimed that Cardinal Cooke had declined chemotherapy. After the cardinal's death, Dr. Cahill was interviewed by Anne Buckley of *Catholic New York* and reassured everyone that the cardinal had accepted chemotherapy "to prolong the productive life of a man who loved every minute of life."[21]

The physician discussed with Bishop Ahern his reason for making this statement. Dr. Cahill told the bishop that if the cause of Cardinal Cooke's canonization was ever begun, he wanted it known for certain that the cardinal had taken every necessary measure to preserve his life. According to Bishop Ahern, Dr. Cahill was afraid that the remark in the news media would cast a shadow on the authenticity of the cardinal's holiness.[22] Bishop Ahern noted that Dr. Cahill was the second person to refer to the possibility that Cardinal Cooke was a saint. The first person had been Monsignor Vincent Kenney, on the night of the cardinal's first diagnosis of cancer many years before.

On August 26, 1983 the first public announcement was made of the terminal illness of Cardinal Cooke. Newspapers in New York City and around the country blurted out the news in the headlines. In the meantime, Cardinal Cooke had summoned Bishop Joseph O'Keefe, vicar general of the archdiocese, and entrusted to him the entire care of the Church of New York. He had written to the Holy Father and was making arrangements to spend whatever time he had left in an atmosphere of prayerful retreat. Those last six weeks of his life were a time of great spiritual activity. The cardinal neither read the newspapers nor viewed the news on television. It seemed something of a surprise to him when this author told him on September 5th that the entire city was praying with him and for him. At that moment, he did not seem to be aware of the immense concern voiced by his fellow New Yorkers.

The cardinal was lovingly cared for by a very competent group of nurses and by his attending physicians. Maura O'Kelly, his housekeeper, was also allowed to be one of those in attendance. It was Maura, a few days before the final diagnosis, who realized how terribly ill the cardinal was when she found him bathed in perspiration and not able to move very well. The cardinal had not wanted special attention paid to his illness at that time, but Maura, on her own initiative, had "gone against the rules" and summoned Bishop Kenney. The bishop, a former secretary of Cardinal Cooke's, was in residence at Holy Family Church. He came up from the church at once, and when he saw the cardinal he told him very gently that he must seek medical advice right away.[23] Father Edwin F. O'Brien was the only secretary in attendance that day because the cardinal's other secretary, Monsignor Charles McDonagh, was on a brief vacation.

When they all assembled on that fateful day there was a good deal of sorrow and grief and crying behind closed doors. The cardinal himself, although deeply affected, seemed to have taken the whole thing in stride. He was mostly concerned about seeing that all the details were properly carried out for the notification of those people who needed to be officially informed. The cardinal was particularly anxious that an appropriate program be worked out for responding to the immense number of letters that poured in. Handwritten notes from world dignitaries were piled on a dresser in the hall outside the cardinal's room. Cardinal Cooke prepared a spiritual schedule by which he was able to offer Mass as the principal celebrant as long as he was able. When this was no longer possible he became a concelebrant in the daily liturgy. On a very limited basis his family, the auxiliary bishops and a small number of friends were permitted to see him, but only after taking very serious precautions. These medical precautions were necessary because the cardinal was extremely vulnerable to infection by reason of his low white blood cell count.

The cardinal recited the rosary and the liturgy of the hours with his secretaries. Much time was spent in personal prayer. He also used his final weeks to compose a large number of letters to many groups. Several of these letters have already been cited in this portrait, and they are all published in a book entitled, *This*

Grace Filled Moment.[24] These letters are illuminated with faith, trust in God, loving union with Jesus and devotion to the Blessed Virgin Mary and the saints.

Maura O'Kelly shares with us the following touching incident — "I didn't say anything to the cardinal for a few days after I heard that he was dying. I couldn't stop crying. I didn't want to cry in the room. I always tried to be cheerful around him. One day he kept looking at me and said, 'Maura, you were always so good and kind to me.' I said back to him, 'Your Eminence, you were always very good to me.' I went over and took his hand and said, 'They told me what's going to happen.' I couldn't stop crying. Tears came to his eyes as he said, 'You've got to be very brave just like my sister.' I said, 'I'm going to miss you terribly. I will never, never forget you.' . . . He accepted death. He was still gentle. He was still kind. He was worried about our feelings after his death. The last time I talked to him was the day before he died."[25]

On September 15, 1981, the Feast of Our Lady of Sorrows, Cardinal Cooke had revised his last will and testament. In it he wrote,

> I thank God for the wonderful gift of the priesthood and for the happiness that I have found united with Jesus in the Church and the service of my brothers and sisters in God's family. . . . With gratitude I accept whatever manner of death God wills for me and despite my unworthiness, with faith in God's grace and plan, I hope for eternal life in the company of the risen Savior. May God bless you with His peace.
>
> All property real and personal of whatever kind or wherever situated that at my death I shall own or be entitled individually or as Archbishop of the Roman Catholic Archdiocese of New York or by virtue of my holding that office, I hereby give, devise and bequeath to the Archdiocese of New York for its corporate purposes.[26]

He nominated as his executors Bishop O'Keefe and Monsignor Joseph Murphy, the chancellor of the archdiocese.

Monsignor Murphy was a close friend and associate of Cardinal Cooke. He lived with him in the cardinal's residence and served as chancellor for many years. Monsignor Murphy has provided us with two of the most revealing clues to Cardinal Cooke's spirituality: two prayer cards that the cardinal kept in his breviary or daily prayer book. According to Monsignor Murphy,[27] these prayers contain the secret of Cardinal Cooke's life and explain the way in which he accepted his illness and death. The first prayer card, entitled *Your Cross*, reads,

> The everlasting God has in his wisdom foreseen from eternity the cross that he now presents to you as a gift from his inmost heart. This cross he now sends you he has considered with his all-knowing eyes, understood with his divine mind, tested with his wise justice, warmed with loving arms and weighed with his own hands to see that it be not one inch too large and not one ounce too heavy for you. He has blessed it with his holy Name, anointed it with his grace, perfumed it with his consolation, taken one last glance at you and your courage, and then sent it to you from Heaven, a special greeting to you, an alms of the all-merciful love of God.

Monsignor Murphy commented, "Cardinal Cooke lived that, day in and day out. It was an overriding influence in his life. That is a very important part of his spiritual story. It explains his equanimity. He lived that. You could see that he was physically suffering, but he was at peace through it all."

The other prayer card was a prayer for generosity. According to Monsignor Murphy it explains the active life of Cardinal Cooke, the obverse of his life of suffering and patience.

> Dear Lord, make me generous. Make me even extravagant in my love for thee and for those thou lovest. My affection

for thee has been measured; make it full. My concern for myself has been selfish; let it lessen. My sharing with others has been limited; make it bountiful. Open my needs to the needs of others. Touch my hands to help them. Dear Lord, make me generous to thee then I shall be surely extravagant with everyone except myself.

On September 25, 1983, the President and Mrs. Ronald Reagan visited the cardinal at 2:30 in the afternoon.[28] Cardinal Cooke had been so ill that day that it seemed unlikely that he would be able to receive them. They were greeted at the door of the residence by Monsignors Murphy and McDonagh and Father O'Brien. As suggested by Cardinal Cooke, the Reagans went to the third-floor chapel, where they were greeted by William Cardinal Baum. A five-minute prayer service was offered consisting of the Twenty-Third Psalm from the Book of Common Prayer, the Lord's Prayer, the Prayer for the Nation and for the Leader of the Nation and the Prayer for the Bishops and Cardinal Cooke. The cardinal also joined in these prayers from his bedroom. Following the prayer service, the President and First Lady accompanied the three priests to the cardinal's room on the second floor. Cardinal Cooke welcomed them and invited them to join him in the final prayer of the service, the prayer of Saint Francis.

The cardinal then took the trouble to introduce the three priests who had accompanied the President and Mrs. Reagan upstairs. Cardinal Cooke expressed regard for the President and thanked him and Mrs. Reagan for coming to visit him. Mrs. Reagan reminded the cardinal that he had come to them in their time of need when the President had been shot.

Then the unexpected happened. As ill as he was, the cardinal had a list of requests for the President. He encouraged the President to pursue the cause of world peace and multilateral disarmament. Mr. Reagan told the cardinal the good news he had heard from the secretary general of the United Nations — President Gemayel of Lebanon reported that a cease-fire had been reached. Cardinal Cooke responded that this was the best medicine he had had in many days. He said it made him feel as good as he had when he was a boy in the bleachers at Yankee Stadium and watched "the Babe" circling the bases after a home run. The cardinal expressed a hope for lasting peace in Lebanon because there were many good forces at work in this important land which he loved. He also spoke of the quest for peace in the world and especially in the Near East. He expressed his belief that Lebanon was the key to peace in the Near East. The cardinal also said that it was very important for the Palestinian people to find a homeland.

Cardinal Cooke went on to thank the President for his strong stand on behalf of the right to life of the unborn. The cardinal suggested that the President would long be known and would be rewarded by God for his courageous pro-life stand. The cardinal went on to speak of the improved conditions of servicemen overseas and to thank him for his stand on tax tuition credits for parochial school children. As the Reagans were leaving, Cardinal Cooke presented the President with a medallion of Saint Patrick's Cathedral and Mrs. Reagan with a Celtic cross.

Monsignor Peter Finn, archdiocesan director of communications at that time, remarked that both President and Mrs. Reagan seemed to be deeply moved by their visit with the cardinal. As they descended the stairs the President kept repeating, "What a remarkable man." In fact, that visit cost the cardinal almost his last ounce of strength. He was extremely ill that evening and there was even some fear that he would die that night.

His Source of Strength

The devotional life of the cardinal during the last few weeks of his life was centered in three areas. [29] The first of these was the

Holy Eucharist. The Real Presence of Christ in the Holy Eucharist had been the center of his life and priesthood. It became the life preserver he clung to as his powers were slipping away. He found his greatest consolation in the daily concelebration of Mass and also in the opportunity to adore the Blessed Eucharist when it was brought to his room. About a week and a half before his death, he was no longer able to concelebrate Mass but continued to receive Holy Communion.

The Sacred Scriptures were also central to his spirituality to the very end. The Xavier Guild for the Blind had recorded the entire Bible on cassette tapes, read by Father Robert I. Gannon, S.J. The cardinal used those tapes frequently. He used them before his terminal diagnosis, when he was required to remain inactive for a few hours to receive the nourishment of a blood transfusion. During the final weeks of his life he listened either to the tapes or to the Scriptures being read by a secretary.

Finally, a strong aspect of his devotional life centered on the Blessed Virgin Mary. He never went to any religious service or event that he did not bring to an end with the recitation of the "Hail, Holy Queen." This beautiful prayer, written a thousand years ago by a monk who was crippled with cerebral palsy, Blessed Herman of Reichenau, was one of the central themes of his life. [30] The cardinal intoned this prayer at the end of every function for those who knew this Latin hymn. So close was this prayer to him that as his body was interred in the crypt in Saint Patrick's Cathedral, the "Salve Regina" — "Hail, Holy Queen" in the original Latin — was sung by all in attendance with deep fervor and meaning. The cardinal had lost his own natural mother at the early age of nine. One suspects that his special devotion to the Blessed Virgin Mary indicated that his spiritual mother had in many ways taken her place during his lifetime.

The Last Days

The following vignette given by Monsignor McDonagh brings to a fitting close our remembrance of the last days of Terence Cooke. Monsignor McDonagh tells the story in his own words.

During the first few days after Cardinal Cooke had shared the seriousness of his medical condition with all the people of the Church of New York a great deal of mail came to the house. The cardinal, with his great attention to detail, tried to make sure that we would respond to all of the mail.

I started to read one particular letter. I looked to the end of the letter to see if it were signed. It was difficult to read because the writing was kind of scrawling. It wasn't signed. At first, I was going to put it aside since we couldn't respond to it. Somehow I kept reading it. It turned out to be a very beautiful letter. It was from a person, from the grammar and spelling, I would say a person who did not have a lot of education, a person who was terminally ill as well. This individual asked that the cardinal be united with him in his terminal illness on the journey to Christ.

In the corner of the envelope was something hard. It was a small cross. At the end of the letter the individual asked that that be a sign of the spiritual union with the cardinal in the crucified Christ. I brought the letter into the cardinal's bedroom and read it to him. The cardinal paused and made that intention of being spiritually united with this person. I handed him the small crucifix. He held it reverently, looked at it, was deeply moved and said, "We adore you, O Christ, and we worship you because by your glorious Cross you have redeemed the world." Then he reverenced the cross with a kiss and gave it back to me. Every time I left the room for the next six weeks we would repeat this prayerful devotion.

I am convinced that this simple incident was a spiritual experience that Cardinal Cooke needed at that point in his illness. I think in those early days they were very, very difficult for him spiritually even though he responded in the way he had to. I think deep down the realization of terminal illness, of having to let go of the things of this world was a difficult experience for him. In that simple experience of perhaps the most humble person in the Church of New York — reminding the cardinal of the reality in which he was involved, the paschal mystery of Jesus Christ — he needed that reminder and I am convinced it brought him a great deal of peace for the next five weeks or more that he spent upon this earth.[31]

It is significant that one of the last utterances of Cardinal Cooke was spoken with his proverbial Irish humor. Dr. Cahill recounted the following incident, "Towards the very last days the very severe abscess which the cardinal suffered from had to be lanced. I explained to him that this would be extremely painful because there was no way to give any pain-reducing medication at that point. I further told him that if I did not lance the abscess he would die in a few hours of blood poisoning. The cardinal agreed with my opinion to lance the abscess. As the boil was lanced he cried out in pain. The nurse in attendance said to the cardinal, 'That's terribly painful, Your Eminence, isn't it?', to which he smiled and gave a weak laugh and said, 'My doctor told me it was going to be painful.' I replied, 'I never told you it would be this bad.' The cardinal laughed again."[32]

During the last two days the cardinal was in a semi-comatose condition. His kidneys had failed and his entire system was beginning to close down. All of New York City was kept aware of the cardinal's physical condition by hourly reports on the radio. At 4:45 in the morning of October 6, 1983, His Eminence Terence Cardinal Cooke peacefully entered into eternal life.[33]

The Final Farewell

The City of New York went into mourning. The headlines in the newspapers proclaimed the greatness of the man and the loss that the entire city felt. The *New York Daily News* carried his motto, "Thy Will Be Done," on the front page. For New Yorkers no explanation of the headline was necessary. Because of the length of his terminal illness, extensive preparations had been made for his funeral. The Cathedral remained open from early morning until midnight, during which time hundreds of thousands of people passed before his open walnut casket. [34] The streets adjacent to the Cathedral were blocked off and police barricades were set up to manage the very long lines of mourners. Although priests and religious were summoned to go into the Cathedral ahead of the line, Tomas Cardinal O Fiaich, then Archbishop of Armagh and Primate of All Ireland, insisted on waiting in line with the people so that he could get some feeling of their sentiments. He reported that during midday he remained in the line for four and a half hours.

The viewing of the cardinal's body was interrupted only by the regular weekend Mass schedule and by a series of special Masses offered in the cardinal's memory: for young people on Saturday afternoon; for various organizations of papal knights and ladies on Saturday evening; for the military vicariate on Sunday afternoon; and the Mass of the Holy Eucharist, attended by the priests and religious of the archdiocese, on Sunday evening. Cardinal Cooke was also remembered at the altar in various churches throughout Rome, especially his titular church of Saints John and Paul, where Timothy Cardinal Manning, cardinal archbishop of Los Angeles, was the celebrant on Saturday. New York Auxiliary Bishop Austin Vaughan was the celebrant that evening in Rome at a Mass held at the North American College, at which the United States ambassador to Italy and the special United States representative to the Holy See were among the invited guests.

On Monday, October 10th, a beautiful autumn afternoon, the archdiocese bid farewell to its beloved cardinal archbishop in a most impressive pontifical Mass of the Resurrection attended by three thousand worshipers, including seven cardinals, seventeen archbishops, eighty-eight bishops, about nine hundred priests, hundreds of religious, and scores of civil and ecumenical dignitaries.[35] The streets outside the Cathedral were filled with tens of thousands more who could not enter but who listened to the service on loudspeakers. All joined with Archbishop Pio Laghi, apostolic delegate to the United States, who was the principal celebrant, in the splendid liturgy which echoed the faith that Cardinal Cooke had lived and now lived more fully in Christ Jesus.

At the end of the Mass, the pallbearers carried the cardinal's simple casket to the archbishop's crypt under the main altar of Saint Patrick's Cathedral. Cardinal Cooke was interred in the crypt with his predecessors, there to await the bodily resurrection at the end of the ages.

CHAPTER ELEVEN

THE SPIRITUAL JOURNEY OF TERENCE COOKE

One of the most outstanding biographies of a saint ever written is *The Hidden Face,* the life of Thérèse of Lisieux, by Ida F. Goerres. [1] The author identifies the temptation of hagiographers, the writers of the lives of holy people, to depict someone as the flowering of a splendid, rich, well-born human spirit — the pinnacle of human nature. Canonization has become in the minds of some "the recognition and proclamation of a hero or genius on the religious plain."

Indeed this may be true of some of the saints, for instance, Blessed Edith Stein. Sanctity may also be the recognition of almost superhuman accomplishments, practical and spiritual, as in the case of Saint Maximilian Kolbe. The temptation to do this increases especially when the individual enjoyed great notoriety so that his good deeds were well-known and his acts of virtue were grist for the media mill.

This temptation, however, is mitigated in the case of Cardinal Cooke because his memory is still so fresh. With the passage of time, the devotion of those who did not actually know the saintly person produces a patina of the mythological which colors his memory. His devotion and his kindly deeds take on a kind of transcendent hue. There are still too many people around who knew, loved and admired Terence Cooke and yet who never thought of him as a saint. Monsignor Patrick J. Sheridan, now vicar general of New York and a friend of the cardinal for almost all his life could honestly say that he never thought of him as a saint. "He was a great guy but he could drive you crazy, because he would only give you part of the reason for making a decision and then tell you that the rest was confidential."[2] Memories like this suggest that it is too early for our subject to become a plaster-of-Paris saint.

However, when people start talking about someone as a saint very soon after the death of the individual, those put in charge of such things are faced with the contrast of the humanity and the sublimity of it all. Questions arise about what personal effects of the individual one should keep for posterity. The Oratorian Fathers in Birmingham, England took the easiest and best way out of this dilemma. They left the study of Cardinal Newman exactly as it was for these hundred years. The whole place may well become a reliquary if he is beatified.

Since the new archbishop had to move into Cardinal Cooke's room, his effects were quickly dispersed. It was our job to try to recover some of these and to decide which ones to keep. We have, for instance, the cardinal's baseball cap and electric razor. Can you imagine these in a relic display? I once saw the false teeth of a canonized saint. What about a half-used bottle of Pepto-Bismol in the cardinal's closet? I drew the line and threw it out. One is much too close to the situation when faced with baseball caps and bottles of medicine to mistake an ordinary man for an angel of light.

On a more serious level, questions persistently come to mind. Are we dealing with some hero from classical antiquity, or an ordinary man? Are we dealing with someone who had unusual mystical qualities like John of the Cross, or a Christian who struggled with ordinary defects and setbacks in the long road of the Christian life? If we are dealing with a very ordinary man who perhaps did extraordinary things, is this person an appropriate subject for a process of canonization? This process does not require a spiritual Hercules or even a wonder worker like Martin de Porres. But it does require an individual of outstanding virtue who consistently struggles to grow in holiness. A cause also requires that the individual be an appropriate model for the Christian people in his or her time. Are we dealing with such a person in Terence Cooke? These questions must be considered on two levels; first, the psychological, and second, the spiritual.

An Extraordinary Man

There is little doubt that while Terence Cooke was not a figure of startling charismatic qualities, he was a man of extraordinary ability in certain areas. On the level of natural talents, he was far more than an able administrator. He was a prodigious worker, willing to do things that few would undertake because of the magnitude of the task. For instance, he not only reorganized the archives of the Cathedral and chancery as a young priest; but three years before his death, he instituted a complete corporate restructuring of the huge archdiocesan organization in order to put it on a sound operational basis.[3] So thankless a task was this that very few people knew or cared that it happened. Countless human beings will profit by the fact that the archdiocese was put in a very sound condition during a time of decline in religious observance.

The cardinal was the farthest thing from a grand leader in the public eye, but he had an extraordinary ability to get people to work together. He did this by kindness and a generous regard for them, which Saint Paul called "charity unfeigned." The cardinal was willing to put himself out and even at times to endanger his health so that other people would feel good about themselves. Archbishop Theodore E. McCarrick, now the head of the Arch-

diocese of Newark, New Jersey, remembers the following incident, which took place when he was vicar of Harlem.

One evening, then-Monsignor McCarrick was walking
through Harlem with Cardinal Cooke when a man came over and
gave the cardinal a live dove. At the time, the cardinal was on
medication that caused his skin to break easily. The dove was
scratching his hands, but because children gathered around he
submitted to the whole thing cheerfully. The cardinal wanted to
be with the children, and they wanted to be with the dove. His
sensitivity to people told him that it was important for the people
of the neighborhood to see their bishop carrying a dove that one of
their number had given him. He wanted to be open to them. It
was a time, as Archbishop McCarrick recalls, that a great deal of
the funds of the archdiocese were given to the poor. [4]

Archbishop McCarrick was the first person to formally petition John Cardinal O'Connor about the possibility of a cause of
canonization for Cardinal Cooke. [5] Archbishop McCarrick had
known the late cardinal very well. Consequently, it is important to
hear directly from him why he made this overture to Cardinal
Cooke's successor so soon after the cardinal's death. When
questioned about why he thought the cardinal might be a candidate for canonization, he said, "More than anything else it was his
kindness. This was a man who really had so schooled himself that
this was heroic. In all the years that I worked with him I never
heard him say a mean thing about anybody. They were tough
times. He was unflappable because there was such a peace and
serenity within him." [6]

Archbishop McCarrick related an incident that happened
when the cardinal visited Immaculata High School in Manhattan.
The archbishop was trying to hurry him along because of another
engagement. When Cardinal Cooke finally got into the car, a
young girl walked over to him. She told him that she was a
transfer student, and she was very upset that the cardinal "had
closed my high school." Cardinal Cooke responded gently,

"Sweetheart, we do the best we can." Archbishop McCarrick commented, "I don't think that I could have done that. I would have gotten mad or defensive. He was so kind. That has to be holy."[7]

Throughout this entire spiritual portrait there has emerged a picture of a man who was extraordinary for his dedication and ability to work, extraordinary because he could do thankless tasks with at least the same enthusiasm that he brought to those which received public recognition. Moreover, he was always kind and calm. The question then emerges — are these ordinary human qualities of a remarkable, well-balanced human being, or are they qualities that reflect the grace of God?

A Holy Man

Our discussion of holiness must begin with a few definitions. By "holy" most people mean devout, pious, dedicated to works of religion. But holiness has another, deeper meaning. To be holy means to be different or transcendent. Holiness is the quality of God that places him beyond all change and all earthly dimensions. When we say that a person is holy in this sense, we mean that the power of the grace of God coming from outside this world is obviously operating within the person to an unusual degree. Surely all who have attempted to follow Our Lord Jesus Christ as disciples have had an experience of holiness which seemed to come from outside themselves, and which was quite beyond any of their own natural powers. This is called actual grace. The question of holiness in relation to someone such as Cardinal Cooke is this — did he make a consistent and profound response to grace?

Anyone who knew Terence Cooke knew that he was a devout man. We have already seen that he never went in or out of the cathedral without a visit to the Eucharistic Presence of Christ in the Blessed Sacrament. He was a man who literally loved to pray. This was true of him as a young man, and it was true till the day of his death. His secretaries record that most often when they traveled with him in the car, they would say the rosary or recite the Psalms in the Liturgy of the Hours. Despite his hectic schedule he would always find time to pray the breviary. [8] The last weeks of his life were spent in a profound period of recollection and retreat that was the culmination of a life of sincere and dedicated religious devotion.

Beyond devotion there is the much more serious and pertinent question of sanctity or inner holiness. In the life of Terence Cooke there is evidence of a consistent and constantly developing response to the grace of God through Our Lord Jesus Christ. This is quite different from the good natural qualities which we have already described, such as patience and kindness, even if these qualities were good to an extraordinary degree. To put it even more exactly, were these natural qualities in their extraordinary degree the result of the work of the grace of God? Were they a response to something which comes from on high, and has neither its origin nor its cause in the behavior of the individual? The only thing that individuals contribute to this grace is their willingness to respond to it so that it can grow. This growth in the life of grace is often described in terms of a journey, an analogy that is consistent with the call of Christ, "Follow me." It may be helpful to review the stages of the spiritual journey briefly before we try to assess Terence Cooke's personal spirituality.

The Spiritual Journey

Most people, when and if they consider the question of spiritual development, think of it as a buffet or even a smorgasbord. Life presents us with a series of haphazard opportunities to be good, bad or indifferent. Once in a while we rise to the occasion and respond to the situation by acting upon the grace that is given to us. If we are doing fairly well for a while, we say that we have made a little progress. This haphazard approach is uninformed and useless in the determination of holiness.

The spiritual journey has been defined in its developmental stages since the beginning of Christianity. As early as the fourth century, Saint Augustine divided the spiritual road into the three stages of purgation, illumination and union with God. A vast and intriguing library of ascetical and mystical theology is available in the Catholic Church to describe these various stages and many sub-stages along the way. [9]

In the broadest terms, these three stages may be described as follows. Purgation, the first stage, is the long period of time when an individual escapes from his or her own self-centeredness and narcissism and overcomes habits which are either seriously sinful or could lead to serious sin. Sometimes those who have grown up in excellent home environments find that they have little tendency toward serious sin but have many forms of narcissism to overcome. Usually the purgative period is a time of darkness and trial when the individual learns, with the help of God, to pass beyond narcissistic and self-centered goals and to begin to be concerned about charity. That is the unselfish love of God and the love of others in God.

The second stage of the spiritual journey is called illumination. It is characterized by a great freedom in the presence of God and ability to do extraordinary things within the parameters of one's own natural gifts. People in the illuminative way are able to spend long periods of time in prayer with relatively few distractions. They enjoy praying. They are also able to be extraordinarily generous and give of their time, talents and treasure with little or no consideration of their own needs.

People in this way invariably accomplish unusual and extraordinary things. If the person is a housewife at home she will become extraordinarily good and kindly to her family and neighbors. Those in some position of responsibility with substantial resources are quite likely to go beyond any ordinary expectations. If someone is put in a position of prestige and power, he or she is very likely either to be extraordinarily successful or, if unsuccessful in human terms, to accomplish great things for the kingdom of God despite failure. Invariably this period of illumination is accompanied by a tranquil spirit and the overcoming of many small faults.

Before a person comes to the final stage of the spiritual journey there is a profound experience of darkness called by Saint John of the Cross "the dark night of the senses." At this point all consolation and earthly supports are taken away. The individual must go through a period of complete purification of self. After this period, there is a time of simple union with God. The consolations of religion are no longer important to the individual; what is important is simply responding to God, giving oneself totally and entirely over to God. This becomes the sole purpose of an individual's life and is manifested by an unusual attitude of charity and humility to others.

Finally, there is a second period of trial called "the night of the spirit." At this time the individual is plunged into great darkness; it seems that the very self is beginning to disappear. Probably most who go through this experience in this world face it at a time of protracted terminal illness. It may be said that for a devout soul, a period of terminal illness can be the opportunity for an immense growth in holiness, because it presents a chance for the individual to surrender self totally and at every level to the will of God. After that time there is the final stage of the spiritual journey called the transforming union with God, a period of the highest spiritual grace, and in fact a period so exalted that relatively few of the mystical writers have had much success in describing it.

For anyone interested in the stages of the spiritual journey, the question arises as to where an individual was on this journey at the time of death. This is not precisely the same as the question of heroic virtue. Heroic virtue can be practiced by a very ordinary person in an extraordinary situation, for instance, martyrdom. Not every canonized saint and certainly not every canonized martyr gives evidence of having arrived at the heights of mystical union with God. Evidence that a person has arrived at the highest stage of mystical experience is not necessary for the process of canonization. What is necessary is that the person consistently practice heroic virtue at his or her level of spiritual development.

The question of where Terence Cooke arrived on the spiritual journey is intriguing. He was not by any means what people would ordinarily call a mystic. He was not a person who lived silently in communion with the other world, nor did he ever write about profound mystical realities as did Bonaventure, John of the Cross and Thérèse. He was an eminently practical man who could deal easily with the things of this world.

It is often difficult to speculate about where a person was in the spiritual journey at the time of death. Being somewhat informed on these things, however, and having been a close confidant of our subject over a period of years, I would cautiously say that it was my impression that during much of his time as Archbishop of New York, he functioned like those who are said to be in the illuminative way.

My reasons for this view are largely based on the data that is given in this book, and on some personal conversations with him. The apparent ease with which Cardinal Cooke followed the Christian life and lived according to the Beatitudes suggests that he was depending very heavily on the gifts of the Holy Spirit in his life. Although a man of balanced and kindly personality, he often went quite beyond what even well-balanced human beings are able to do. His remarkable career as Archbishop of New York during times of great turmoil, and his willingness to defer constantly to the needs of others, along with his profound attraction to prayer, would, I believe, lead any objective and informed observer to conclude that he was in the illuminative way. A reading of the nineteenth century classic on the spiritual life of an active Christian, *The Soul of the Apostolate*, [10] would suggest that it was precisely this kind of spiritual development that permeated the life of Terence Cooke.

In the last years of his life, a darkness came down upon Terence Cooke. This was the darkness of the certitude of physical death. On several occasions during the terminal phase of his illness, he remarked to people that he had not expected to live as long as he did. Although he apparently accepted the knowledge of his terminal illness and of its outcome with equanimity, one has to assume that this was accomplished at considerable personal price.

Cardinal Cooke was a very private man. He did not allow others into the inner sanctum of his heart. He felt a responsibility to make everyone feel better and to be optimistic and upbeat. Perhaps it was only his closest associates who had some indication of what was going on when he received the final news that he would be dead within a few weeks. His secretaries and housekeepers were able to see that he had to struggle with this news for a few days, while he busied himself with the final arrangements for the transition of the responsibilities of the archdiocese, and planned all the good works he wished to do in what he called that "grace-filled time." The cardinal was obviously also under stress. It is not too much to say that like Our Lord Jesus Christ, he was pulled in two directions. During the agony in the Garden, the Son of God said to the Heavenly Father, "Not my will but thine be done." If it is possible for the Son of God to experience a conflict between the totally acceptable human desire to live and the divine will that he also possessed, shall we expect that an ordinary mortal man would not have felt such a conflict with the certitude of death immediately in front of him?

Those who have cared for the terminally ill have recognized in some an extraordinary spiritual fervor which shines out in them after they accept the inevitability of death. Perhaps in the case of a relative or friend you may have noticed a transformation, a rising of the spirit, a flaming up of grace which had not been seen there before. Those who cared for Cardinal Cooke in his last days on earth observed this phenomenon. [11]

Cardinal Cooke had many reasons to be conflicted about his death at the time it came. He had held off death for years. He still had many unfinished tasks to do for the Church and the archdiocese. Moreover, he deeply enjoyed doing what he had been called to do. He enjoyed making people happy. To the external observer, he almost seems to have led a charmed life. Now, despite his struggle to live, he was dying.

From his public letters and statements, from the testimony of those around him, there is every evidence that he spent those last days in complete and total acceptance of the divine will. This is the ultimate criterion of Christian holiness.

When Cardinal O'Connor proposed the opening of the cause of canonization of Cardinal Cooke and asked me to consider being the promoter, I spent a few weeks considering this question: From what I knew of Terence Cooke, was there enough evidence of heroic virtue and of personal spiritual growth to warrant such a cause? I pondered this carefully and prayerfully, and in the light of what I knew of him on a fairly intimate basis.

The more I thought and prayed, the more I came to the conclusion that Cardinal Cooke was an outstanding example of an ordinary man doing extraordinary work by the grace of God. He was not and never pretended to be a great heroic figure. He was one of us. He was one of us who had consistently, and with as much dedication as anyone can muster along the way, given himself to the Gospel. In his "ordinariness," he was extraordinary. He carried the very familiar burden of an illness that is all too common. One out of every five readers of this book will encounter this disease — cancer. But he accomplished extraordinary things while he was ill with an all too ordinary disease.

As you scan the brief outline of the spiritual life which is given above, I would ask you to pose for yourself the question: "Was this man advanced on the spiritual journey?" I cannot be sure that he came to the highest reaches of that journey because he was such a private person. There is little doubt in my mind, however, that in the last weeks of his life he did attain to the third level of that journey, namely, union with God. I do believe that by the time Terence Cooke closed his eyes in death, he was close enough to the divine reality and the transcendent light within that he scarcely noticed the difference. It is true of those who have made great progress in the spiritual life, according to Saint Bonaventure, that they come to live in the vestibule of heaven. [12] From every description that one has, the second floor of the cardinal's residence on the corner of Madison Avenue and Fiftieth Street in Manhattan was, for a short time in the early autumn of 1983, a vestibule of heaven.

CHAPTER TWELVE

THE CAUSE OF
TERENCE CARDINAL COOKE

One day, as the present writer was attending an ecclesiastical event a bishop from another state[1] who had once lived in New York approached me and said, "I hear you want to make Terry Cooke a saint." I responded that I did believe he led a saintly life and that we were interested in investigating the possibility of promoting his cause. The bishop, who obviously wished to be challenging, said, "Terry wasn't a saint. He was a great guy, but he wasn't a saint."

I replied, "I'm delighted to hear you say this because I need to find some people who can be witnesses against him. I'll sign you right up." The bishop responded, "I don't want to be a witness against him, but listen, Terry was a wonderful guy, but he was a saint like my mother and father were saints." I asked the obvious question, "Were your mother and father saints?" He responded, "Of course they were saints. They were very holy people." I replied, "You won't be very helpful as a witness against the cause."

The introduction of a cause of canonization is a sensitive thing. People will often begin speaking about the cause of a person while he or she is still alive. This is especially true if the life of the person has been accompanied by extraordinary signs, for

231

instance, known healings of the sick or unusual mystical signs like the stigmata. On the other hand, there are very holy people whose lives are totally devoid of these phenomena. They live apparently ordinary lives and do ordinary things; it is only after their death that the extraordinary quality of their holiness is recognized.

Examples of this kind of person are Saint Thérèse of Lisieux and Saint John Neumann, the bishop of Philadelphia. No one who attended the funeral of Thérèse of Lisieux would have imagined that she would be a canonized saint. In fact, one of the sisters in the community commented at the time of her death that the reverend mother would have difficulty finding something to write about Thérèse in the community chronicle. It was only after her death that the heroic quality of her sanctity began to be recognized.

As we have already noted, some of the people who knew Cardinal Cooke very well were thinking of the possibility of his canonization even before he had died. One of the most distinguished of these people was Dr. Kevin Cahill, his personal physician. As we have mentioned, Kevin Cahill publicly stated that he thought about the possibility of beatification and canonization while the cardinal was dying.

Other people have reported that they prayed to Cardinal Cooke immediately after his death or shortly after his funeral. A woman who knew Cardinal Cooke for many years, Mrs. Hazel Komonchak, wrote to the cardinal at the time of his terminal illness, telling him that they should pray for each other. At that time she was also suffering from cancer. After the cardinal's death she began to pray to him. She writes, "The day he died will always be very vivid to me. As I heard it over the TV, I cried so hard that my granddaughter came running to see what was the matter. My faith in his prayers is still strong, and I have interceded for a number of friends who have been at death's door, and his prayers have been heard. My advice is ask Cardinal Cooke to intercede."[2]

The unprecedented outpouring of concern and affection at the time of the cardinal's death also suggested to other people that he had an unusual holiness. A remarkable example of this is a letter from a man who was visiting from South America.

> I am an Argentinian, Catholic, married with three beautiful children, a working man, and a resident of Buenos Aires, Argentina. With great sacrifice I support my family and cover all the expenses associated with maintaining a home. Only God and I know the many trials and tribulations I've had to endure in order to avoid serious financial difficulties.
>
> My work requires that I regularly travel outside my country. On these trips I visit the local churches to be in this way closer to God and feel that I am in His company, for many times I have been alone. It was during one of these trips to New York, in October of 1983, that I decided to visit the Cathedral of Saint Patrick (which I already knew) when I found out that His Eminence Terence Cardinal Cooke was being mourned, reposing at the Cathedral, and that he had died on October 6th. I paid my respects to him and prayed for the eternal repose of his soul, and as I always do, for my job and the well-being of my family. There was something about His Eminence that attracted me. I did not know him during his life. I was barely beginning to know him when he was called by God.
>
> Thus began my devotion to His Eminence. From that moment on my life began to change. I began to meet new people, very kind people who helped me advance my career and in turn allowed me to fix-up my home which was in a poor state of disrepair for lack of money. Excellent business opportunities keep coming my way, and the love and affection of my wife and children, which never waiver, are at its peak.
>
> I feel a great relief, a feeling which I had not experienced in a very long time. Now I look to the future with greater confidence and optimism.

> All of this I owe to Terence Cardinal Cooke whom I have
> already incorporated in my life for ever and I hope that I will
> have the grace to meet him when God calls me too. My
> whole family share my devotion to His Eminence. I pray to
> him constantly and I know that he is always by my side.
>
> I am convinced that he is a saint, that God gave me the
> opportunity to know him and to be in his company to the last
> day of my life. [3]

Several people had mentioned the possibility of a cause for
Cardinal Cooke to his successor, then-Archbishop John J. O'Connor. He received a letter from the bishop of Metuchen at that
time, the Most Reverend Theodore McCarrick, now Archbishop
of Newark. The letter was a formal petition to Archbishop O'Connor to introduce the cause of Cardinal Cooke.

The Possibility of a Cause

Cardinal O'Connor then publicly announced that he was
interested in the possibility of a cause for Cardinal Cooke. The
announcement was received with considerable enthusiasm. The
present author was appointed to investigate the possibility of a
cause on August 6, 1985. Since it was impossible for me to give
the required amount of time to this cause, Cardinal O'Connor, at
my request, approved the establishment of the *Cardinal Cooke
Guild* to respond to the interest shown in the cause and to keep
track of the various reports and favors received through the
cardinal's intercession.

The Cardinal Cooke Guild

One of Cardinal Cooke's closest friends and helpers over the
years was Sister Aloysius McBride of the Carmelite Sisters of the

Aged and Infirm. Sister Aloysius, (known to most people as Mother Aloysius till this custom of her community was changed) had known the cardinal as a young priest. He had assisted her in the works of her community, which was founded in New York by Mother Angeline Teresa in 1929 to care for elderly persons who are no longer able to care for themselves.

Cardinal Cooke and Sister Aloysius had worked together on many projects, and the cardinal relied on her for much help until the end of his life. Although it was an exception without parallel, Mother Michael Rosaire, superior general of the Carmelite Sisters, agreed to release Sister Aloysius to organize the Guild, which would encourage prayer and support for the cause. The procedures and practices followed by the Guild are those which have been adopted by many groups interested in causes of canonization, particularly of members of religious communities.

The response to the Guild was literally phenomenal. Within a few years over fifteen thousand people have pledged their support to the Guild, which entirely underwrites the cost of the cause of Cardinal Cooke. Volunteers perform much of the basic work; it is not unusual for volunteer workers to put in thirty hours a week. Interestingly enough, the volunteers are drawn from different religious denominations, because support for the cardinal's cause has been widespread among many Protestant and Orthodox Christians as well as among Jewish people.

Part of the explanation for the phenomenal response to the Guild was the popularity of Cardinal Cooke himself. But it is surprising that many of the members of the Guild did not know the cardinal personally. They had heard about him from the media during his life, and they had come to believe by a kind of intuition that he was a very holy man.

The co-author of this biography and the archivist of the cause, the Reverend Terrence L. Weber, is a Lutheran pastor. He has already told us in the introduction why he became interested in the possible cause of the cardinal. Pastor Weber's interest is not an isolated phenomenon; many persons of other religious denominations have also offered their support for the cardinal's cause.

Significantly, people often show interest in the Guild because of the effect that Cardinal Cooke had on their lives, even when they did not personally know him. It is difficult at times to comprehend how a person became so involved. The Guild received a letter from a woman who was contemplating returning to the Church after many years. She writes, "It is because of Cardinal Cooke that I am returning to the Catholic Church. He has drawn me to it. I believe that he has interceded for me. I believe he is a great saint of the Church. For this reason I accept the communion of saints and I pray for his canonization every day. All my resentment toward and struggles with the Catholic Church are gone. All I desire is to remain in and grow in the Catholic faith. For my change of heart I do believe that it was the intercession of Cardinal Cooke."[4]

Signs of Intercession

There are two crucial elements in any cause for canonization. These two elements must arise spontaneously and cannot be the result of the influence of outsiders. One of them is the reputation of holiness, and the other is called "the reputation of signs." The reputation of holiness must stand on the life and experience of the individual. We have already seen in this biography that a significant number of people who knew Terence Cooke well considered him a person of real holiness and deep Christian spirituality.

The reputation of signs means that gradually it has come to be believed that through the intercession of the individual with almighty God, Divine Providence has granted extraordinary graces of a spiritual or a physical nature. This is a difficult thing to deal with because the individual, in all sincerity, may be operating on the suggestions of the unconscious mind. It may also be that the apparent favor or sign is merely a coincidence in either the moral or physical order.

As a person trained in a natural science, I found it both intriguing and unsettling to move into this area. As one who has written in the area of spirituality and religious experience, I was well aware that people may effect psychosomatic or psychogenic changes in their own lives by merely desiring to do so. This phenomenon could make it appear that an extraordinary grace had been granted, when in fact there was simply the ordinary action of grace in conjunction with a person's will to recover.

In order to deal with this phenomenon, the Congregation for the Causes of Saints has set up extremely rigid criteria for the declaration of any favor as a miracle. According to the present practice of the Sacred Congregation, a miracle must be the instantaneous or rapid disappearance of a life-threatening or other serious pathology without adequate treatment, without medical explanation and without relapse. Since most people at the present time receive significant medical treatment, it has often been difficult to present to the Holy See evidence of a miracle. [5] Indeed, an unexplained cure through the power of God may actually have taken place, but it may not be possible to determine this because the person has received considerable medical assistance.

In reporting the following cases, we are in no way indicating that they were miraculous. Our purpose is to indicate the gradual increase in the number of people who believe that through the prayerful intercession of Cardinal Cooke (sought in private prayer) Divine Providence has granted blessings to them. We often ask others to pray for us when they are alive. There is nothing to keep a person from praying to someone who is dead to intercede for them with the Lord.

Perhaps the easiest reports to deal with are those that relate to signs of moral or spiritual blessings. In no way can anyone ascertain that such an occurrence was a miracle, but it can be established that those involved felt that God had granted special graces through the intercession of an individual. One of the graces that people often report they prayed for in the case of Cardinal Cooke is a peaceful and happy death, since he had been ill for so long. On October 8, 1984, the late Monsignor Harold Engel, wrote to the Guild. The reader may recall that Monsignor Engel was Cardinal Cooke's supervisor for a number of years in the Catholic Youth Organization.

> Unusual and very premature as is this letter, I feel that I should put it in writing at this time. Because of my close relationship with the cardinal, some time after his death I found myself praying to him and asking for his help. A woman in whose case I was greatly interested had been suffering from a serious malignancy and had undergone many operations. Because of the nature of his final illness I finally decided to ask his help for this woman. For many months I included this intention to him, God willing, in daily prayer. About a week ago I realized she was pretty far gone, a fact too that she was quite aware of. At that time I told her I was going to ask him to ask God to call her "home." Since then I had made this my explicit intention, and hoped that he would try to bring it about by his first anniversary. This morning I offered my Mass for her, and soon I received word that she had died. I feel so strongly that Cardinal Cooke was part of this that I am forced to record it. This woman died two days after the first anniversary of the death of Cardinal Cooke. [6]

Someone not familiar with the progress of potential causes of canonization may find the account of a psychological or moral change somewhat unconvincing. However, these changes make profound differences in people's lives. They are often just as important as a physical cure. The Guild receives a good many reports of this kind. They are impossible to verify with absolute certainty. However, the seriousness of the individuals and the conviction that they have been assisted by the cardinal's prayers is of real interest.

Sometimes the reports are humorous. One day we received a phone call from a woman in her early sixties who was quite excited that her husband had given up drinking through her prayers to Cardinal Cooke. She immediately wanted this favor reported to the Holy See. When I explained to her that it would not qualify for a miracle, she was most disappointed and responded, "I don't care what the pope thinks! It's good enough for me."

Some of the most meaningful favors reported, while pertaining to medically verifiable problems, deeply affected the lives of individuals convinced them that the cardinal had helped them. A police officer and his wife had been trying for twelve years of marriage to have a child. Medically, they were never told that they could not have children, but they had been constantly disappointed. In early August of 1985, Carol told her husband, Matthew, that she had a feeling that a baby was coming. They spent a whole week of "not getting their hopes up" and doing a great deal of praying to Cardinal Cooke. On August 12th, the day before the doctor confirmed the good news, the couple attended a funeral Mass in the Bronx. The husband writes that "many thoughts ran through my mind as I prayed, or maybe it was more like one Bronx boy talking to another. I asked that the Lord would send us the child we longed for. I left the church with a great feeling of peace, a feeling of strength to accept whatever the Lord had in store for us."[7]

Actually, the little child was born in a very dangerous situation. The pregnancy had gone well, but during labor it was determined that the placenta had ruptured from the uterine wall and the baby was seriously in danger. Surgery was performed immediately and Matthew Terence entered the world at 12:01 on

April 28, the anniversary of Cardinal Cooke's elevation to the cardinalate. This was also the birthday of Matthew's great aunt, Sister Aloysius McBride.

The reader may suspect that these are coincidences. It goes without saying that that is possible. However, such unusual coincidences form a chain of events, most improbable events at times, which makes the reader conclude that other than ordinary discernible causes are in operation.

There are times, however, when we go beyond the conclusion of the mere possibility of a divine intervention. A statement of the possibility of unusual causality is not sufficient. More must be said if one is to be honest. For example, there are situations in which even educated medical personnel not associated with the Church at all will use the word "miracle."

The author recalls the day very well in November of 1987. I received a distressing phone call from one of the former students of our spirituality program. Her daughter, Alison, who was at that time sixteen years old, had been diagnosed as having acute AML leukemia. Her chances for survival were estimated to be no better than twenty percent with chemotherapy. Her anguished mother on the telephone asked me to send any information I had on Cardinal Cooke. The family was determined to intercede with the cardinal every day privately for the recovery of their daughter. A large number of friends were enlisted at the same time to participate in this veritable crusade of prayer. Leaflets that related to the cause of canonization of Cardinal Cooke were distributed among their friends. Although risky, chemotherapy was considered essential for any chance of survival. On the day after the first dose of chemotherapy, Alison entered a profound medical crisis and had to be placed in intensive care. So severe was her reaction to the chemotherapy treatment that she had to be given massive amounts of blood. During the next two weeks, Alison received five hundred units of blood. Several times her parents were summoned to the hospital to bid her farewell. None of the staff thought she would pull through. Her mother writes us,

> During this time we prayed constantly to Cardinal Cooke. We had a piece of his clothing given to us by Father Benedict. We prayed with this in mind. The rosary was said every day. Prayers for the canonization of Cardinal Cooke were recited after the rosary. On December 8th, Alison began to respond. In the morning she was as close to death as anyone had seen her, and by evening she was asking to have the television put on in her room. [8]

Her parents consider this a miracle. When asked what he had done in these last critical hours, her doctor said, "I did not do anything, but Alison is better." Because of her extremely bad reaction to the chemotherapy, Alison could not be given the entire course of treatment. She received her last mild treatment on April 16, 1988. Her maintenance therapy was stopped after only one and a half treatments because the medication caused her to develop hepatitis. At this bout her doctors stated flatly that the leukemia would return without further chemotherapy. Her mother continues, "We prayed constantly to Cardinal Cooke. There was no return of the AML leukemia, which usually returns within six months." Contrary to all expectations, Alison has had no signs of leukemia since November of 1988. Her hepatitis has also disappeared. Her mother writes, "We feel these definite favors were granted to us through the intercession of Cardinal Cooke."

One of Alison's physicians, who are both Jewish, did not hesitate to say "the hand of God was operating" in this case. [9] Because of the severe complications involved further chemotherapy was impossible. It is medically predictable that without chemotherapy there would be a return of leukemia in six months. Alison's parents were told this by both specialists. It is impossible not to note that in this case, hundreds of people were aware of the family's intention to ask for a favor through the intercession of Cardinal Cooke. Today, Alison is primarily in excellent health and a freshman at a prestigious Catholic university.

The Judgment of the Church

It goes without saying that no responsible person in the Church can describe any of these occurrences as miraculous. If indeed the cause of Cardinal Cooke is presented and makes progress, two miracles certified by two medical panels as clinically inexplicable will eventually be required. [10] These miracles must satisfy very stringent requirements; they must be supported by objective testimony and by empirical data. Those interested in this cause must be completely docile and await the judgment of the Church as regards the heroic qualities of the virtue of Cardinal Cooke. This is true even though individual acts of heroism can be identified in his life. To be considered for canonization, a person must consistently and over a long period of time lead a life of heroic Christian virtue. Miraculous cures are then seen as separate signs of divine approbation.

Of course, no decision can be made on the sanctity of Terence Cooke without the long process which the Church wisely prescribes to protect the title of "saint." This designation is only given after it has been established that the individual has practiced all the Christian virtues to a heroic degree for a long time. The title of "saint" does not imply perfection because we are all poor sinners, even the saints. The difference is that the saints know this awesome fact far better than the rest of us do.

Heroic virtue means that the person has tried to follow Christ with complete heart, soul, mind and strength. The Church also declares that this person has arrived at the final destiny of the human soul in the kingdom of God, in which Christ has promised a place for us. In his superb book, *Fundamentals of the Faith*, Professor Peter Kreeft gives an excellent summary of what a saint should be. He describes a saint as "a realist who knows that he or she is a sinner. A saint's dedication to God is heroic, and along with this he or she experiences joy even in the greatest suffering — at times, a heroic joy."[11]

A saint consistently puts the will of God first in life regardless of the cost, be it humiliation, injustice or rejection. The saints say with Saint Paul, "I have learned, with whatever state I am, to be content. I know how to be abased and I know how to abound" (Philippians 4:11-12). A saint is always open to others, is patient and kind, and is absolutely determined to do God's will as it is manifested. The saint is the enemy of the world, the flesh and the devil. For that reason the saint often appears to be out of line with the rest of the world. The saint is able to recognize Christ where He is hidden and loves to visit the sick, the dying, the poor, even to listen to the mentally ill. The saint seeks Christ hidden away out of the limelight. The saint is willing to serve and to beg, to wash the feet of the disciples. The saint is pressed on by the charity of Christ as by an obsession.

Saints can be bothersome because they don't see the same things that the rest of us see or evaluate things the same way. They try to put all things into the perspective of the reign of God on earth. All this time they appear in their own eyes to be failing. Cardinal Newman says of the saints that their virtues and good qualities seem to them to be "all dust and ashes." He notes that saints appear to the rest of us to be like the common run of humanity, but they are inwardly fighting secret battles, winning secret victories and studying how to make progress in the kingdom of God.[12]

Yet the saints are all poor sinners. More than anyone else, a saint will tell you that he or she is a nothing, a zero, an empty place, a vacuum without Christ. The saints see this emptiness in themselves, and they strive not to live by the common rules of self-seeking. Saints make mistakes. Saints can be stubborn. Saints can become myopic. Like all the rest of us they fall and fail. But secretly saints are rising in the kingdom of God.

Was Terence Cooke one of these people? Or was he simply a good man who stumbled along the way as best he could? The cleric who complained at the time of his appointment as archbishop that New York did not need another businessman, never really knew the real Terence Cooke, the inner, personal, private Terence Cooke. Those of his critics who actually knew him will maintain that he was at times indecisive, while those who know better recall that he did not act at times because he simply did not know what to do. The fact is that when he was unsure, he prayed and asked others to pray that he would be guided correctly. Some will say that he should have been more direct, confrontational, prophetic, if you will. This simply was not his personality. We have seen in this spiritual biography that such qualities, however desirable, were not fostered by his family or his experiences in adult life.

Cardinal Cooke often spoke of his appointment as Archbishop of New York as an example of God choosing the weak to confound the strong. He never thought of himself for a moment as a great charismatic leader, as a towering Moses in the wilderness. Terence Cooke was an ordinary man who was given an extraordinary task in a most difficult time. Even his critics will admit that a towering, heroic leader would not have done well in the period of transition and confusion in which Cardinal Cooke served. Indeed, it may well be that Providence, which placed him in the midst of that confusing time, called him away from it when his work was done and other qualities in a leader were needed.

We dare not spend too much time on the critics. No one ever had more critics than the Savior of the World. The question is: did Terence Cooke, all his life, seek constantly to do God's will as best he could do it? Did his life manifest the works of faith, hope and love? Did he share these gifts of grace with others around him? Did he accept and use the mysterious gifts of the Holy Spirit, especially courage, counsel, prudence, and even wisdom, while enduring a particularly exhausting physical illness? Did he give his best without yielding any quarter to his illness? Did he seek his strength from God, his consolation from Christ, his virtues from the Spirit and his support from Our Lady and the saints? Did he give a moving witness to his contemporaries? Did he treat his brothers and sisters, without exception, with love?

I have answered these questions for myself. You must answer them for yourself. The officials of the Church will study his life and answer for themselves. Only time will tell what the Lord's answer will be, and how it will be communicated to the Church. In the meantime, those of us who knew Terence Cooke well will continue to consider it a great grace of God that we were privileged to know a man who so consistently, generously and graciously sought only to be a servant of God.

One of the friars was distressed at the number & weight of the sufferings borne by St. Frances. He suggested that Frances pray to God for a temporary reprieve. "Doing God will is consolation enough, and more than enough for me" Frances gently chided the concerned Friar,

We strive to find our consolation in accepting God's will.

Hunger — To love and be loved —

Hunger for Community Person not Institution (Product Service).

Socrates — "the nearest way to glory is to strive to be what you wish to be thought to be".

From Cardinal Cooke's personal notes.

FOOTNOTES

All interviews have been fully transcribed from a tape recording and are part of the Cardinal Cooke Archives located at Saint Joseph's Seminary in Yonkers, New York.

Chapter One

1. Interview with Miss Katherine T. Cooke on May 13, 1984. Terence MacSwiney died on October 25, 1920 — only six months before the birth of Terence Cooke. On July 22, 1989 Miss Cooke died in the privacy of her Manhattan apartment.
2. Terence Brown, *Ireland: A Social and Cultural History* (Ithaca: Cornell University Press, 1985), p. 51.
3. Private conversation with former Israeli ambassador to the United Nations, Abba Eban, on January 2, 1990.
4. Interview with Katherine T. Cooke.
5. Interview with Bronx neighbors.
6. *Collection of Private Letters of Terence Cardinal Cooke*: "Letter to Father Louis Martorella" (Cardinal Cooke Archives: New York, hereafter referred to as CCA:NY September 30, 1939).
7. Interview with Sister Anthony, O.P. on November 11, 1984.
8. Interview with Katherine T. Cooke.
9. *Ibid.*
10. Interview with The Most Reverend Joseph T. O'Keefe, Bishop of Syracuse, New York on April 4, 1988.
11. Interview with Monsignor Edward T. Dugan on October 14, 1989.
12. Cf. *Collection of Private Letters.*
13. *Collection of Private Papers of Terence Cardinal Cooke:* "Love of God and Neighbor" (CCA:NY, June 3, 1936).
14. *Ibid.*: "Meet General Smuts" (CCA:NY, 1938).
15. Florence D. Cohalan, *A Popular History of the Archdiocese of New York* (United States Catholic Historical Society: Yonkers, 1983), pp. 215-263.
16. Anthony R. Rhodes, *The Vatican in the Age of the Dictators, 1922 - 1945* (New York: Holt, Rinehart and Winston, 1974), pp. 219-254.
17. Cf. Robert I. Gannon, S.J., *The Cardinal Spellman Story* (Garden City: Doubleday, 1962).
18. Cf. John Cooney, *The American Pope* (New York: Times Books, 1984). An excellent review of this book was done by Monsignor John Tracy Ellis, *Catholic Historical Review* LXXII (October, 1986), pp. 676-681.
19. Interview with The Most Reverend Patrick V. Ahern, Episcopal Vicar of Staten Island on May 13, 1986.
20. cf. Joseph L. Lichten, *A Question of Judgment* (Washington: National Catholic Welfare Conference, 1963).
21. *Collection of Private Papers*: "Campaigning for Christ" (CCA:NY, undated).
22. *Ibid.*
23. *Ibid.*
24. Interview with Monsignor John J. Gillen on October 14, 1986.

247

Chapter Two

1. Interview with Katherine T. Cooke.
2. Interview with Monsignor Edward T. Dugan.
3. *Collection of Private Notes of Terence Cardinal Cooke*: "Methods of Perfection" (CCA:NY, 1942).
4. *Ibid.*: "Sanctity - Perfection" (CCA:NY, undated).
5. Interview with Father William Reisig on May 13, 1984.
6. *Ibid.*
7. *Collection of Private Notes*: "The Virtue of Fortitude" (CCA:NY, December 6, 1943).
8. *Ibid.*
9. *Ibid.*
10. *Ibid.*: "Publican and Pharisee" (CCA:NY, undated).
11. *Ibid.*
12. *Ibid.*: (CCA:NY, January 25, 1945).
13. *Ibid.*: "Humility" (CCA:NY, January 22, 1945).
14. *Collection of Letters of Testimony*: "Letter from Father Joseph Leinhard, S.J." (CCA:NY, April 16, 1987).
15. *Collection of Private Notes*: (CCA:NY, March 7, 1945).
16. Interview with Katherine T. Cooke.
17. *Collection of Private Notes*: (CCA:NY, May 13, 1945).
18. *Ibid.*: (CCA:NY, undated).

Chapter Three

1. *Collection of Private Letters*: "Letter from Francis Cardinal Spellman" (CCA:NY, December 11, 1945).
2. Diagnosis was "anaseikonia," a slightly different retinal image in each eye and the confused image caused difficulty in focusing.
3. *Basic Biography of Terence Cardinal Cooke* (Archdiocese of New York, 1978).
4. Private conversation with Sister Julia Valleau, O.P. on October 14, 1989.
5. Private conversation with Sister Genevieve James, O.P. on October 14, 1989.
6. Interview with Sister Rose Mary Commerford on December 18, 1986. (When Father Cooke was at Saint Agatha's Home, Sister Rose Mary was known as Sister Mary Raymond).
7. Interview with Mr. Thomas D. Maloney on November 19, 1987.
8. *Collection of Private Letters*: "Letter to Monsignor Patrick A. O'Boyle" (CCA:NY, October 31, 1947).
9. *Ibid.*: "Letter to Monsignor Christopher Weldon from Monsignor John McClafferty" (CCA:NY, June 14, 1948).
10. *Ibid.*: "Memo to Monsignor Christopher Weldon" (CCA:NY, March 29, 1948).
11. *Ibid.*: Personal observations of Dorothea Sullivan in a letter to Mrs. Charles Ridder of *Catholic News* (CCA:NY, April 25, 1969).
12. *Collection of Private Papers*: Questionnaire (CCA:NY, June 20, 1949).
13. Interview with Sister Elizabeth White on October 16, 1987.
14. *Collection of Letters of Testimony*: "Letter from Mary Bierbauer" (CCA:NY, Winter 1987).
15. *Ibid.*: "Letter from Barbara Johnson" (CCA:NY, May 15, 1986).
16. *Collection of Private Letters*: "Letter from Father Thomas Lacey" (CCA:NY, May 30, 1951).

17. Interview with Monsignor Harold S. Engel on April 30, 1987.
18. *Ibid.*
19. *Ibid.*
20. *Collection of Private Papers*: "Surrender to the Will of God" (CCA:NY, June 1952; October 26-31, 1952; June 26, 1953).
21. *Ibid.*: "Rule of Life."
22. *Ibid.*: "The Catholic Approach to Social Work."
23. *Ibid.*
24. *Ibid.*
25. *Ibid.*: "Consequences of the Love of God" (CCA:NY, undated).
26. *Ibid.*
27. *Ibid.*
28. *Ibid.*
29. *Ibid.*: "The Forgotten Virtue - Hope" (CCA:NY, undated).
30. *Ibid.*
31. *Ibid.*
32. *Ibid.*
33. *Ibid.*
34. Interview with Monsignor Harold S. Engel.
35. *Ibid.*
36. *Collection of Private Letters*: "Letter to Cardinal Spellman" (CCA:NY, August 11, 1950). Matter refers to a letter sent to all diocesan priests on July 24, 1950.
37. *Ibid.*: "Letter from Monsignor James J. Lynch" (CCA:NY, February 25, 1954).

Chapter Four

1. Refurbishing of the seminary chapel was completed in 1983.
2. *Collection of Private Papers*: "Joy and Holiness" (CCA:NY, February 1956).
3. *Ibid.*
4. *Ibid.*
5. *Ibid.*
6. *Ibid.*: "How Sisters Encourage Vocations" (CCA:NY, November 9, 1961).
7. *Ibid.*
8. Cf. Paul Blanshard, *American Freedom and Catholic Power* (Boston: Beacon Press, 1949).
9. Interview with Mr. Bernard Carroll on October 30, 1986.
10. *Ibid.*
11. *Collection of Private Papers*: "Sympathy" (CCA:NY, 1954).
12. *Ibid.*
13. *Basic Biography*. Michael Cooke died under the care of the Dominican Sisters of Saint Rose of Lima at Rosary Hill. Throughout his life, Cardinal Cooke was deeply devoted to these Sisters. Since the establishment of the Cardinal Cooke Guild they have been very generous regarding his cause.
14. Terence Cooke lived at the cardinal's residence from January 1957 until his death in October 1983.
15. *Basic Biography*.
16. Interview with Katherine T. Cooke.
17. *Collection of Private Papers*: (CCA:NY, c. June 1967).
18. Interview with Bishop Patrick V. Ahern.

19. *Ibid.*
20. *Collection of Homilies of Terence Cardinal Cooke*: Homily at Mass of Thanksgiving upon returning from the Sacred Consistory of April 30, 1969 in Rome (CCA:NY, May 7, 1969).
21. *Collection of Private Letters*: "Letter from Pope Paul VI" (CCA:NY, September 15, 1965).
22. *Ibid.* (CCA:NY, March 2, 1968).
23. Interview with Katherine T. Cooke.
24. Interview with Bishop Patrick V. Ahern.

Chapter Five

1. Pope Paul VI, *Message of the Holy Father to Priests at the Conclusion of the Year of Faith* (Rome, 1968).
2. *Collection of Public Letters of Terence Cardinal Cooke*: "Letter to Pope Paul VI" (CCA:NY, March 8, 1968).
3. *Collection of Private Papers*: "The Perfection of a Priest" (CCA:NY, c. 1953).
4. Personal letter from Monsignor Eugene V. Clark on January 10, 1990.
5. Interview with Bishop Patrick V. Ahern.
6. Interview with The Most Reverend Theodore E. McCarrick, Archbishop of Newark, New Jersey on May 30, 1988.
7. *Collection of Homilies*: Chrism Mass 1977 (CCA:NY, April 5, 1977).
8. Pope John Paul II, *A Letter to All the Priests of the Church on the Occasion of Holy Thursday* (Rome, 1979).
9. *Collection of Homilies*: Chrism Mass 1977.
10. Private conversation with Father William Reisig on December 20, 1989.
11. Interview with Katherine T. Cooke.
12. Interview with Monsignor Charles G. McDonagh on October 14, 1989.
13. Interview with The Reverend Jerome Vereb, C.P. during the summer of 1986.
14.. The attempted assassination of Pope John Paul II took place in Vatican Square on May 13, 1981 by Turkish terrorist, Mehmet Ali Agca.

Chapter Six

1. *Collection of Homilies*: Installation Mass (CCA:NY, April 4, 1968).
2. Private conversation with Peggy Cooke.
3. Dr. Martin Luther King, Jr. was assassinated on April 4, 1968 in Memphis, Tennessee by James Earl Ray.
4. *Collection of Public Statements of Terence Cardinal Cooke*: "Assassination of Dr. Martin Luther King, Jr." (CCA:NY, April 5, 1968).
5. *Collection of Homilies*: Memorial Mass for Dr. Martin Luther King, Jr. (CCA:NY, April 6, 1968).
6. Interview with Bishop Joseph T. O'Keefe.
7. William Geist, "For Harlem Church, Cooke 'Made Difference,'" *New York Times*, (CCA:NY, October 10, 1983).
8. *Collection of Public Letters*: "Letter to the Black Community" (CCA:NY, October 2, 1983).
9. *Ibid.*: "Letter to the Hispanic Community" (CCA:NY, September 2, 1983).
10. *Ibid.*: "Letter to Saint Paul's Church, East Harlem" (CCA:NY, September 16, 1983).
11. *Servicio de Exequias* (CCA:NY, October 9, 1983).

12. Interview in *New York Times* with Archbishop Iakovos (CCA:NY, October 7, 1983).
13. Interview with The Reverend John Andrew on August 15, 1989.
14. Rabbi Marc Tanenbaum, "Reflections of Cardinal Cooke," *New York Times* (CCA:NY, Fall 1983).
15. *Ibid.*
16. *Collection of Public Letters*: "Letter to the Irish-American Community" (CCA:NY, September 30, 1983).
17. *Ibid.*
18. Interview with Monsignor Peter G. Finn on March 12, 1986.
19. Interview with Mr. Michael Flannery on June 15, 1989.
20. Private conversation with Father Benedict J. Groeschel on September 5, 1983.
21. Interview with Michael Flannery.
22. *Ibid.*
23. Interview with Monsignor Charles G. McDonagh on May 26, 1989.
24. At the onset of World War I, the Holy See established the Military Diocese on November 24, 1917 to provide pastoral care to the men and women of the Armed Forces of the United States. Bishop Patrick Hayes, later cardinal archbishop of New York, was appointed the first military bishop. On September 8, 1957, the Holy See decreed that the Archbishop of New York should always be the military bishop. With the installation of John Cardinal O'Connor as Archbishop of New York in 1984, this custom changed. (Cf. *Cohalan*, pp. 218-219, 286).
25. *Collection of Homilies*: Pastoral Visit to Vietnam (CCA:NY, Christmas 1968).
26. *Ibid.*
27. *Ibid.*
28. *Collection of Homilies*: Pastoral Visit to Bethlehem (CCA:NY, Christmas 1971).
29. *Collection of Pastoral Letters of Terence Cardinal Cooke*: "Letter on Peace" (CCA:NY, May 19, 1972).
30. *Ibid.*
31. *Ibid.*
32. *Ibid.*: "Letter for Respect Life Month" (CCA:NY, October 9, 1983) The complete text of this Pastoral Letter is contained in appendix III.
33. Personal letter from Monsignor Eugene V. Clark.

Chapter Seven

1. *Collection of Homilies*: Chrism Mass 1977.
2. Interview with Miss Maura O'Kelly on July 13, 1989.
3. *Ibid.*
4. *Ibid.*
5. Private conversation with Miss Margaret Wallace on July 13, 1989. Miss Wallace died on February 17, 1990.
6. *Collection of Letters of Testimony*: "Letter from Sister Aloysius McBride, O. Carm." (CCA:NY, March 23, 1984).
7. *Collection of Public Statements*: "Election Day 1977" (CCA:NY, October 10, 1977).
8. The list of the cardinal's accomplishments described in this section were taken from the *Basic Biography*, published by the archdiocese in 1978. Many of his accomplishments from 1979 until 1983 were taken from the files of Catholic Charities, with the assistance of Monsignor James Murray.
9. Personal letter from Monsignor Eugene V. Clark.

10. *Ibid.*
11. Interview with Bishop Joseph T. O'Keefe.
12. *Ibid.*
13. Interview with Bishop Joseph T. O'Keefe.
14. Personal letter from Monsignor Eugene V. Clark.
15. Interview with Bishop Joseph T. O'Keefe.
16. *Ibid.*

Chapter Eight

1. *Collection of Homilies*: Chrism Mass 1977.
2. Patrick Cardinal Hayes was the fifth Archbishop of New York from March 10, 1919 until his death on September 4, 1938.
3. The Most Reverend John J. Hughes was the fourth Bishop and first Archbishop of New York from December 20, 1842 until January 4, 1864.
4. The Most Reverend Michael Augustine Corrigan served as New York's third Archbishop from October 10, 1885 until his death on May 5, 1902.
5. Interview with Monsignor Florence D. Cohalan on June 27, 1988.
6. Interview with Archbishop Theodore E. McCarrick.
7. *Ibid.*
8. In a summary of his life and work prepared for distribution, Cardinal Cooke allowed this term to be used of himself. Its meaning refers to his use of organizational techniques and administrative procedures to efficiently manage the complex archdiocese. It cannot be determined whether or not the cardinal coined this term himself, but he did approve of its use in describing his work.
9. Interview with Monsignor Joseph P. Murphy on January 15, 1987.
10. Interview with Monsignor Eugene V. Clark on June 23, 1988.
11. Interview with Sister Anthony, O.P. on November 11, 1984.
12. *Basic Biography.*

Chapter Nine

1. *Collection of Homilies*: Chrism Mass 1977.
2. *Ibid.*: Installation Mass (CCA:NY, April 4, 1969).
3. Personal recollection of Father Benedict J. Groeschel.
4. Interview with Monsignor Michael Wrenn on October 31, 1989.
5. Interview with Archbishop Theodore E. McCarrick.
6. *Collection of Public Statements*: "Letter to Pope Paul VI after publication of *Humanae Vitae*" (CCA:NY, July 31, 1968).
7. John Harvey, *The Homosexual Person* (San Francisco: Ignatius Press, 1987), pp. 235 ff.
8. Cf. *Insight: A Quarterly of Gay Catholic Opinion* (New York: Publication of Dignity, Spring-Winter 1977). This publication has been discontinued.
9. Two popular books have been written on the subject because of the initiative of Cardinal Cooke. Father Harvey's thorough study, *The Homosexual Person*, and my own book, *The Courage to be Chaste*, which is dedicated to the members of Courage, but addressed to all single people wishing to live chaste lives.
10. Personal recollection of Father Benedict J. Groeschel.
11. Cf. Sexaholics Anonymous, P.O. Box 300, Simi Valley, California 93062: SA Literature.

12. Interview with Bishop Joseph T. O'Keefe on October 19, 1989.
13. All of the information in this section concerning the abortion issue comes from an interview with Monsignor James J. Murray on July 13, 1989 unless otherwise indicated.
14. *Collection of Public Statements*: "Bishops' Response to Abortion Law" (CCA:NY, April 10, 1970).
15. *Collection of Pastoral Letters*: "Letter on Abortion" (CCA:NY, December 2, 1970).
16. Personal letter from Monsignor Eugene V. Clark.
17. *Collection of Public Letters*: "Letter from President Richard M. Nixon" (CCA:NY, May 5, 1972).
18. *Collection of Public Statements*: "Speech to the American Health Congress" (CCA:NY, August 8, 1972).
19. *Ibid.*
20. *Ibid.*: "Tenth Anniversary of Legalized Abortion" (CCA:NY, January 16, 1983).
21. Tim Stafford, "The Abortion Wars," *Christianity Today*, (Volume 33, Number 14, October 6, 1989), p. 20.
22. In a letter to Father Benedict J. Groeschel on August 14, 1989, Robert Drinan writes, "I am of course opposed to abortion and have said on countless occasions that I agree totally with the Second Vatican Council which indicated that abortion is virtually the same as infanticide. I recently wrote that it is appalling that there are now at least fifty million abortions each year that we know about throughout the world."
23. Interview with The Most Reverend James T. McHugh, Bishop of Camden, New Jersey on October 21, 1989.
24. *Ibid.*
25. *Collection of Pastoral Letters*: "Letter for Respect Life Month" (CCA:NY, October 8-9, 1983).
26. *Ibid.*
27. *Ibid.*
28. Frank Lombardi, "Interview with Terence Cardinal Cooke," *New York Sunday News*, (CCA:NY, December 20, 1981), pp. 8-9, 19.
29. Video, "Who Was Terence Cooke?" This video cassette was produced in 1985 by Archdiocesan Instructional Television.
30. Interview with Monsignor Charles G. McDonagh on May 26, 1989.
31. *Collection of Public Statements*: "Statement on Being Appointed Archbishop of New York" (CCA:NY, March 8, 1968).
32. Thomas à Kempis, *The Imitation of Christ* (Brooklyn: Confraternity of the Precious Blood, 1954), p. 115.
33. *Collection of Public Statements*: "Annual Clergy Conference" (CCA:NY, May 7, 1971).
34. *Ibid.*: "Return from Rome after the Sacred Consistory" (CCA:NY, May 7, 1969).

Chapter Ten

1. *Collection of Homilies*: Chrism Mass 1977.
2. Interview with Bishop Patrick V. Ahern.
3. Cf. Jean-Pierre de Caussade, *Abandonment to Divine Providence* (New York: Doubleday, 1975).
4. Joseph Cardinal Ratzinger, *Behold the Pierced One* (San Francisco: Ignatius Press, 1986), pp. 37-42.

THY WILL BE DONE

5. *Collection of Public Letters*: "Letter to the Chaplains in the Military Vicariate" (CCA:NY, September 30, 1983).
6. *Ibid.*: "Letter to Pope John Paul II" (CCA:NY, August 25, 1983).
7. Interview with Bishop Patrick V. Ahern.
8. *Ibid.*
9. Personal letter from Monsignor Eugene V. Clark.
10. Interview with Dr. William F. Robbett on March 10, 1988.
11. *Ibid.*
12. *Ibid.*
13. *Ibid.*
14. *Ibid.*
15. Personal letter from Dr. William F. Robbett on February 1, 1990.
16. Interview with Dr. William F. Robbett on March 10, 1988.
17. *Ibid.*
18. Interview with Dr. Thomas Fahey on June 8, 1988.
19. *Ibid.*
20. *Ibid.*
21. Anne Buckley, "Interview with Dr. Kevin Cahill," *Catholic New York*, (CCA:NY, October 13, 1983).
22. Interview with Bishop Patrick V. Ahern.
23. Interview with Maura O'Kelly.
24. John Reardon, Robert Stewart, and Anne Buckley, eds., *This Grace Filled Moment* (New York: Rosemont Press, 1984).
25. Interview with Maura O'Kelly.
26. *Last Will and Testament of Terence Cardinal Cooke* (CCA:NY, September 15, 1981).
27. Interview with Monsignor Joseph P. Murphy.
28. The information used in writing this section comes from various sources. Immediately following the presidential visit, Monsignor McDonagh wrote a detailed account including the topics of discussion between the President and the cardinal. We have also quoted Monsignor Peter Finn whom we interviewed on May 12, 1986. Both he and Monsignor McDonagh were eyewitnesses to the visit of the Reagans. On August 9, 1989, former President Reagan was interviewed by Pastor Weber and corroborated the information concerning his visit with Cardinal Cooke.
29. Interview with Monsignor Charles G. McDonagh.
30. Cf. Benedict J. Groeschel, *Stumbling Blocks or Stepping Stones* (New York: Paulist Press, 1987).
31. Interview with Monsignor Charles G. McDonagh.
32. Anne Buckley, "Interview with Dr. Kevin Cahill."
33. The time of the cardinal's death is noted on the death certificate. Also, in the cardinal's annual date book, the entry is made for October 6, 1983: "4:45 a.m. — Passage of His Eminence Terence Cardinal Cooke to Eternal Life."
34. The members of the New York City Police and Fire Departments provided an honor guard. Members of Religious Communities of Women kept vigil each night in the Cathedral with groups rotating throughout the night.
35. Figures used were taken from statistics provided by *Catholic New York*.

Chapter Eleven

1. Cf. Ida F. Goerres, *The Hidden Face* (New York: Pantheon, 1959).
2. Interview with Monsignor Patrick J. Sheridan on March 29, 1988.
3. Interview with Bishop Joseph T. O'Keefe on April 4, 1988.
4. Interview with Archbishop Theodore E. McCarrick.
5. Archbishop McCarrick's letter, then Bishop of Metuchen, New Jersey, was dated March 17, 1984. This was the day before Cardinal O'Connor was installed as the successor of Cardinal Cooke.
6. Interview with Archbishop Theodore E. McCarrick.
7. *Ibid.*
8. Personal letter from Monsignor Eugene V. Clark.
9. For a brief summary of the classical teaching on spiritual life, the reader may consult my book, *Spiritual Passages,* (New York: Crossroads-Continuum, 1983). A more extensive description can be found by R. Garrigou-Lagrange, *The Three Stages of the Interior Life* (Saint Louis: B. Herder, 1947).
10. Cf. Dom Jean-Baptiste Chautard, *The Soul of the Apostolate* (Trappist, Kentucky: Abbey of Gethsemani, 1946).
11. Interview with Monsignor Edwin F. O'Brien on November 13, 1989.
12. The same mystical doctor in telling us how this is accomplished gives us an insight which fits Cardinal Cooke so well. Bonaventure writes, "If you should ask how these things come about, seek grace, not instruction; desire, not intellect; the cry of prayer, not pursuit of study; the spouse, not the teacher; God, not man; darkness, not clarity; not light but the wholly flaming fire which will bear you aloft to God with burning affections." *The Mind's Road to God,* translated by George Boas (New York: Bobbs Merrill, 1953), p. 45.

Chapter Twelve

1. This chapter deals with some sensitive issues. Some of the sources quoted wish to remain anonymous. We will identify them as Jane or John Doe. Their true identity and testimony, however, are known to the authors of this book.
2. *Collection of Letters of Testimony:* "Letter from Mrs. Hazel Komonchak" (CCA:NY, July 1988).
3. *Ibid.:* "Letter from Ricardo Pettinato" (CCA:NY, December 14, 1987).
4. *Ibid.:* "Letter from Jane Doe" (CCA:NY, February 20, 1988).
5. Miraculous cures are accepted even if the illness was not life-threatening and even if some therapy was applied.
6. Collection of Letters of Testimony: "Letter from Monsignor Harold S. Engel" (CCA:NY, October 8, 1984).
7. *Ibid.:* "Letter from Matthew and Carol Kirk" (CCA:NY, August 11, 1986).
8. *Ibid.:* "Letter from Jane Doe" (CCA:NY, November 15, 1988).
9. Private conversation with Dr. Michael Harris on November 7, 1989.
10. According to canon law, one miracle is required in the causes of non-martyrs with a view to the beatification; in all causes one miracle is required for canonization and this miracle must have happened after the beatification of the person in question.
11. Peter Kreeft, *Fundamentals of the Faith* (San Francisco: Ignatius Press, 1988), pp. 239 ff.
12. John Henry Cardinal Newman, as cited in *The Soul Afire,* ed. H.A. Reinhold, (New York: Doubleday, 1973), p. 258.

A P P E N D I X   I

SIGNIFICANT DATES AND EVENTS

HIS EMINENCE TERENCE JAMES CARDINAL COOKE, D.D.
METROPOLITAN ARCHBISHOP OF NEW YORK
AND MILITARY VICAR

March 1, 1921	Born to Margaret and Michael Cooke
March 13, 1921	Baptized in Corpus Christi, Bronx
July 1, 1930	Margaret Cooke, cardinal's mother, dies
April 24, 1932	Confirmed in St. Benedict's, Bronx
March 17, 1945	Ordained to the Office of Deacon
December 1, 1945	Ordained to the Sacred Priesthood of Jesus Christ by Francis Cardinal Spellman
June 18, 1949	Assigned to Catholic Charities
January 13, 1954	Appointed Procurator of St. Joseph's Seminary
January 12, 1957	Appointed Secretary to Cardinal Spellman
August 1957	Elevated to Papal Chamberlain
June 1, 1958	Appointed Vice-Chancellor of Archdiocese of New York
November 21, 1958	Elevated to Domestic Prelate
May 27, 1961	Michael Cooke, cardinal's father, dies
June 15, 1961	Appointed Chancellor of Archdiocese of New York
June 27, 1964	Elevated to Prothonotary Apostolic
November 11, 1964	First cancer diagnosis
February 13, 1965	Appointed Vicar General of Archdiocese of New York
December 13, 1965	Episcopal Ordination as Auxiliary Bishop to Francis Cardinal Spellman and Titular Bishop of Summa
December 2, 1967	Francis Cardinal Spellman dies
March 8, 1968	Appointed Archbishop of New York

257

April 4, 1968   Installed as Seventh Archbishop and Tenth Bishop
                         of New York
                         Martin Luther King, Jr. assassinated
June 1968   Pope Paul VI issues *Humanae Vitae*
April 30, 1969   Elevated to Cardinalate by Sacred Consistory
July 28, 1971   Mary Gannon, cardinal's aunt, dies
April 21, 1973   Joseph Cooke, cardinal's brother, dies
November 24, 1975   Second cancer diagnosis
August 6, 1978   Pope Paul VI dies
September 3, 1978   Installation of Pope John Paul I
September 28, 1978   Pope John Paul I dies
October 22, 1978   Installation of Pope John Paul II
October 2-3, 1979   Papal Visit of John Paul II to New York
August 24, 1983   Informed of terminal condition
August 26, 1983   Publicly announced terminal condition
October 6, 1983   Entered Eternal Life at 4:45 a.m.
October 10, 1983   Funeral Mass of the Resurrection
                         Interred in the Archbishop's Crypt
August 6, 1984   Possibility of Cause of Canonization
                         announced by Archbishop John J. O'Connor
October 15, 1984   Cardinal Cooke Guild organized

PASTORAL MESSAGE ON PEACE TO THE PEOPLE OF NEW YORK

May 19, 1972

*T*he recent developments in Vietnam, the escalation of military activity both by North Vietnam and by our own nation, have placed in harsh perspective a conflict over which so many of us have agonized for so long. Just when the conflict seemed on the verge of ending, hostilities have flared anew and our hopes for a quick solution have been placed in jeopardy. Therefore, I am moved to speak again, not just for an end to this terrible war, but for the prevention of future wars and for peace in the world, and to propose some positive recommendations.

One should not speak simplistically of so complex an issue as the war in Southeast Asia. No issue within memory has so divided and even polarized our people and there is certainly no consensus on how the conflict should be ended. All of us in the Archdiocese of New York have been praying in a special way during this month of May that the Lord would grant a speedy end to this war and a return home for all the men and women who have been separated from their loved ones.

My relationship with the Catholic men and women in the military services in their assignments throughout the world has

259

made it clear to me how much they miss home and how deeply they appreciate the presence of their Chaplains and count on them for guidance in their religious and moral lives while they are apart from their families and their local congregations. They see these dedicated religious men as visible reminders of their continued relationship with God wherever they are and however sorely beset by temptation. I know from personal experience how much they long for peace and how great are the difficult burdens which they carry in this awful struggle.

I also share profoundly the concern of my fellow Americans for all prisoners of war and those who are missing in action. I have always been and I am now willing to go anywhere to talk to anyone about the possibility of securing the release of our captive American servicemen.

In the pressing search for peace this is not the moment when anything positive can be gained by dissecting the decisions of the past. Historians of the future will be better able to assign the praise or blame, wisdom or folly. The task confronting our country now is to bring this war to a speedy end.

For my part, I do not think that our national purpose in Vietnam has all along been ignoble, selfish and dishonorable. On the contrary, I am convinced that our country committed itself to struggle to help our fellowmen achieve the blessings of peace and liberty against the forces of tyranny and oppression.

Yet, within the family of man all wars are to be deplored whether they are fought for just causes or ill. What is clear is that we must work for peace and for an end to war and that those on all sides who have responsibility over the conduct of political, military and economic power must strive for an end to hostilities and for a solution which seeks decency and justice for all.

There is no doubt that on both sides during this long and terrible war there have been tragic incidents calling for grave moral concern. The scars of the long years of conflict in Vietnam are so very visible. They are to be seen not only in the suffering peoples and the ravaged land of that unfortunate part of the world, but also here at home in the shrill impatience and the strident discord that characterizes the partisans of the extremes on both sides of this difficult question. The war has divided families, has destroyed friendships, has successfully aborted dialogue in so many areas of American life.

Many millions of Americans are perplexed and disheartened, and find themselves caught between extreme viewpoints. They know that they do not see the facts so clearly as to lead them to a judgment of condemnation, and yet they have been so wearied by the continuous crises here and in Southeast Asia that they feel that this war has gone on too long and we must soon have an end to it. We must take every step to end it as quickly as possible.

But just as it takes two sides to make war, so it takes two sides to end war and to make peace. Both sides must hasten, not to escalate but to negotiate, and both must bring to the peace table good will and a firm resolve to reach an agreement. I share the anguish that afflicts everyone in this present crisis and I long for a peaceful solution. What are we to do, then, we who are united in our determination to bring about the end of this and all wars? I offer three proposals.

First, I propose that all of us should pray — and across this nation countless millions of Americans do believe in the power of prayer. Now this is the time to turn to God, who in His unsearchable way, guides the destinies of man and to beg for His help. God will not be deaf to the pleas of suffering people, of people who want to do what is right, but who are baffled by the problem which is beyond their power to resolve. It is my firm conviction that if all of us unite in prayer each in his own way and according to his own belief we shall find our path out of the confusion that afflicts us. We have been pulled so far apart it is only the Lord who can bring us all together. Only the Lord can truly bring that reconciliation that will bind up the wounds of families and friends and generations. We share the agony of this awful war, let us share the cry that goes up to God to help us.

Secondly, let those who are involved in the peace negotiations in Paris take seriously the words of Pope Paul who recently pleaded "that on both sides the operations of war come to an end, and that noble and generous proposals for rapid and sincere and effective negotiations for a cease-fire and for peace might prevail over every other interest and that in this way an honorable and peaceful solution will be made possible."

But if prudent hopes for peace are to continue to be frustrated in Paris and if the four parties cannot find a peaceful solution very soon, then I recommend that we turn for help to that organization which is equipped to step in and find a solution. The United Nations was created for such a purpose and it does afford the possibility of impartial intervention. It has the moral influence, if we support it, to call all parties to agreement. We all remember the high hopes for which the United Nations was created more than twenty-five years ago, hopes for a better, more just and stable world. If these hopes have not been fulfilled to the extent of our expectations, it is largely because the nations of the world have failed to entrust to the United Nations the problems which they themselves could not resolve. This may well be the time for us to call upon the United Nations to exercise its peace-making and peace-keeping functions for the common good of the family of nations.

Thirdly, even before the current conflict is ended, let us face the problem of war itself and begin to develop an instrumentality to prevent future wars. Even though all the guns are not yet silent and the bombs and the rockets still do their ugly work, we must now think of building and preserving a lasting peace guaranteed not by the precarious balance of terrible armaments, but in some other way by an effective covenant of the nations which share this small planet — Earth. It seems incomprehensible to me that nations with enough resources in talent and technology to harness nuclear power and to challenge the world of space cannot harness those talents and resources to prevent war and give peace a chance.

Therefore, I recommend that our nation establish a Commission to mobilize our finest resources in the cause of lasting peace — to bring scholars and scientists and men of every relevant discipline together in the service of all mankind to study and to plan for the prevention of war. There is no cause more noble or more important to this battered world, and there is no moment like the present to launch this hope for the future.

It was at the United Nations seven years ago that Pope Paul uttered the memorable cry "War Never Again!" Three words that express the deepest yearnings in the hearts of men! Can anyone doubt that in this nuclear age we have reached a crossroads of history, a point of no return, where war is no longer an acceptable alternative for nations in order to settle disagreements. The elimination of war, and ultimately of the very capacity to wage it — is an imperative for the survival of the human race. We are confronted by a frighteningly unwanted timetable. The clock ticks on and the bomb which might explode at any time could destroy all of us, friend and foe alike. It is not in the least alarmist to say that if we do not, with deliberate speed, develop the means of war-prevention and make impossible the waging of war by any nation on this earth, we run the risk of witnessing, in our time, the very end of human history.

The challenge is enormously difficult. It will require prayerful study, persevering dialogue, the careful planning of restraints, the development of the technology and the diplomatic initiatives which will be necessary. Because the task is so difficult and will take unparalleled effort we have all the more reason to approach it without delay. War is the problem men must solve and we must begin to solve it now!

Is it asking too much of America that she take the first step forward and then call upon the other nations of the world to come together in this quest to end war? It is undoubtedly the priority of our era, and the nation which seizes the initiative to accomplish it will earn the gratitude of all mankind.

Only God, our Father, can complete the work we long to begin today! Let us lift up our hearts and pray with confidence for an end to the war in Vietnam and for the development of adequate means to prevent wars in the future and to establish Peace on Earth.

Sincerely yours in Christ,
✠ Terence Cardinal Cooke
Archbishop of New York

PASTORAL LETTER FOR RESPECT LIFE MONTH

October 8-9, 1983

Dear Friends in Christ:

*H*ow often we speak of "the gift of life," God's "gift of life" to us, His sons and daughters. What a beautiful phrase! How filled with meaning it is! In the Book of Genesis, we read of the origin of this gift: "So God created man in His own image, in the image of God He created him; male and female He created them."

It is at times when life is threatened — such as times of serious illness — that the Lord gives us a special grace to appreciate "the gift of life" more deeply as an irreplaceable blessing which only God can give and which God must guide at every step. From the beginning of human life, from conception until death and at every moment between, it is the Lord Our God who gives us life, and we, who are His creatures, should cry out with joy and thanksgiving for this precious gift.

We are made in God's image and likeness, and this fact gives a unique dimension to "the gift of life." We have even more reason to be grateful. It is tragic that in our time, concepts which are disastrous to the well-being of God's human family — abortion, euthanasia and infanticide — are falsely presented as useful and even respectable solutions to human, family and social problems. Human life is sometimes narrowly viewed in terms of being inconvenient or unwanted, unproductive or lacking arbitrarily imposed human criteria.

From the depths of my being, I urge you to reject this anti-life, anti-child, anti-human view of life and to oppose with all your strength the deadly technologies of life-destruction which daily result in the planned death of the innocent and the helpless. Together we must search for ways to demonstrate this conviction in our daily lives and in our public institutions. In doing so, we must never be discouraged or give up. Too much is at stake — "the gift of life" itself.

The "gift of life," God's special gift, is no less beautiful when it is accompanied by illness or weakness, hunger or poverty, mental or physical handicaps, loneliness or old age. Indeed, at these times, human life gains extra splendor as it requires our special care, concern and reverence. It is in and through the weakest of human vessels that the Lord continues to reveal the power of His love.

For the last ten years, I have served as Chairman of the Bishops' Committee for Pro-Life Activities in the United States. With God's help, I have tried to encourage and promote a *Respect Life* attitude throughout our nation. I have pleaded with you to pray and to be active in the many efforts for the enhancement and the protection of human life at every stage of existence.

In October, as we observe *Respect Life Month,* I call on you to rededicate your efforts for the sanctity of all human life and to work to counteract the contemporary threats to life. I urge you to increase and to strengthen the programs in our parishes and communities for the poor, the elderly, the handicapped, the rejected, the homeless, the suffering, the unwanted, the unborn. I ask you to focus attention again on the Pastoral Plan for Pro-Life Activities and on the three elements of education, pastoral care and public policy which are necessary if we are to work for and defend the most defenseless members of society.

At this grace-filled time in my life, as I experience suffering in union with Jesus, Our Lord and Redeemer, I offer gratitude to Almighty God for giving me the opportunity to continue my apostolate on behalf of life. I thank each one of you, my sisters and brothers in the Archdiocese of New York and throughout our nation, for what you have done and will do on behalf of human life. May we never yield to indifference or claim helplessness when innocent human life is threatened or when human rights are denied.

With you, I entrust our efforts to the care of Our Lady who, from the moment of her Immaculate Conception to the present, has been the refuge for the poorest and most forgotten among God's people. I assure you of a special share in the prayerful offerings of my sufferings to the Father, in union with Jesus and through the Spirit of Love Who is ours in abundance.

May God bless you always and give you His peace.

Devotedly yours in Christ,
✠ Terence Cardinal Cooke
Archbishop of New York

INDEX